Contents

A LITTLE HISTORY OF LITERATURE

JOHN
SUTHERLAND

A LITTLE
HISTORY
of
Literature

YALE UNIVERSITY PRESS
NEW HAVEN AND LONDON

Illustrations by Sarah Young

For information about this and other Yale University Press publications please contact:

U.S. Office:	sales.press@yale.edu	www.yalebooks.com
Europe Office:	sales@yaleup.co.uk	www.yalebooks.co.uk

Set in Minion by Yale University Press
Printed in the United States of America

Library of Congress Cataloging-in-Publication Data

Sutherland, John, 1938-
  A little history of literature / John Sutherland.
    pages cm
Includes bibliographical references and index.
  ISBN 978-0-300-18685-7 (alk. paper)
  1. Literature—History and criticism. I. Title.
  PN511.S746 2013
  809—dc23

2013024200

A catalogue record for this book is available from the British Library

10 9 8 7 6 5 4 3 2 1

CHAPTER 1

What is Literature?

Imagine that, like Robinson Crusoe, you are marooned for the rest of your days on a desert island. What one book would you most want to have with you? That is a question asked on one of the longest-running and most-loved programmes on BBC radio, *Desert Island Discs*. Broadcast also on the BBC's World Service, it is listened to across the globe.

The question is one of two that are put to that week's guest, after we have heard snatches of the eight pieces of music they would take to the island. The castaway is allowed one luxury – what will it be? Answers are usually very ingenious: at least a couple of guests have chosen cyanide pills, for instance, and another chose the Metropolitan Museum of Art in New York. Then they are asked which book they would like, in addition to the Bible (or any other equivalent religious volume) and the works of Shakespeare, which are already on the island – presumably left by the previous occupant, who chose the pill.

I've listened to the programme for fifty years now (it's been running since 1942) and much more often than not, the guest chooses a great work of literature to keep them company for the rest of their lonely lives. In recent years, Jane Austen, interestingly, has been the most popular author (more of her, and of Robinson Crusoe, later). And on virtually every one of the thousands of programmes aired, the chosen book has been a work of literature that the castaway has already read.

This points to some important truths about literature. First, obviously, that we regard it as one of the most important things in our lives. Secondly, that although we're said to 'consume' literature, unlike the food on our dinner plate it is still there after we have consumed it. And, in most cases, it's just as appetising as it was the first time round. My own choice, when on the programme some years ago, was a novel, Thackeray's *Vanity Fair*, which (since I'd spent years editing and writing about it) I must have read at least a hundred times. Yet still, like my favourite music, it gives me pleasure whenever I revisit it.

Re-reading is one of the great pleasures that literature offers us. The great works of literature are inexhaustible – that is one of the things that makes them great. However often you go back to them, they will always have something new to offer.

What you are holding is, as the title says, a 'little history', but literature is not a little thing. There is hugely more of it than any of us will read in a lifetime. At best what we can put together is an intelligent sample, and the most important decision to make is how to assemble our selection. This little history is not a manual ('Read this!') but advice, along the lines of, 'You may find this valuable, because many others have, but, at the end of the day, you must decide for yourself'.

For most thoughtful people, literature will play a big part in their lives. We learn a lot of things at home, at school, from friends, and from the mouths of people wiser and cleverer than ourselves. But many of the most valuable things we know come from the literature we have read. If we read well, we find ourselves in a conversational relationship with the most creative minds of our own time and of the past. Time spent reading literature is always time well spent. Let no one tell you otherwise.

What, then, is literature? It's a tricky question. The most satisfactory answer is found by looking at literature itself; most conveniently at the very first printed works we come into contact with over the course of our lives – 'Children's Literature' (written, one should note, *for* children, not *by* them). Most of us take those first faltering steps into the world of reading in the bedroom. (We learn to write, most of us, in the classroom.) Someone we love reads to us, or with us, in bed. So begins the lifelong journey through all those pages that lie ahead.

As we grow up, the practice of reading for pleasure – which typically means reading literature – stays with us. Many of us will go through life taking a novel to bed with us. (Or we may listen to *Book at Bedtime*, another long-running BBC radio programme.) How many of us, in our youngest days, will have naughtily gone on reading by torchlight under the bedclothes in our pyjamas? The garments (our 'armour', in a sense) which we put on to face the outside world – the 'real world' – are more often than not tucked away across the bedroom inside a wardrobe.

Thanks to the numerous TV, film and stage adaptations of the book, many children and adults know the story of the four young Pevensies who find themselves evacuated to a house in the country. It is wartime in 1940s Britain. Under the care of kindly Professor Kirke (the word 'kirk' means 'church' in the Scots language: literature is always bringing in these little symbolic elements), they are safe from the nighttime raids of the London Blitz. The real world has become very dangerous for children; mysterious aircraft, for reasons not fully understood, are trying to kill people. Explaining to young children the politics, or the history, or the point of it all would be difficult. Literature, with its ability to communicate to all ages, can help.

In the story, while exploring the Kirke mansion one rainy day, the children discover an upstairs room with a large wardrobe. The youngest, Lucy, ventures into the wardrobe by herself. I suspect everyone knows what she discovers inside, from whatever version of *The Lion, the Witch and the Wardrobe* they remember. Lucy finds herself in what could be called an 'alternative universe' – a universe of the imagination; but as real, essentially, as the London she left. And quite as violent as that burning city. Narnia is not a safe place, any more than lions or witches are generally safe for human beings to hang out with.

As it's narrated, Narnia is not Lucy's *dream*, something inside her head, a 'fantasy'; it is actually *there*, as much a thing outside her wakeful self as the wooden wardrobe, or the looking-glass through which Alice goes into Wonderland, in Lewis Carroll's children's story published eighty-five years earlier. But to understand how Narnia can be both real and imaginary, we need to know how to process literature's complex machinery. (Children pick up the knowledge as quickly and intuitively as, in their earliest years, they pick up the complex machinery of language.)

The Lion, the Witch and the Wardrobe is an 'allegory' – that is to say, it pictures something in terms of something else; it depicts something very real in terms of something wholly unreal. Even if the universe expands for ever, as astronomers nowadays tell us it might, there will never be a Narnia in it. That world is a fiction; and its inhabitants (even Lucy) are mere figments (fictional inventions, that is) of the creative imagination of the author C.S. Lewis. But nonetheless we feel (and Lewis certainly meant his reader to feel) that a solid core of truth is contained in Narnia's manifest untruths.

Ultimately, then, we could say that the purpose of *The Lion, the Witch and the Wardrobe* is theological, a matter of religion. (Lewis was, in fact, a theologian as well as a story-teller.) The story makes sense of the human condition in terms of what the author suggests are larger truths. Every work of literature, however humble, is at some level asking: 'What's it all about? Why are we here?' Philosophers and ministers of religion and scientists answer those questions in their own ways. In literature it is 'imagination' that grapples with those basic questions.

That early bedtime reading of *The Lion, the Witch and the Wardrobe* transports us through the wardrobe (and the printed page) to a greater awareness of where and what we are. It helps make sense of the infinitely perplexing situations in which we find ourselves as human beings. And, as an added bonus, it does so in ways that please us and make us want to read more. Just as the Narnia stories helped explain the world to us, as children, so our adult reading connects us to other adult lives. Re-reading *Emma*, or a Dickens novel, in middle age, we are surprised and delighted to find much more in it than when we read it at school. A great work of literature continues giving at whatever point in life you read it, and from whatever sources it comes from. In the following chapters we'll see again and again how privileged we are to live in a golden age when, thanks to modern translation services, not just 'literature' but 'world literature' is available to us to read. Many of the great writers who appear in the following pages would be green with envy at the abundance and availability we enjoy today. So although we'll look at literature from far and wide, the kaleidoscope you'll encounter in this book has one thing in common: you're now able to read it all in English (and I hope, one day, you will).

There have been those, from the ancient Greek philosopher Plato onwards, who believe that the charms of literature and its spin-off forms (theatre, epic and lyric in Plato's day) are dangerous – particularly for the young. Literature distracts us from the real business of living. It traffics in falsehoods – beautiful falsehoods, it is true, but for that reason all the more dangerous. The emotions inspired by great literature, if you agree with Plato, cloud clear thinking. How can you think seriously about the problems of educating children if your eyes are bleary with tears after reading Dickens's description of the death of angelic Little Nell? And without clear thinking, Plato believed, society was in peril. Give that child Euclid's *Geometry* to read in bed at night, not Aesop's animal fable about Androcles and the Lion. But, of course, neither life nor human beings are like that. Aesop's fables had already been teaching Plato's contemporaries important lessons – and delighting them, into the bargain – for two hundred years, and two and a half millennia later they do the same for us today.

How best, then, to describe literature? At its basic level, it is a collection of unique combinations of twenty-six small black marks on a white surface – 'letters', in other words, since the word 'literature' means things made of letters. Those combinations are more magical than anything a conjuror can pull out of his top hat. Yet a better answer would be that literature is the human mind at the very height of its ability to express and interpret the world around us. Literature, at its best, does not simplify, but it enlarges our minds and sensibilities to the point where we can better handle complexity – even if, as is often the case, we don't entirely agree with what we are reading. Why read literature? Because it enriches life in ways that nothing else quite can. It makes us more human. And the better we learn to read it, the better it will do that.

CHAPTER 2

Fabulous Beginnings
MYTH

Long before we began to think of literature as something written down and printed, there was something which – on the principle 'If it walks like a duck and quacks like a duck, it's a duck' – we could still call literature. Anthropologists, who study humankind from the ancient past to the present day, call it 'myth'. It originates in societies which 'tell' their literature, rather than writing it. The awkward and contradictory term 'oral literature' (that is, 'spoken literature') is often used. We don't have a better term.

The first point to make about myth is that it is not 'primitive'. In fact it is very complex. The second point is that, taking the long view, written and printed literature are relatively recent arrivals – but myth has been with us forever. It makes sense to suppose that as a species we are somehow wired, inside ourselves, to think mythically, just as linguists nowadays argue that we are genetically wired, at a certain period of our lives, for language. (How else, as toddlers, could we learn something as complex as the language we're hearing?) Myth-making is in our nature. It's part of who we are as human beings.

What this means in practice is that we instinctively make mental shapes, patterns, from everything that goes on around us. As babies, we are born, one philosopher said, into 'a great blooming, buzzing confusion'. Coming to terms with that frightening confusion is one of humankind's greatest enterprises. Myths have been a way of helping people make sense of our world. When we began to write, literature would do the same.

Here's an elegant little mind game, set up by the critic Frank Kermode, which demonstrates the point I'm making about being 'wired' to think mythically. If you put a wristwatch to your ear, you will hear tick-TOCK, tick-TOCK, tick-TOCK. 'Tock' will be stressed more than 'tick'. Our minds, receiving the signal from our ear, 'shape' the tick-tick into tick-TOCK – into, that is, a tiny beginning and a tiny ending. That, essentially, is what myth does. It creates a pattern where none existed, because finding a pattern helps us make sense of things. (It also helps us to remember them.) And what is most interesting in that little 'tick-TOCK' example is that no one teaches you to hear that narrative shape. It's natural to do so.

One way, then, of thinking about myth is that it makes sense out of the senselessness in which, as human beings, we all find ourselves. Why are we here, and what are we here 'for'? Typically, myth supplies an explanation through stories (the backbone of literature) and symbols (the essence of poetry). Let's try a mind game. Suppose you are one of the first people to try growing crops on the land, 10,000 years ago. You know there are periods when nothing grows. Nature dies. Then, after some time, the earth comes back to life. Why? What explanation can you come up with? There is no scientist around to explain it. But you have, somehow, to 'make sense' of it.

Seasonal rhythm is vital to agricultural communities – 'a time to plant, and a time to pluck up that which is planted', as the Bible puts it. Any farmer who doesn't know those 'times' will starve. The mysterious cycle of the earth's annual death and rebirth inspires 'fertility myths'. These myths are often dramatised in terms of kings or rulers who die only to be resurrected. It creates a reassuring sense that although things change, in a larger way they stay the same.

One of the oldest (and most beautiful) poems in English literature, *Sir Gawain and the Green Knight*, opens, vividly, at the Christmas festivities in the court of King Arthur. It is the deadest time of year. A stranger, who is decked out in green from head to toe, bursts in on horseback. He imposes certain trials on those present, and gives them to understand that bad things will happen if the right things are not done. He is a version of the Green Man, the pagan god of vegetation: himself holding a holly bough, he represents the green shoots which (God willing) will sprout in spring. If, that is, mankind is watchful.

Let's explore that tiny beginning and ending of the tick-TOCK pattern, this time in a more literary example: the familiar and much-told myth of Hercules. Early versions of the story are found on decorated Greek vases, from around the sixth century BC. A recent version can be found in the *Iron Man* films. The legendary strong man of myth meets a giant, Antaeus, stronger than even he is, with whom he is obliged to fight. Hercules throws the giant to the ground. But every time Antaeus makes contact with the earth, he becomes stronger. Hercules finally wins by grabbing his opponent in a bear-hug and lifting him in the air. Uprooted, Antaeus withers and dies.

What is significant is that the story moves from beginning to end very satisfactorily (as do all the 'labours' of Hercules). It has a plot: there is an opening situation (the hero, Hercules, meets a giant, Antaeus), a complication (Hercules fights Antaeus, and is losing), and a resolution (Hercules realises how to beat his opponent, and wins). The fight in which the hero has to outsmart his much stronger opponent, as Hercules outsmarts Antaeus, will be familiar to every lover of James Bond films. The myth, like every Bond film, has a 'happy ending'. In simple and complicated ways, we find that kind of 'plotting' everywhere in narrative literature.

There is another element to myth. Myth always contains a truth, which we understand before we can clearly see it or explain it. To help prove that point, let's look at the oldest – and many would say the noblest – work of literature that we have, the poems known as the *Iliad* and the *Odyssey*. Tradition has it that they were created by an ancient Greek author, known only as 'Homer', probably around 3,000 years ago.

The poems are about a long war between two great powers, Greece (as it would become) and Troy. There was such a war – archaeology has established it. But creating the work when he did, Homer was never too far away from the bare-bones 'myth'. The hero of the poems, Odysseus (also known by his later Latin name, Ulysses), has many adventures on his way back from the war (a journey that takes him ten years). In one of them he and his shipmates are captured and imprisoned in a cave by a one-eyed giant called Polyphemus. This monster's single eye is in the middle of his forehead. When he feels hungry, he eats one of the captives in his cave – usually for breakfast. Odysseus, the most cunning of heroes, gets Polyphemus drunk and stabs him in his eye, blinding him, so that he and his crew can escape.

What 'truth' can we see buried in this myth? It lies in that single eye. You have probably had the experience of arguing with someone who can't or won't see 'both sides of the question' – someone who just holds to one viewpoint. It's hopeless. You'll never change their mind. All you can do is find some way of escaping – and preferably in a less violent way than Homer's hero.

You may be thinking that this all sounds rather primitive ('the thought of savages', as some belittle it). But myth always contains within it that grain of truth which is as relevant for us now as it was for the time when it was written. And mythic thought lives on, thrives even, long after you might think modern society and science had left its explanations hopelessly behind. It is, if you look carefully, woven into the fabric of contemporary literature, even if the eye does not immediately see it.

Here is one, fairly recent, example of the ways in which myth is woven into our culture. In the period between James Cameron's Oscar-winning film *Titanic*, in 1997, and the centenary anniversary of the great liner's launch, on 12 April 2012, there was huge fascination with everything about the wreck in Britain and the USA. This fascination seemed, on the face of it, a little odd. Some 1,500 people had died when the ship went down. It was a horrible event. But the death toll pales in comparison with the millions of deaths and casualties caused by the First World War just a few years later. Why had people never forgotten the shipwreck? The answer may well be in the name of the vessel: *Titanic*.

In ancient myth, the Titans were a tribe of giant gods. Their parents were the earth and sky and they were the first race on earth to have human form. After a long time enjoying their status as the most powerful species on earth, the Titans found themselves locked in a ten-year war with a new race of gods who had reached an even higher stage of evolution than they had. Although the Titans were giants possessed of gigantic strength, that was pretty well all they had: brute force. This new race, the Olympians, had much more: intelligence, beauty and skill. They were, essentially, more like humans (like us, we might think) than forces of nature.

Despite their massive strength, the Titans, as the myth goes, went under. Their defeat is the subject of one of the greatest narrative poems in the English language, John Keats's *Hyperion*, which he wrote around 1818. In the poem, the Titan Oceanus contemplates his conquering successor, Neptune, who has replaced him as God of the Sea, and realises that:

'tis the eternal law
That first in beauty should be first in might

For the un-beautiful Titans, their day is over. But, Oceanus prophesies:

Yea, by that law, another race may drive
Our conquerors to mourn as we do now.

The White Star Line vessel that went to the bottom of the ocean in April 1912 was named the *Titanic* – accompanied by the ritual bottle of champagne cracked across its bow, itself a mythic act called 'libation' – because it was one of the largest, fastest, most powerful vessels ever destined to cross the Atlantic. It was thought to be unsinkable. But those who named it must have felt a certain uneasiness. Was it not tempting fate to name a ship *Titanic*, recalling what had happened to the Titans?

One reason we are so fascinated by the disaster is because we suspect, irrationally, that the sinking of the *Titanic* contains a message for us. (Millions of dollars have been spent exploring the vessel underwater and there has always been interest in 'raising' it.) The event is telling us something, warning us about something that we really should try to understand. Do not be overconfident, seems to be the message within what has become a myth for our age. The Greeks have given us a name for that overconfidence: *hubris*. It's echoed in the phrase 'Pride comes before a fall', and is a common theme throughout literature.

The courts of inquiry, after the *Titanic* disaster, laid the blame, rationally enough, on lax regulation, inadequate iceberg monitoring, poor construction, and criminally insufficient lifeboat space. All this was true. But in his famous poem, 'The Convergence of the Twain (*Lines on the loss of the "Titanic"*)', Thomas Hardy, one of our greatest but most pessimistic writers (whose poetry we look at in detail in Chapter 24), saw deeper, more cosmic, mythic forces at work. (The 'creature' in his lines is the ship.)

> Well: while was fashioning
> This creature of cleaving wing,
> The Immanent Will that stirs and urges everything
>
> Prepared a sinister mate
> For her – so gaily great –
> A Shape of Ice, for the time far and dissociate.

The Admiralty came up with one verdict, based on nautical science. The poet came up with another verdict, based on a mythic understanding of the world. In the next chapter, let's consider how myth – the bedrock of literature – evolves into epic.

CHAPTER 3

Writing for Nations
EPIC

The word 'epic' is used widely but very loosely nowadays. In the newspaper I've just put down, for example, I find a soccer match (one of the very few, alas, in which an English team has won a major sporting title) described as an 'epic struggle'. But in terms of literature, 'epic' has, when properly applied, an anything but loose meaning. It describes a very select, very ancient, set of texts that carry values which are 'heroic' in tone ('heroic' being another word we tend to use too loosely). They show mankind, we may say, at its most manly. (The gender bias in that remark is, unfortunately, appropriate: an 'epic heroine' is almost always a contradiction in terms.)

When we think seriously about epics we encounter an intriguing question. If this is such great literature, why don't we write it any more? Why have we not done so (successfully, at least) for many centuries now? The word is still with us; the literature, for some reason, isn't.

The most venerable epic that has survived through the ages is *Gilgamesh*, whose origins can be traced back to 2000 BC. The narrative originated in what is now called Iraq (then called Mesopotamia), the cradle of Western civilisation. This 'fertile crescent' was also where wheat was first cultivated, enabling mankind's great move from hunter-gatherer to an agricultural way of life. This, in turn, made cities possible – made us possible, we may say.

Like some other epics, the surviving text of *Gilgamesh* is incomplete, dependent as it is on clay tablets not all of which have endured the passage of thousands of years. The hero is first encountered as the King of Uruk. He is part-god, part-man, and has built, to glorify himself, a magnificent city over which he tyrannises brutally. He is a bad, despotic ruler. The gods, to mend his ways, create a 'wild man', Enkidu, as strong as Gilgamesh but nobler in character. The two wrestle, and Gilgamesh wins. They then become comrades and embark on a series of quests, adventures and ordeals together.

The gods, always unpredictable, infect Enkidu with a fatal illness. Gilgamesh is distraught at the death of his dearest friend. Now fearing death he travels the world to discover the secret of immortality. A divinity who can grant him his desire sets him a test: if he wants to live for eternity he can, surely, stay awake for a week. Gilgamesh tries, but fails, accepts the fact that he is mortal, and returns to Uruk a better and wiser ruler. And, in course of time, he will die.

The themes of this very old story – the building of civilisation by heroism and the domestication of the savage legacy in our human nature – is common to all literary works that merit the title 'epic'.

Historically, epic evolves out of myth. One can usually see the joins between the two narrative forms quite clearly. In the great British epic, *Beowulf*, for example, the hero – a 'modern' (eighth-century modern, that is) warrior – is shown slaying 'monsters': Grendel and his mother, who live deep in a dark pool and emerge at night to slay any human they find. Beowulf himself is later slain by a dragon. Dragons are mythic, as are monsters like the Grendels. Warriors, like Beowulf and his comrades, are historical. Their armour and weaponry can be found, exactly as the epic poem describes them, in the ship-burials in which heroes and kings like Beowulf were sent to their final rest. The most famous of such ship-burials, the one excavated at Sutton Hoo in Suffolk, is on display in the British Museum. You won't find dragon bones buried with the swords, helmets, chain-mail and shields.

British literature is founded on this 3,182-line Anglo-Saxon poem. It was probably composed in the eighth century, drawing on old fables that went even further back into the mists of time. It was brought to England in some earlier form by invading Europeans, then it was recited orally for centuries, with countless variations, before being transcribed by an unknown monk (who made some tactful Christian insertions) in the tenth century. Monasteries were institutions that archived the nation's earliest writings and nurtured learning and literacy. *Beowulf*, as the text has come down to us, stands at a junction point between pagan and Christian, between savagery and civilisation, between oral and written literature. It's hard work to read but important to know what it means, historically.

Epics in their earliest oral form typically happen at just such transitional moments in history. That is to say when 'society', as people know it, is taking its first 'modern' shape – becoming, recognisably, the world in which they now live. Epics celebrate, in heroic narrative, certain fundamental ideals. And, more specifically, they mark the 'birth of nations'.

Let's return to *Beowulf*, and its opening lines; first in the original Old English, then in modern English translation:

Hwæt. We Gardena   in gear-dagum,
þeodcyninga,   þrym gefrunon,
hu ða æþelingas   ellen fremedon.

Lo! we have learned of the glory of the kings
who ruled the Spear-Danes in the olden time, how
those princes wrought mighty deeds.

Although the poem is in 'Old English', and circulated in England for centuries, it is set in 'Daneland', which is another way of saying 'a land far, far away'. But what is clear is that this great poem starts by metaphorically raising a national flag: the flag of the Spear-Dane kingdom. In the poem, Beowulf, a princely-hero from 'Geatland' (now Sweden), comes to save an embryonic civilisation from being destroyed by the Grendels. Had he not succeeded – by quite extraordinary, self-sacrificing heroism – the modern world of the Anglo-Saxons and all the other European nations would never have existed. They would have been killed at birth by horrible ancient monsters. Civilisation, the epic tells us, had to fight to the death to come into being.

A further important point needs to be added here. Literary epics – those, that is, which are still read centuries (millennia, in some cases) after they were composed – chronicle the birth not of 'any' nation, but of nations that will one day grow to be great empires, swallowing up lesser nations. In their later maturity empires cherish 'their' epics as witness to that greatness. Epics certify it. Linguists love the following conundrum: '*Question*: What's the difference between a dialect and a language? *Answer*: A language is a dialect with an army behind it.' What, then, is the difference between a long poem about a primitive people's early struggles and an epic? An epic is a long poem with a great nation behind it – or, more precisely, in front of it.

Consider the most famous of all: the epics originating in what we now know as Greece, Homer's *Iliad* and *Odyssey*. We know nothing about Homer's life, and never will. Legend has it he was blind. Some have suggested he was a woman. But since ancient times his name has been attached to these greatest of poems. What are they about? In the *Iliad*, a beautiful Greek woman, Helen, becomes the lover of a handsome young foreign prince, Paris. Their love is complicated by the inconvenient fact that she is married. The two of them elope to his homeland, Troy (located where Turkey is now). It's a romance, you say – a love story. But viewed objectively, it is about the clash of two emergent city states: Greece (as it will become) and Troy; two maritime trading nations in a world not big enough for the both of them. In the Trojan War, one nation must burn. It will be the 'topless towers of Ilium' (as the Elizabethan dramatist Christopher Marlowe put it): Troy goes up in flames so that Greece can rise to greatness from its ashes. Had it been the other way around, world history would have been very different. We would have had no Greek tragedy; some would say, no democracy (a Greek word) either. Our whole 'philosophy of life' would have been different.

Homer's sequel to the *Iliad*, the *Odyssey*, is more mythic than the preceding epic story. As we saw in Chapter 2, over ten eventful years the Greek hero Odysseus returns from the Trojan War to his minor kingdom, Ithaca. On his journey, after escaping from the one-eyed giant Polyphemus, he and his crew are stranded on an island where the beautiful sorceress Circe tries to cast spells over them, and are threatened by the sea-monsters Scylla and Charybdis. Finally Odysseus contrives to make it back to Ithaca and save his own marriage to the ever-faithful Penelope. Stability (after much slaughter) is restored. Civilisation can grow. Empires can rise. That is a dominant theme of Homer's two epics.

The *Iliad* and *Odyssey* remain the most readable (and filmable) of stories. But at their centre, these epic narratives look at how ancient Greece – what we like to call the cradle of modern democracy, our world – came into being. Epics are the offspring of 'noble and puissant [powerful] nations', as the poet John Milton called them. (Milton is the author of what many see as the last great epic in British Literature, *Paradise Lost*, composed in the mid-seventeenth century when Britain itself was becoming 'puissant' – a world power. See Chapter 10.)

Could Luxembourg, or the Principality of Monaco, however gifted its authors, host an epic? Could the multinational European Union have one? Such states can create literature, great literature, even. But they cannot create epic literature. When the Nobel Prize-winning novelist Saul Bellow asked his insulting question, 'Where is the Zulu Tolstoy, where is the Papuan Proust?' he was, essentially, making the point that only great civilisations have great literature. And only the greatest of those great nations possess epics. Great world power is at their centre.

The following is a list of some of the world's most famous epics, and the great nations or empires from which they sprang.

Gilgamesh (Mesopotamia)
Odyssey (ancient Greece)
Mahābhārata (India)
Aeneid (ancient Rome)
Beowulf (England)
La Chanson de Roland (France)
El Cantar de Mio Cid (Spain)
Nibelungenlied (Germany)
La Divina Commedia (Italy)
Os Lusíadas (Portugal)

Saul Bellow's own nation, the USA, is missing from the list. Should it be included? No nation has been more powerful. But historically speaking, the United States is a young country – juvenile in comparison with Greece, or Britain (which once owned a considerable part of it). Its frontier struggles, as modern American civilisation spread westward, can be seen as having inspired some versions of epic, in the form of the films of D.W. Griffith (*Birth of a Nation*, 1915) and westerns (John Wayne and Clint Eastwood are undeniably 'heroic' cowboys). Some have argued that Herman Melville's novel *Moby-Dick* (1851), which recounts Captain Ahab's doomed quest for the (mythic?) white whale, is not merely 'the Great American Novel' but 'the American Epic'. In modern polls George Lucas's *Star Wars* film series is often voted the great modern epic. But what we see here is less actual epics than the aching sense that the USA may have come too late on the world-scene ever to have one. A real one, that is. It still tries.

Traditionally, literary epic has four elements: it is long, heroic, nationalistic and – in its purest literary form – poetic. Panegyrics (extended hymns of praise) and lament (songs of sadness) are main ingredients. The first half of *Beowulf* is an extended celebration of the youthful hero's prowess in defeating Grendel and his mother. The second half laments Beowulf's death, in old age, having incurred fatal wounds in defeating the dragon that terrorises his kingdom. He has secured his country's future with his life. The death of the hero is, very often, a climax moment in epic narratives.

Typically, we may say, epic is set in a great age that has passed, at which later ages look back nostalgically, with the sad sense that epic greatness – heroism and honour – is a thing of the past, but that without it, we would not be where we are. It's the kind of complex feeling literature often elicits.

The great epics are still highly enjoyable to read, although most of us will be obliged to read them at one remove, in translation. In many ways, epics are literary dinosaurs. They once dominated, by virtue of sheer size, but now they belong in the museum of literature. We can still admire them, as we admire the other mighty works of our national ancestors, but, sadly, we seem no longer able to make them.

CHAPTER 4

Being Human
TRAGEDY

Tragedy, in its full literary form, represents a new highpoint (some would argue the highest ever reached) in the long evolution of literature: the imposition of 'form' on the raw materials of myth, legend and epic. Why do we still read and watch drama that was written 2,000 years ago, in a language few of us understand, for a society which might as well be on another planet for all the resemblance it has to ours? The answer is simple: tragedy has never been done better than when Aeschylus, Sophocles, Euripides and other ancient Greek dramatists did it.

What, though, do the terms 'tragedy' and 'tragic' actually mean? A jumbo-jet falls out of the sky. It happens rarely but, alas, it happens. Hundreds of passengers are killed in the event, which makes headlines in national newspapers. The *New York Times* has on its front page 'Tragic accident: 385 dead'. The *New York Daily News* has the more sensational 'Horror at 39,000 feet: Hundreds slain!' Neither headline would strike readers of either paper as unusual.

But, ask yourself, is a *horrible* event the same thing as a *tragic* event? This question was given exquisitely precise treatment in a play written some two-and-a-half millennia ago. The play was composed by Sophocles, who was writing for an Athenian audience. It would have been performed in the open air, in daylight, in an amphitheatre – a solid-stone 'theatre in the round' with raked seating – by actors wearing masks (called 'personae') and elevated footwear (called 'buskins'). The persona may have acted as a megaphone, and the buskins made the actors visible even to those in the very back seats. (The acoustics of the theatres where they performed were better than you will find on Broadway or in London's West End. If you go to the best-preserved of the ancient theatres, at Epidaurus, a guide will sit you in the farthest row of stone seats, go to the centre of the acting area, and strike a match. You can easily hear it.)

Sophocles' masterpiece, *Oedipus Rex* ('Oedipus the King'), recounts the following story, based on an ancient Greek myth. Things that happened in the past are now 'coming to a head'. It is foretold by a priestess at Delphi – famous for her power of foreseeing what is to come, but equally famous for the enigmatic nature of her prophesies – that a son, born to the king and queen of Thebes, Laius and Jocasta, will kill his father and marry his mother. The infant is destined to be a monster. Thebes will be better off without him – even though he is the couple's only child and his death will pose tricky problems as to who will be the next king. Baby Oedipus is put out on a mountainside to perish. But the baby does not die. He is rescued by a shepherd and, by a series of accidents, his true birth wholly unknown, he is eventually adopted by another king and queen, in Corinth. The gods seem to be taking an interest in him.

Grown to adulthood, Oedipus himself consults the oracle because he is worried that people are saying he is not his father's son. The oracle warns him that he is doomed to kill his father and to incestuously marry his mother. Assuming that the oracle is referring to his adoptive parents, Oedipus flees from Corinth and heads for Thebes. At a crossroads, he meets a chariot coming the other way. The charioteer pushes him off the road. Oedipus hits out at him, and in turn the other driver strikes Oedipus hard on the head. A furious fight ensues, and an enraged Oedipus kills the other man, not knowing that he is his father, Laius. It's road rage, a heat-of-the-moment deed.

Oedipus continues his journey to Thebes, unaware of what lies in wait for him. First is the Sphinx, a monster that lives on a mountain and is terrorising the city. The Sphinx poses a riddle to every traveller to Thebes. If they cannot answer correctly, they die. The riddle is: 'What walks on four feet in the morning, two in the afternoon and three at night?' Oedipus answers correctly, the first person ever to do so: it is 'man'. The baby crawls on all fours. The adult walks on two legs. The old man walks with a stick. The Sphinx kills itself. A grateful Thebes elects Oedipus their king. Once crowned, Oedipus consolidates his hold on the throne by marrying the mysteriously widowed Queen Jocasta. They are unaware, both of them, what has happened to Laius and the awful thing they are doing.

Oedipus proves to be a good king, a good husband, and a good father to the children he and Jocasta have. But, years later, a terrible and mysterious plague afflicts Thebes. Thousands die. Crops fail. Women cannot bear children. This is the point at which Sophocles' play begins. There is, clearly, another curse on the city. Why? A blind soothsayer, Tiresias, reveals the awful truth. The gods are punishing the city for Oedipus's crimes of patricide (killing his father) and incest (marrying his mother). The horrible details are finally disclosed. Jocasta hangs herself. Oedipus blinds himself with his wife's brooch-pins. He lives what remains of his life as a beggar, the lowest of the low in Thebes, attended in his wretchedness by his faithful daughter, Antigone.

To return to the question with which we started, what makes *Oedipus Rex* tragic, as opposed to merely horrible? Why is the death and suffering of all those unidentified Thebans not more tragic than the story of a single man who survives, albeit disabled and broken in spirit?

These questions were addressed by one of the greatest of literary critics, Aristotle, another ancient Greek. His study of tragedy – specifically *Oedipus Rex* – is called the *Poetics*. The title does not mean that Aristotle is exclusively concerned with poetry (although

Oedipus Rex and many of its translations are written in verse) but with what one could call the mechanics of literature: how it works. Aristotle sets out to answer that question, using *Oedipus Rex* as one of his main examples.

Aristotle begins with an illuminating paradox. Imagine, for example, the following. You meet a friend who is just coming out of a theatre showing Shakespeare's *King Lear* (a play strongly resembling *Oedipus Rex*). 'Did you enjoy it?' you ask. 'Yes,' she says, 'I've never enjoyed a play so much in my whole life.' 'You cold-hearted thing!' you retort. 'You enjoy the spectacle of one old man being tormented to death by his devilish daughters, another old man being blinded on stage. You tell me you *enjoyed* that? Perhaps you should go to a bullfight next time.'

It's nonsense, of course. Aristotle makes the point that it is not *what* is depicted in tragedy (the story) which affects us, and gives us aesthetic pleasure, but *how* it is depicted (the plot). What we enjoy (and it's quite correct to use the word) in *King Lear* is not the cruelty, but the art, the 'representation' (Aristotle calls it 'imitation', *mimesis*).

Aristotle helps us understand what it is that makes a play like *Oedipus Rex* work as tragedy. Take that word 'accident'. In tragedy, we are led to understand as the play progresses, there are no accidents. It is all foretold – which is why oracles and soothsayers are so central to the action. Everything fits and falls into place. We may not see that at the time, but we will later. As Aristotle puts it, when we see a tragedy acted the events should strike us as 'necessary and probable' as they unfold. What happens in tragedy *must* happen. But actually seeing what lies behind the unfolding of the predestined course of events is, typically, too much for flesh and blood to bear. When Oedipus sees how things have worked out, because he now understands, they *had* to work out that way, he fulfils another of the soothsayer's claims – that he is (metaphorically) blind – by literally blinding himself. Humankind cannot bear too much reality.

With Aristotle's assistance we can take apart Sophocles' perfectly constructed tragedy, as a mechanic might dismantle an automobile engine. Tragedy, he decrees, must address itself to personal histories of noble men, who actually existed. Royalty is an ideal subject (there was, in earlier times, actually a king called Oedipus). The idea of a slave or a woman being a tragic hero is, Aristotle says, absurd. The tragic play, Aristotle insists, must concentrate our attention on 'process' – there must be no distractions. Any violence must take place off-stage and, ideally, the tragedy must – as in *Oedipus Rex* – narrate the final phase of the tragic process. Tragedy is concerned with what in chess is called the 'endgame': consequences.

The modern French playwright Jean Anouilh (1910–87), discussing his adaptation of another of Sophocles' plays (about Oedipus's daughter, Antigone), described the tragic plot as a 'machine', all the component parts working with each other to produce the final effect, like the 'movement' of a Swiss watch. What gets the machinery moving? Aristotle says that there must be a trigger and the tragic hero must pull it. He calls that trigger *hamartia* which is usually translated, awkwardly, as 'an error in judgement'. Oedipus triggers the tragedy that will ultimately destroy him by losing his temper and killing that infuriating stranger at the crossroads. He is hot-headed (so is Laius, his father – it runs in the family). That is his *hamartia*, or error in judgement, which starts the machine, just as a key starts the engine in a car – a car that drives off and has a fatal crash. It is terrifying because we all are guilty of such errors in our everyday lives.

Aristotle is particularly shrewd on how the audience collaborates, if the play is working as it should, in the full experience of tragic performance. He notes how emotionally powerful tragedy can be – pregnant women have been known to give premature birth, he says, while watching tragedy, so overwhelming was the tragic effect. The specific emotions that tragedy brings about, he says, are 'pity and fear'. Pity, that is, for the tragic hero's suffering, and fear because, if it happens to the tragic hero, it can happen to anyone – even us.

The most controversial of Aristotle's arguments is his theory of *catharsis*. This word is untranslatable (we usually use Aristotle's own term) and it is best understood as a 'tempering of the emotions'. Let's go back to our audience leaving the theatre after watching a tragedy like *King Lear* or *Oedipus Rex*, performed well. The mood will be sober, reflective – people will be in a sense exhausted by what they have seen on stage. But also strangely elevated, as if they had gone through something like a religious experience.

We don't have to take everything Aristotle says as critical gospel – let's say he gives us a toolkit. But why does *Oedipus Rex* still work for us, separated as we are by all those centuries? We don't, for example, agree for a minute with Aristotle's social views on slaves and women, or his political views that only kings, queens and the nobility matter in the history of nations.

There are two plausible answers. One is that the play is so wonderfully well constructed. It is a thing of aesthetic beauty – like the Parthenon, or the Taj Mahal or a Da Vinci painting. Secondly, although the store of human knowledge has expanded hugely, life and the human condition are still very mysterious to the thinking person. Tragedy confronts that mystery, examines the big questions: What is life all about? What makes us human? In its aims, tragedy is the most ambitious of literary genres. Aristotle has no doubt that it is, as he tells us, the 'noblest'.

CHAPTER 5

English Tales
CHAUCER

English literature – as we know it – starts with Geoffrey Chaucer (*c.* 1343–1400), 700 years ago. But I'll rephrase that sentence. Not 'English literature' but 'literature in English' starts with Chaucer. It was a long time before England had a language that unified the speech and writing practice of the whole population – and Chaucer marks the point where we can see it happening, around the fourteenth century.

Compare the two following quotations. They are the opening lines of two great poems written, in what we now think of as England, at almost exactly the same time, toward the end of the fourteenth century:

> Forþi an aunter in erde I attle to schawe,
> Þat a selly in siȝt summe men hit holden …

> When that Aprilis, with his showers swoot,
> The drought of March hath pierced to the root …

The first quotation is by someone known only as the 'Gawain Poet', and is the opening of *Sir Gawain and the Green Knight*, a semi-mythic tale set in the reign of King Arthur (discussed in Chapter 2). The second is by Chaucer and is the opening couplet of *The Canterbury Tales*.

Most readers – unfamiliar with Anglo-Saxon poetic diction, its two-stress rhythms, half-lines and vocabulary sometimes as alien as Klingon – will make heavy weather of the *Gawain* example. Only a few of the words hint that it is a kind of English. The second extract (with the information that 'swoot' means 'sweet') is, for the modern reader, broadly understandable – as is the whole poem, its rhymes and rhythms. With a few words translated for us, most of us can handle the poem in the various early forms in which it was transcribed. And it's more enjoyable in the original. It speaks to us, as we say.

Fine poem though *Gawain* is, its retention of the language and style of Old English stands at a literary dead end. Those people to whom it once spoke are long gone. There was no future for writing like that – beautiful as the poem is to those today who trouble to learn the dialect in which it is written. Chaucer's 'new' English is at the threshold of centuries of great literature to come. He was hailed as 'Dan' Chaucer by his follower, the great Elizabethan poet Edmund Spenser – 'Dan' is short for Dominus, 'Master'. The leader of the pack. Chaucer was, Spenser said, 'the source of English undefiled'. He gave our literature its language. And he himself was the first to do great things with it, opening the way for others to do great things.

It is significant that we know who Chaucer actually was and can see him, as we read, in our mind's eye. Literature, after him, has 'authors'. We do not know who composed *Beowulf*. It was probably the work of many anonymous hands and minds. Nor do we know who the 'Gawain Poet' was. It could have been more than one person. Who knows?

Much had changed in the regional kingdoms and fiefdoms (estates controlled by lords) of Britain during the half-century that separates *Beowulf* from *The Canterbury Tales*. It wasn't just

'English' that had happened, but 'England' itself. The British Isles were conquered by William, Duke of Normandy, in 1066. 'The Conqueror', as he is called, brought with him the apparatus of what we recognise as the modern state. The Normans continued the unification of the land they had invaded, installing an official language, a system of common law, coinage, a class system, Parliament, London as the capital city, and other institutions, many of which have come down to us today. Chaucer was this new England's pioneer author, and his English was the London dialect. One can still hear the old rhythms and vocabularies of Anglo-Saxon literature, even in his verse, but it is subterranean, like a drumbeat reaching us from vibrations in the ground.

So who was this man? He was born Geoffroy de Chaucer, his family name derived from the French *chausseur*, or 'shoemaker'. The family had, over the centuries, risen well above the cobbler level and their Norman-French origins. In Geoffrey's time they had connections with, and received favours from, the court. Luckily, under Edward III the country was more or less at peace – although occasional forays were made into France, now a foe with whom England would be at odds for 500 years. Geoffrey's father was in the import/export wine trade. This line of work meant intimate contact with continental Europe, whose literatures (well ahead of England's at the time) would later be drawn on extensively by Geoffrey.

Chaucer may have officially or unofficially attended one of the great universities or he may have received his impressive education from home tutors. We don't know. What is clear is that he came into manhood extraordinarily well read and fluent in several languages. As a young man he craved adventure and embarked on a military career. (One of his two great poems, *Troilus and Criseyde*, is set in the background of the greatest war in literature – that between the Greeks and Trojans.) In France the young English soldier was taken prisoner and ransomed. In later life his favourite thinker was the Roman poet Boethius who wrote his great treatise, *The Consolation of Philosophy*, in prison. Chaucer translated it from the original Latin, partly via a French version, into English, and absorbed its thinking, particularly on the uncertainty of 'fortune' – life's ups and downs.

On his return from the wars he married and settled down. His wife, Philippa, was nobly born and brought him money as well as status. His private life is a matter of persistent debate. From his often bawdy writings, however, we can assume that Geoffrey Chaucer was not puritanical by nature. The term 'Chaucerian' has become proverbial for someone who enjoys life to the full.

His early career was assisted by friends at court. Patronage was how you got on in those days. In 1367 the king settled a generous life pension of twenty marks on him for his service as 'our beloved Valet' (courtier). Today we would call Chaucer a civil servant. In the early 1370s he was employed in the king's service abroad. He may well have met the great Italian writers, Petrarch and Boccaccio, in Italy – then the literary capital of the modern world. Both would go on to be major influences on his own writing.

In the mid-1370s Chaucer was appointed Controller of Customs in the Port of London. This was the highpoint of his professional life. Had he continued to rise in the world it is unlikely that we would have *The Canterbury Tales*. But in the 1380s, his fortunes declined. His friends and patrons could no longer help him. Now a widower, and out of favour at court, he retired to Kent, where he wrote *The Canterbury Tales*, his great Kentish poem. He had, at this stage of his life, apparently nothing to do but enjoy life as best he could in his provincial retirement.

The Canterbury Tales and *Troilus and Criseyde* are two supremely great poems. Both were momentously innovative. They changed literature. *Troilus* takes Homer's great epic, the *Iliad*, which Chaucer had picked up from Italian sources, and turns the war story into a love story – a full-blown romance. While the great battle rages outside the walls of Troy, one of the Trojan princes, Troilus, falls madly in love with a widow, Criseyde. Their relationship – as the code of 'courtly love' requires – must be kept secret from the world, in part to preserve its purity. She, however, betrays him. It destroys Troilus. Affairs of the heart, the poem intimates, can even overshadow great wars. How many future plays, poems and novels can we see anticipated in that plot?

The Canterbury Tales remains, for modern readers, the best entry-point into Chaucer. Its format was in all likelihood taken from a more modern source than that for *Troilus*, Boccaccio's *Decameron*, in which ten refugees from plague-ravaged Florence tell each other tales (100 of them, no less) to while away the weary days of their quarantine. *The Decameron* is written in prose. *The Canterbury Tales*, although most of it is written in easy-flowing verse, can, like Boccaccio's book, be read now as a kind of early novel – or bundle of small novels. (See Chapter 12 for more on early novelish works in literature.)

Each of Chaucer's tales is entertaining in its own way, and together they compose a small world, or 'microcosmos'. The eighteenth-century poet, John Dryden (England's first poet laureate – see Chapter 22), said it contained 'God's Plenty'. All life is there, from the lofty courtly love woes of 'The Knight's Tale' through the bawdy high jinks of the lower-class pilgrims' stories, to the orthodox religious advice given by the Parson. Unfortunately not all the poem is there, in the text we now have. Chaucer wrote his poem a century before the invention of printing presses. We have the poem in imperfect form as it survived in various manuscript transcriptions, none by Chaucer himself.

The narrative opens in April 1387. Twenty-nine pilgrims (including Chaucer, who remains entirely on the edge of things) gather at the Tabard Inn on the south bank of the Thames in London. They intend to make the four-day, 100-odd-mile 'pilgrimage', by horse, in company, to the tomb of the martyr Thomas Becket in Canterbury Cathedral. Their host at the inn, Harry Bailey, appoints himself their guide on the journey, and – to foster togetherness and harmony – decrees that each of the pilgrims shall tell two stories on the way to Kent, and two on the way back. This would mean around 116 tales. That design was never completed, and perhaps it was never meant to be or, more likely, that Chaucer died before he had the chance. What has come to us are twenty-four tales, some fragmentary. It's tantalising, but more than enough to get a sense of the work's huge achievement.

Chaucer's pilgrims comprise a mirror of society at the time –

strikingly, in many of its features, like our own society. It is not a 'Christian' poem, despite its being centred on an act of devotion. The point Chaucer makes is that Christianity is a flexible creed which can contain all types of people in a generally secular social framework. You can be both 'worldly' and 'religious'. Not every day of the week is Sunday. At the time Chaucer was writing, it probably seemed a radically new idea.

Among the pilgrims are a number of ecclesiastics (church people), male and female: a Friar, a Monk, a Prioress, a Summoner, a Pardoner (whom Chaucer particularly despises for 'selling' forgiveness of sins) and a Parson (whom Chaucer reveres). These churchmen and women do not, on the whole, much like each other. Nor is the reader led to like all of them.

At the bottom of the social heap are a Cook, a Reeve (a land agent), a Miller and a Shipman (a common sailor). A notch above them are a Merchant and a Franklin – members of the emergent bourgeois class. Both are rich. Likely even richer (well-off enough to have made three trips to Jerusalem) is the 'Wife of Bath'. A self-made woman, she has prospered by the manufacture of cloth (*toile de Nîmes* – denim). A veteran widow of five marriages, both battered and educated by her husbands, she is female pluck personified. A feisty woman, she picks fights with her fellow pilgrims (notably the celibate Clerk) on the subject of marriage. She knows more than most about that particular institution – precisely five times more than the Clerk.

Above this mercantile 'middle class' are members of what we would now call the professions: a doctor (the Physician), a lawyer (the Man of Law) and an academic (the Clerk – someone who makes a living with his reading and writing skills). Each of the pilgrims is sharply characterised in the 'General Prologue' and a shorter prologue to each tale. They live vividly in the reader's imagination. In the overall structure of the tales there emerge a number of debates: on marriage (should a wife be submissive or assertive?), on destiny (how can this pagan concept be combined with Christianity?) and on love (does it – as the Prioress's motto puts it – 'conquer all'?).

The pilgrim of highest 'degree' (social class) and, for that reason, the first tale-teller, is the Knight. His tale, set in ancient Greece, steeped in the codes of courtly love and Boethius's ideas about patiently suffering all misfortune, is appropriately 'chivalrous' – that is, knightly. It is followed, almost immediately, by a *fabliau*, or bawdy tale, told by the Miller. The love he chronicles, about an old carpenter, his young wife, and some mischievous young men, is anything but courtly. Texts of *The Canterbury Tales* were routinely censored for young readers until well into the twentieth century (including my own school copy, as I still, somewhat resentfully, recall).

Many changes are rung throughout the two-dozen tales, concluding, appropriately, with a high-minded and earnest sermon by the Parson, after which the reader can depart in peace and having been thoroughly entertained. Dryden was right. All life is there. Our life as well.

CHAPTER 6

Theatre on the Street
THE MYSTERY PLAYS

In the late fifteenth and early sixteenth centuries the world of literature saw the emergence of both printing and the modern theatre. These two great machineries, the page and the stage, would be where great literature happened over the next four centuries. In this chapter we shall look at the early stirrings of drama in England. Not on the stage but in the streets of England's most vibrant towns.

Where does theatre *really* begin? If you asked Aristotle, he would have said, look at your children. It originates in the make-up, or wiring, of human beings themselves. It's one of the things that makes us human. In the third chapter of his great critical treatise, his *Poetics* (see Chapter 4), he writes:

> Imitation is natural to man from childhood, one of his advantages over the lower animals being this, that he is the most imitative creature in the world, and learns at first by imitation. And it is also natural for all to delight in works of imitation.

By 'imitation' (*mimesis*) he means 'play-acting'. When an actor comes on stage as, say, Richard III, he is pretending to be that character. He is not the king whose body was dug up in a car park in Leicester in 2013. And that pretence, or 'imitation', is at the very heart of drama. It points to one of the strangest aspects of theatrical experience – for those on both sides of the footlights.

Of course we know, if we think about it, that Ian McKellen or Al Pacino (both of whom have played Richard III to huge applause) are who they are, while they are (the word 'are' gets slippery at this point) the Richard III they are 'playing'. We know the actor is McKellen or Pacino, and so does he. But while we are watching the play are we, the audience, 'carried away'? Do we, as the poet, critic and philosopher Samuel Taylor Coleridge put it, in a wonderful phrase, 'suspend disbelief' – choose to be fooled? Deliberately 'not know' what we know? Or do we remain aware of the fact that we are sitting in a cinema or theatre, with other people, watching a person with make-up on their face reciting words written by someone else? It depends on the play you are watching. But the point to be made is that our experience of drama also requires certain skills in us, as the audience, as to how to respond, appreciate and judge the performance. The more you go to the theatre, the better you get at it.

Theatres began long before the erection of the great wooden structures on London's south bank in Shakespeare's day, with their grand names like the Globe and the Rose. These new Thameside theatres could hold up to 1,500 people – most standing. But the theatre which preceded them, and the plays that were put on, had audiences of tens of thousands and entertained whole populations in the streets, both standing and walking.

Plays depicting biblical stories moved outside to the streets in several European countries in the Middle Ages. In England they were called 'mystery' plays. The French word was *mystère*, but in England 'mystery' could also mean your trade or profession, from the French word *métier*. The plays evolved out of popularised religious ritual, particularly what happened at Easter when, traditionally, congregations were free to 'enact' large parts of the service. They peaked in popularity in the period before Shakespeare and his fellow dramatists came on the scene.

It was the guilds (the early trade unions) which sponsored and performed in the mystery plays. They sprang up in the prosperous towns and cities of an increasingly urbanised England – at a time when all emerging European countries were becoming more urban – but outside the hugely urbanised capital. They were 'provincial' not 'metropolitan'. This tension in literature between what is produced by London (England's literary and theatrical 'world', as it likes to think of itself) and places outside London ('the sticks', as some Londoners like to call it), is with us to the present day. The mystery plays were very 'outside London'. And proud of it.

In England's large cities the guilds nurtured the skills (and tricks) of their trades. Membership was strictly controlled. Members tended to be literate as well as skilled. The bulk of the population at the time was not (or at best was semi-) literate. The guilds passed their skills on through a master-apprentice system which survives to present times. They also held a monopoly over trades – you couldn't, for example, work as a builder ('mason') or a carpenter unless you belonged to the right guild and paid your 'dues'. So they became rich and powerful. But they retained a strong sense of civic duty to the communities that had made them rich and powerful.

In the medieval period the most important Book was the Bible. Without it, for people of the time, existence was meaningless. But much of the population could not read their own language, let alone the Latin of the standard Bible. Books were still hugely expensive even after the invention of printing in the late fifteenth century. The guilds took it on themselves to evangelise – spread the good word – by street entertainment. Drama served that purpose perfectly.

Annually, on some particular holy day in the Christian calendar (usually the feast of Corpus Christi), dramatic 'cycles' (that is, the whole biblical narrative) would be staged. Each guild would sponsor a wagon, or 'float'. Typically they would choose an episode from the Bible which fitted with their profession. The pinners (nail-makers), for example, would tell the story of the crucifixion, while the bargemen might tell the story of Noah and the Flood. The established Church was generally tolerant of all this. Indeed some clergymen, who would have been by far and away the most literate members of their community, probably helped write the plays. The guild stored lavish costumes, props and scripts for repeated use. Prompt-copies have survived for several of the city-based cycles, notably those of York, Chester and Wakefield.

The mystery plays were immensely popular in their day – and it was, historically, a fairly long day: two centuries long. There is no question but that the young Shakespeare saw them during his childhood in Stratford, enjoyed them, and was influenced by them for the rest of his life. He occasionally refers to them in his plays as something his audience would have been familiar with as well.

A particularly fine example of the mystery-play genre is the *Second Shepherds' Play* in the Wakefield Cycle. It is not a catchy title, but it is great drama, early as it may be. It was probably composed around 1475 and performed, with elaborations and topical adaptations, for many decades thereafter annually on the feast of Corpus Christi in May or June. The Yorkshire town of Wakefield was enriched in the Middle Ages by the wool and leather trades. Sheep and cattle grazed on the grassy hills around the town, which had good communication with the rest of the country and could get its wares to markets in the big cities. Wakefield also had a reputation for particularly enjoying itself at fairs and other public events and was nicknamed 'Merry Wakefield'. The citizens liked a good laugh, and the *Second Shepherds' Play* supplied it.

The entire Wakefield mystery cycle encompasses thirty plays, beginning with the Creation in Genesis and winding up with the hanging of Judas in the New Testament gospels. There are two shepherds' plays, celebrating the product (wool) that was the town's principal source of prosperity. The second play opens with three shepherds on the Bethlehem hills (definitely Yorkshire rather than Palestine hills) watching their sheep by night.

December is a bitterly cold month to be out tending sheep. The first shepherd angrily bemoans the weather, and goes on to rail against the oppressions, including taxes, that poor folk like them-selves must bear while the rich are snug, well-fed and warm in their beds. (Taxes were imposed by the guilds as well as the town authorities. It's a little in-joke.)

> We're so burdened and banned,
> Over-taxed and unmanned,
> We're made tame to the hand
> Of these gentry men.
> Thus they rob us of our rest, may ill-luck them harry!
> These men, they make the plough tarry,
> What men say is for the best, we find the contrary –
> Thus are husbandmen oppressed, in point to miscarry,
> In life,
> Thus hold they us under
> And from comfort sunder.

It's an extraordinary outburst. And it speaks to us with a directness and force which carries across the centuries and resonates to the present day. Talk to citizens standing outside the job centre in Wakefield today and they might well complain in much the same way as does their distant predecessor, the first shepherd. And certainly with the same rich Yorkshire accent.

The play, however, does not continue in this angry vein. There follows a hilariously comic episode. Mak, another shepherd, has stolen one of the lambs that his three comrades have been out all night guarding, frozen to their bones. Mak takes his booty home and hides it in a crib, disguising it as a newborn baby.

The other shepherds come to Mak's cottage (like the three kings in the biblical story) to give the baby a silver piece – a very sizeable sum for them. After much comic knockabout they discover what exactly the 'newborn' in the crib is. Sheep-stealing was a capital crime, punishable by death (hence the proverb, 'As well be hung for a sheep as a lamb'). But it is Christmas, a time for the forgiveness of sins. That mercy, the play implies, is what Christ died for. The shepherds merely toss Mak in a blanket.

The play then reverts to familiar religious doctrine. The Angel of the Lord appears and instructs the three good shepherds to worship the true newborn, who is lying between two animals in a Bethlehem manger.

The *Second Shepherds' Play* is a highpoint of this pioneering form of street theatre. But the same energy, vivacity and 'voice of the people' animates all the cycles. They died out, as a vital part of town life, in the late 1500s and there is some uncertainty as to why. One reason may be that reformers never liked them. Did they evolve into something much greater than themselves, the London theatre of the seventeenth century, dominated as it would be by Shakespeare? Or did they wither away under the pressures of urbanisation, mass movements of population, the decay of the guild system, the construction of permanent theatres ('out of the wet') in towns, and easier access to the Bible in its printed form? The Bible found other ways of getting to the people over the following centuries. Mystery plays were no longer needed.

Whatever the answer, there is one important conclusion to be drawn from the two-centuries-long flowering of this street theatre. Namely the fact that the way in which we respond to literature on the stage – whether that stage is a trundling procession of carts or the boards of a modern theatre – is very different from the way in which we respond to printed literature on the page.

You can pick up a book any time and put it down when you want. It is different in a theatre: the curtain goes up at a precise moment and comes down at specifically timed intervals. The audience does not move from its seats while watching the play. People, even in the twenty-first century, tend to 'dress up' to go to the theatre. They generally do not, as when watching TV, eat meals or talk during the performance; if you so much as rustle sweet wrappers, or, worse still, your mobile goes off, you will get furious glances. The audience tends to break into laughter at the same moments and they applaud at the end.

Not to labour the point, but all this reminds us that we are in a kind of church. Congregation, audience – what's the difference? Reading – 'curled up with a book' – is one of our most private activities but in a theatre we consume literature publicly: as a community. We experience and respond collectively. That's a great part of the pleasure of theatre. We are in company.

Some of the mystery plays that have come down to us, like the *Second Shepherds' Play*, are as great, in their way, as anything in the history of British drama. But most of the mystery-play material is, for the modern playgoer, of more historical than literary interest. Nonetheless, it has huge significance. It reminds us where theatre started and what fuels its lasting appeal. Even today, although we no longer have to stand out in the street to enjoy it, drama is 'community' literature. Literature of the people.

CHAPTER 7

The Bard

SHAKESPEARE

Any poll to decide the greatest writer in the English language would come up with the same result. No contest. But how did Shakespeare come to be so? A simple question, but it admits of no simple answer.

Some of the best literary-critical minds in history (not to say generations of theatre-goers) have tried, but no one has been able to explain convincingly how an early school-leaver, the son of a high-street tradesman, born and brought up in the backwater of Stratford-upon-Avon, whose principal interest in his career seems to have been gathering enough money to retire, became the greatest writer the English-speaking world has known, and, many argue, ever will know.

We shall never be able to 'explain' Shakespeare and it's foolish to try. But we can certainly appreciate his achievement and – although the picture is infuriatingly incomplete – we can trace the outline of his life for any hints it might give as to what made him the greatest writer in the English language.

William Shakespeare (1564–1616) was born some six years into the reign of Queen Elizabeth I. The England he grew up in was still in the throes of the turmoil left by the reign of the previous monarch, Mary I, nicknamed 'Bloody Mary'. Under her it had been dangerous to be Protestant, under Elizabeth it was dangerous to be Catholic. Shakespeare, like others in his family, cautiously walked a tightrope between the two faiths (although some people want to claim him as a lifelong secret Catholic). He kept strictly off the subject of religion in his drama. It was literally a burning topic – say the wrong thing and you could burn at the stake.

At the centre of this burning issue was the question of who would succeed to the throne. As Shakespeare entered the dramatic profession, Elizabeth, born in 1533, was an ageing monarch. The Virgin Queen had no heir elect nor even a clearly apparent heir. A vacuum in the succession was dangerous. Every thinking person in the country asked themselves the question, 'What comes after Queen Elizabeth?'

The most significant political question in much of Shakespeare's drama (particularly in the history plays) is: 'What is the best way to replace one king (or, in Cleopatra's case, queen) with another?' Different answers are examined in different plays: secret assassination (*Hamlet*); public assassination (*Julius Caesar*); civil war (the *Henry VI* plays); forced abdication (*Richard II*); usurpation (*Richard III*); legitimate bloodline succession (*Henry V*). It was a problem Shakespeare wrestled with until his last play (as we think it is), *Henry VIII*. England itself would wrestle with the problem a lot longer and would undergo the horrors of a civil war while trying to find a way through.

Shakespeare's father was a moderately prosperous glove-maker and alderman in Stratford. He was probably more inclined to Catholicism than his son. William's mother, Mary, was higher-born than her husband. She, we may assume, planted a desire to rise in the world in the mind of her clever son. Young William attended the Stratford grammar school. Ben Jonson, a fellow dramatist (and friend) famously cracked that Shakespeare had 'small Latin, and less Greek'. But by our standards he was formidably well educated.

He left school in his teens and for a year or two probably worked for his father. He may have been arrested for poaching.

Aged eighteen he married a local woman, Anne Hathaway, who was eight years older and several months pregnant. The marriage would produce two daughters and a son, Hamnet, who died in infancy and who is commemorated in Shakespeare's most famous, and gloomy, play.

It has been argued that the Shakespeares' marriage was unhappy – the recurrence in the plays of difficult, cold and domineering women such as Lady Macbeth is cited as evidence, as is the fact that the couple had, for the time, few children (three). But the fact is we know little of Shakespeare's private life. Even more frustratingly, we know absolutely nothing about the remainder of his formative years, between 1585 and 1592. He may have left Stratford and found employment as a country schoolteacher. Another theory about the so-called 'lost years' is that he was in the north of England, working as a tutor for a noble Catholic family, absorbing their dangerous creed. A third speculation is that he joined a troupe of travelling players, and picked up the dramatic skills evident in even his very earliest plays.

He resurfaces in the early 1590s as a rising figure in the London theatre scene, writing plays and acting. He found a medium suited to his extraordinary talent. There was a thriving network of theatres on the south bank of the Thames alongside the bull-baiting arenas and taverns – outlaw territory compared with the north bank, with its inns of court, St Paul's Cathedral, Parliament, and royal residences.

Just as importantly, there was an existing, but still immature, literary medium for Shakespeare to adapt to his own huge talent. His predecessor Christopher Marlowe (1564–93), in plays such as *Dr Faustus*, had innovated the so-called 'mighty line': blank verse. What is it? Consider the following lines – probably the most famous lines in English literature. (Hamlet is thinking about killing himself, unable to bring himself to do what the ghost, his father, has told him to do – kill his stepfather.)

To be, or not to be, that is the question:
Whether 'tis Nobler in the mind to suffer

The Slings and Arrows of outrageous Fortune,
Or to take Arms against a Sea of troubles,
And by opposing end them …

The verse is unrhymed (hence 'blank'). It has the suppleness of everyday speech, but the dignity ('mightiness') of poetry – tease out, for example, the complexity of 'taking arms against a sea of troubles'. It's also something that Shakespeare handled particularly brilliantly – a 'soliloquy': that is, someone totally by themselves, talking to themselves. But is Hamlet actually talking, or thinking? In his 1948 film adaptation of the play, Laurence Olivier (the greatest Shakespearian actor of his time) did it as voice-over, his lips not moving, his face locked in a fixed expression. Shakespeare perfected this way of getting inside the minds of characters on stage. All his great plays – particularly the tragedies – hinge on soliloquy: what is going on inside.

By 1594 Shakespeare had risen to the top of the London theatrical world – as an actor, a shareholder, but most spectacularly as a playwright who was changing the whole idea of what plays could do. He would go on to live for many years in London (his family meanwhile were kept out of the way in distant Stratford), dabbling at times in commerce and adding substantially to his net worth. Over a twenty-year career he penned some thirty-seven plays (occasionally with collaborators) as well as many poems. Notable among the latter is his sonnet sequence, composed in the 1590s – probably during a summer when the open-air theatres were shut, as they often were, during outbreaks of plague.

The sonnets offer rare insights into Shakespeare the man. Many are addressed as love poems to a young man, others to a possibly married woman ('the Dark Lady'). It's possible Shakespeare may have been bisexual, as – it is sometimes argued – he was both Catholic and Protestant in religion. That is something else we shall never be entirely sure about.

Shakespeare's drama moves through identifiable phases, although exact dates of composition and performance of individual plays are uncertain; as are the texts of his plays – none was printed under his supervision in his lifetime. Earliest in his artistic career are the history plays, concerned primarily with the so-called 'Wars of the Roses', the previous century's conflict for the English throne that was finally won by Elizabeth's Tudor forebears.

Shakespeare, in making brilliant drama (still in his twenties), falsifies history outrageously. His magnificent Macchiavellian Richard III, for example, is nothing like the actual historical monarch. 'Good drama, bad history' is the motto of the Shakespeare package. He was always aware, too, of pleasing the monarch: a Scottish king comes to the throne, on Elizabeth's death, in 1603? Soon after, Shakespeare produces a fine play about Scottish kings, *Macbeth*, pandering, at the same time, to James I's known fascination with witchery.

Shakespeare's mid-career comedies are, all of them, set outside England. Italy and the imaginary Illyria are typical locations. They are, among much else, noteworthy for the space they give powerful women (Beatrice in *Much Ado About Nothing* comes to mind). On the other hand there are things, even in the sprightly early comedies, which the modern audience finds hard to swallow. Along with feisty Beatrice there is Kate, in *The Taming of the Shrew*, who is humiliated and brutalised into wifely subservience (forced, publicly, once 'tamed', to be willing to place her hand beneath her husband's foot). Quite literally, trampled on.

It's hard, too, to be entirely comfortable with the 'happy ending' of *The Merchant of Venice* in which the Jew, Shylock, finds his daughter abducted (by a gentile lover) and his wealth forfeited, and is forced to convert – in the face of losing everything – to Christianity. It takes some very fine poetry indeed to make us happy with those resolutions as good ones.

Shakespeare was fascinated by the Roman Republic – a state without kings or queens. That particular issue (touching on his unceasing interest in monarchy) is chewed over – without easy solution – in *Julius Caesar*. Caesar seems likely to become ruler: to protect the republic, is Brutus ('the noblest Roman of them all') morally right to assassinate him? *Coriolanus* sets up a similar problem: would the warrior-hero be right to invade Rome in order to save Rome? Is rebellion right or wrong? Shakespeare never quite decided (it's right in *Richard II*, for example, but wrong in *Henry IV*). In *Antony and Cleopatra* Marc Antony gives up a world empire for love: is 'the world well lost', or is he a lovesick fool?

So wonderful are Shakespeare's middle- and late-period plays – such as *Much Ado About Nothing* and *Measure for Measure*, in which he seems to be redefining drama as well as writing it – that sceptics have wondered how a man who left school in his early teens (not a famous school, at that) could possibly have written them. Other candidates have been suggested, drawing on the little we know about Shakespeare's life. None of the 'alternative Shakespeares' is, however, plausible. The balance of proof remains in favour of the glove-maker's son from Stratford. The genres Shakespeare cultivated in his maturity – comedies, tragedies, problem plays, Roman plays and romances – show a gradual progression in language and plot complexity. And, in the comedies particularly, a darkening of mood.

In 1610, at the height of his career (and still in his forties) Shakespeare, now wealthy, retired from London to live as a gentleman in his native Stratford, proudly displaying his family coat of arms. Alas, he did not live long. He died in 1616, probably of typhus – although a popular (and improbable) legend suggests alcohol as the cause of his premature demise.

The towering achievement of Shakespeare's art are the four tragedies: *Macbeth*, *King Lear*, *Hamlet* and *Othello*. Their greatness, too, is coloured by the ever darkening cloud of gloom that hangs over Shakespeare's late period, possibly the effect of having lost his only son, Hamnet, in 1596. Take, for example, Macbeth's final soliloquy, as he realises he faces his final battle:

> Life's but a walking shadow, a poor player,
> That struts and frets his hour upon the stage,
> And then is heard no more. It is a tale
> Told by an idiot, full of sound and fury,
> Signifying nothing.

It's wonderfully complicated. Here is an actor telling us – as Shakespeare says elsewhere – that the world is a stage: just like the Globe. That bleak negativity of the last word ('nothing'), which hits the ear like a door slamming, is echoed in the most tragic of the tragedies when the aged Lear – himself on the brink of death – comes on stage carrying the corpse of his beloved daughter, Cordelia, in his arms:

> And my poor fool is hang'd! No, no, no life!
> Why should a dog, a horse, a rat, have life,
> And thou no breath at all? Thou'lt come no more,
> Never, never, never, never, never!

The five-times repeated word would, in other contexts, be wholly banal, banal, banal, banal, banal. The dreadful climax of *King Lear* it is so powerful that the greatest Shakespearian critic we have had, Samuel Johnson, could not bear to watch the scene in the theatre nor read it on the page.

Is Shakespeare the greatest writer of the English-speaking world? Indubitably. But he is not, taken in the round, the easiest, or the most comfortable. That, of course, is part of the greatness.

CHAPTER 8

The Book of Books
THE KING JAMES BIBLE

Although we do not automatically think of it as literature, nor is it normally read in that spirit, the King James Bible is the most-read work in the English literary canon. (The word 'canon', incidentally, comes from the Roman Catholic Church's catalogue of 'works which ought to be read'. The Church also drew up a stricter catalogue of books which must *not* be read – the *Index Librorum Prohibitorum*.)

The King James Bible (KJB) is still, worldwide, the most popular version of the Bible. Every American motel has one, in the bedside drawer, thanks to the indefatigable Gideons Society. But it's not simply the fact that it is so easily come by. What has made the KJB a Bible of first choice is that it is so wonderfully written. It was first published in 1611 – around the same time as Shakespeare's great tragedies. It, like them, stands as an example of the English language at its highest pitch of eloquence, subtlety and beauty. It can be admired for that reason, even by those who are not religious, or even atheists. There have been many other translations of the Bible – some, admittedly, are more accurate than the KJB and more up-to-date in their vocabulary. But the KJB, uniquely, is the one version that has universally been valued for its expression. And that expression – even more than Shakespeare's – has soaked into our own expression and, it could be argued, even our ways of thinking.

What is meant by the 'literary quality' of the KJB is easier shown than described. Compare the following lines – they are among the best known in the New Testament and come from the Lord's Prayer, as set down by Matthew. The first is from the KJB, the second from one of the most recent American translations of the Gospels.

> Our Father which art in heaven, Hallowed be thy name.
> Thy kingdom come. Thy will be done in earth, as it is in heaven.
> Give us this day our daily bread.
> And forgive us our debts, as we forgive our debtors.

> Our Father in heaven, help us to honor your name.
> Come and set up your kingdom, so that everyone on earth
> will obey you, as you are obeyed in heaven.
> Give us our food for today.
> Forgive us for doing wrong, as we forgive others.

There are clear differences of meaning here. Is 'doing wrong' the same as 'debts'? Legally, they are not. You can be in debt (with a mortgage, for example) but doing no wrong. Obviously it is a personal judgement as to which translation works best for you. But no one with any 'ear' for literary quality would deny that the first quotation is the more beautiful of the two, by any standard of literary judgement. Moreover, it evokes images: 'Give us this day our daily bread' is 'visual' in a way that 'Give us our food for today' just isn't.

One reason we may find it hard to think of the KJB as literature is because it was produced by what we would call a committee. The KJB is known as the 'authorised' version, but it was not 'authored'. Nonetheless, as a little investigation makes clear, there was a single genius behind it – what Shakespeare would call 'an onlie begetter'.

And it was not, despite the title of the book, King James. Who that author was we shall come to in a moment.

The publication of the King James Bible in English was motivated principally by politics. It would, James hoped, consolidate the Reformation – England's break-away from the Roman Catholic Church – by supplying a core text for Protestant worship that was starkly different from Rome's Latin Bible and religious service. It would stabilise the country while asserting its independence from the Pope. It would be the 'English' Bible, and in the best English that England could manage.

Before the sixteenth century, the Bible was only available in Latin. Most Christians had to take what they were told on trust. Martin Luther, who published the first reliable vernacular (meaning in the language of the people) version of the New Testament in Germany in 1522, believed that the Bible should be the property of all men and women. Trust God, not the self-appointed 'interpreters' of God, he argued. It was revolutionary stuff.

English translations followed Luther's initiative. The most significant, and by far the most literary, was that of William Tyndale (c. 1491–1536) from 1525 onwards. 'Tyndale's Bible' comprised the New Testament and the first five books of the Old Testament (the so-called Pentateuch). God's word, Tyndale believed, like Luther, should be understandable by every English man and woman. It was, at the time, as radical an idea in England as it had been in Germany.

Who was this man, William Tyndale? Little is known of his early life. Even his surname is uncertain; he sometimes appears in documents as 'Hichens'. He attended Oxford University and, on graduating in 1512, enrolled to do advanced study in religious studies, supporting himself as a private tutor. But from the outset of his career William Tyndale was driven by two much higher aspirations – both mortally dangerous at the time. In the 1520s, England was still a Catholic country, with Henry VIII at its head. But Tyndale was committed to defying Rome, and everything associated with Roman Catholicism: 'papistry', as it was called. He yearned to translate the scriptures into English, his native tongue.

His aim, he said, was that even the ploughman should have access to God's word in ploughman's English.

In 1524, Tyndale went to Germany. He may have met his mentor, Luther – it's nice to think he did. Over the next few years, in Flanders, he worked on his translation of the Bible direct from the Hebrew and Greek sources. Copies of his New Testament were the first to be shipped to England, and circulated widely despite the authorities' attempts to destroy them. He fell out with Henry VIII on the issue of the King's divorce, but returning to his home country was never advisable – it would probably endanger his life. In Europe, his activities drew the attention of the fiercely anti-Protestant Charles V, Holy Roman Emperor. Never one to make things easy for himself, he also fell out with the local authorities in Flanders. He was betrayed, arrested, and imprisoned in the castle of Vilvoorde, north of Brussels, on vague charges of heresy. The account of his trial and death is given in the propagandistic, but nearly contemporary, *Foxe's Book of Martyrs* (1563). It is extraordinarily moving, and powerful evidence of how an author, like Tyndale, would go to the stake for what he believed in and what he had written.

What John Foxe tells us is that 'Master Tyndale' was offered a lawyer to defend him. He refused, saying he would defend himself, in his own language. Those of his captors who had conversed with him and heard him pray were of the belief 'that if he were not a good Christian man, they knew not whom they might take to be one'. He is said to have converted not merely his keeper, but his keeper's wife and daughter, to his new idea of what religion was, and should be.

William Tyndale would never get a fair trial, and was given no opportunity to argue his case. Charles V simply ordered that the troublesome fellow be executed. This, he instructed, should be done in the cruel fashion laid down for heretics: burning alive at the stake. The sentence was carried out at Vilvoorde in October 1536. Humanely (in the unspeakably brutal circumstances), and in defiance of the emperor's command, his executors strangled Tyndale before his body was burned, to spare him pain. His last words on earth, reportedly, were: 'Lord, open the King of England's eyes.' Henry VIII's eyes never were opened. He never could stand those who opposed his marital arrangements.

Henry VIII, in his momentous break with Rome, had meanwhile commanded the preparation of a Great Bible in English, and allowed the Tyndale Bible to form the backbone of the text. Between this first English Bible and the KJB of 1611, there intervened the reign of the fanatically Catholic Mary I, who proscribed such Protestant texts as heretical. The five years of Mary's rule (1553–58) ushered in a new period of religious terror. When the accession of Elizabeth saw a return to Protestantism, English translations, including Tyndale's, were again tolerated.

Elizabeth's successor, James, who ruled Scotland as James VI before becoming King James I of England, had long wanted to authorise a new, official English Bible. The increasingly powerful, and politically disobedient, Puritan sect also called for a translation without the inaccuracies they had found in previous versions. James outlined his great project at the Hampton Court Conference of 1604. It was made clear from the first that the eventual authorised version would not belong to any sect, denomination, elite or special interest group (certainly not to William Tyndale) but would be the property of the king, the head of the established church. It would forge a link between earthly and spiritual power, politics and religion, while splitting England, forever, from Rome's authority. In short, it would make the monarch's hold on the throne more secure. To this day newly 'authorised' versions of the Bible in Britain may be printed only by licence of the English Crown.

The Authorised Version was the work of six learned companies, combining the expertise of some fifty scholars. Despite this amassed brainpower – more of an army than a committee – it has been estimated that 80 per cent of the King James version is verbally unaltered from Tyndale's translation of eighty years earlier. A comparison of the opening lines of Genesis, first as translated by Tyndale, and then as they appear in the KJB, will make the point obvious:

In the begynnynge God created heaven and erth.

The erth was voyde and emptie and darcknesse was vpon the depe and the spirite of god moved vpon the water

Than God sayd: let there be lyghte and there was lyghte.

And God sawe the lyghte that it was good: and devyded the lyghte from the darcknesse

and called the lyghte daye and the darcknesse nyghte: and so of the evenynge and mornynge was made the fyrst daye

In the beginning God created the heaven and the Earth.

And the earth was without forme, and voyd; and darkenesse was upon the face of the deepe. And the Spirit of God mooved upon the face of the waters.

And God said, Let there be light: and there was light.

And God saw the light, that it was good: and God divided the light from the darkenesse.

And God called the light, Day, and the darkness he called Night. And the evening and the morning were the first day.

So it goes for five Old Testament books more. William Tyndale's determination had been fully vindicated and he would have had an unanswerable charge of plagiarism – word-for-word imitation – to bring against those six companies of scholars in a modern law court.

In addition to making the book of books accessible to the ploughman and everyone else, as Tyndale had wanted, the 1611 Authorised Version triumphantly achieved the goals James had set down for it. It cemented the structure of the established church in England, which would, with the monarchy and Parliament, be one of the foundation stones of what was to become the modern British state. It also served to create a version, or 'dialect', of the English language which was heard by the population at least once a week (James made church-going compulsory). The weekly lessons read from the Authorised Version permeated the intellectual and cultural fabric of England – particularly its writers – for hundreds of years to come. It's not always audible and not always visible, but it's always present.

In our respect for the Authorised Version – the only truly great work of literature in English for which we can thank a king – we should never forget William Tyndale. He is an author of equal standing, one might claim, with the greatest in his language. And that does not exclude Shakespeare.

CHAPTER 9

Minds Unchained
The Metaphysicals

Ask poetry-lovers who is the finest creator of short 'lyric' poems in English literature and chances are the name that comes up time and again will be John Donne (1572–1631). Donne led a school of poets called the 'Metaphysicals'. Ignore that name, by the way: no one has satisfactorily been able to work out why these poets should be so called. If you need to be precise it's best to settle, as do most literary historians, for 'school of Donne'. But 'Metaphysicals' has a more interesting sound to it.

Donne did not write for the opinion of posterity – at least, not the verses for which he is nowadays most admired, the love poems he wrote as a young man. In his later years – his 'penitential years', as his friend and biographer, Izaak Walton, called them – when he regretted the wildness of his youth, he had become a respectable churchman and did his best to suppress these early works. He would, he said, be glad to see their 'funeral'.

Donne hoped in later life that he would be most admired for his religious poems, which are indeed wonderful – particularly the so-called 'Holy Sonnets', of which the most famous is 'Death Be Not

Proud' in which the poet defiantly asserts that the true Christian need not fear death, but should confront it as an enemy to be fought and defeated. This is how the poem (fourteen lines long, like most sonnets) opens:

> Death be not proud, though some have called thee
> Mighty and dreadfull, for, thou art not soe,
> For, those, whom thou think'st, thou dost overthrow,
> Die not, poore death, nor yet canst thou kill me.

'Thou' and 'thee' sound old-fashioned now, but back then they were informal ways of addressing someone of lesser standing than yourself, like a child or servant; 'you' was used more formally. Here, then, these words indicate disrespect. It is a confrontational opening challenge – come on and fight me, then, if you think you're so tough – which hinges, as does much of Donne's poetry, on a paradox, something that means two things simultaneously. Here the paradox is that those whom death 'thinks' it kills actually go on to eternal life. Death, as we would say, is a loser, and always will be.

Donne also hoped to be remembered for his sermons and solemn meditations on religious subjects. Brilliantly written as they are, few people nowadays read them in their entirety, although parts of the sermons can be read for pure literary pleasure. (Donne, however, would probably be angry that we were treating his work in this way.) The following wonderfully long, looping sentence from his 'Meditation XVII' is a good example of Donne taking a religious truth and expressing it in a way that hits home as only truly great literature can. (I've kept the original spelling here which, I think, adds to the effect.)

> No man is an Iland, intire of itselfe; every man is a peece of the Continent, a part of the maine; if a Clod bee washed away by the Sea, Europe is the lesse, as well as if a Promontorie were, as well as if a Manor of thy friends or of thine owne were; any mans death diminishes me, because I am involved in Mankinde; and therefore never send to know for whom the [funeral] bell tolls; It tolls for thee.

Everyone will die: there is no way out of this world alive. Yet we should see it not as a personal tragedy, but something that connects us, intimately, with the fate of every other person on earth. Put that way, as I've put it, it's trite. As Donne puts it, it's wonderful.

Great as the religious verse and prose is, it is the early *Songs and Sonnets*, written in Donne's wild youth, which have been most influential and are nowadays most often included in anthologies. They were originally circulated in manuscript form for the enjoyment of a small group of similarly clever, intellectually daring friends. Donne's was a highly refined branch of poetry. It is challenging – at times fearsomely so. Modern readers may feel at times that they are not reading the poems, but solving difficult puzzles. Approached in the right way, that adds to the pleasure.

The Metaphysicals were deeply learned but, above all, 'witty'. Wit – meaning smartness – was the essence of their project. And none of the group was wittier than John Donne. The device they most valued was what they called the 'conceit' – the daring idea or 'concept' that no one had ever come up with before. Often these conceits bordered on the extravagantly far-fetched. As always in literature it's something easier demonstrated than described. A prime example is Donne's short poem 'The Flea', written, we assume, in his youth:

> Mark but this flea, and mark in this,
> How little that which thou deniest me is;
> It suck'd me first, and now sucks thee,
> And in this flea our two bloods mingled be.

What is the poet getting at here? One must unravel the poem a bit to solve the puzzle. The unnamed young lady to whom the poem is being addressed is, we gather, stubbornly resisting the poet's urgent overtures that she surrender to him. For his part, the poet is using all the resources of his poetry as an instrument of winning her over.

Donne asks what their coming together would mean, and explains it by the insignificance of a flea. A tiny thing. Nothing of great consequence. He urges his request by pointing to the flea that he has just seen (and probably crushed between his thumbnails, spurting blood). The flea, he presumes, has sucked on both their bodies – so their bodily fluids have already been united. Elsewhere in the poem there are hints, verging on the outrageous, of the Anglican communion service and the communion wine, representing Christ's blood.

Why, the poem wittily argues, shouldn't the two of them be united if their blood has already run together? We do not know if the young woman to whom this poem was addressed was persuaded to give in to her witty lover or not. But few objects of youthful desire can have received a finer literary compliment. And we, hundreds of years later, can enjoy it simply as a poem.

After Donne's death and the victory of the Puritans under Cromwell in the English Civil War (1642–51), poems celebrating 'libertine' (immoral) love were sternly censored and discouraged. That included poems such as 'The Flea', since the young man and woman are clearly not married. The eighteenth century which followed – called the 'Augustan Age' of literature for its fashion of imitating of refined classical (Latin and Greek) models – disapproved of the intellectual recklessness of the metaphysical imagination. For them, the moral impropriety did not matter. It was just, in a literary sense, too wild.

Samuel Johnson, the most authoritative of Augustans, complained that in Donne's poetry 'the most heterogeneous ideas are yoked by violence together'. By that he meant, for example, linking a flea's blood with religious imagery. In another famous example Donne compared separated lovers as being like a pair of compasses, joined at the head. It was 'indecorous' – it lacked polish. It was all over the place. Johnson believed that poetry should follow rules, not flout them.

Despite such objections, the reputation of the Metaphysicals has risen over the centuries since they were writing. They came to be regarded as an increasingly significant movement in the development of English poetry, not merely in themselves but for the influence they exercised on their modern successors. It was the great twentieth-century poet T.S. Eliot who most effectively argued for the greatness and importance of his seventeenth-century predecessors. A poet such as Donne had what Eliot recognised as an 'undissociated sensibility'. What Eliot meant by this very strange phrase was that for Donne and his school, there were no such things as 'poetic subjects' which could be written about and 'unpoetic subjects' which could not be written about. A poet could write about fleas as lyrically as he or she could write about nightingales or turtle doves. Eliot valued metaphysical poetry for its ability to unite high and low. All life is in their verse; nothing is excluded. That was a lesson poets like himself could carry away with them.

Even in later years, when he was respectably married and later the Dean of St Paul's in London, Donne's verse – now sacred, not libertine, in tone – is marked by breathtaking intellectual daring. Johnson's 'violence' of the imagination is there to the end. Literally the end. On his deathbed, Donne wrote a poem about his approaching death called 'Hymn to God, My God, in my Sickness'. It is not a young woman he now addresses, but his Maker whom he will, in an hour or two, meet face to face. The poem is, among other things, a rehearsal for his singing for the rest of eternity in God's angelic choir – he is not in the chamber of death, but a kind of vestry, about to enter the church proper. Here are the first three verses:

> Since I am coming to that Holy room,
>   Where, with Thy choir of saints for evermore,
> I shall be made Thy music; as I come
>   I tune the instrument here at the door,
>   And what I must do then, think here before;
>
> Whilst my physicians by their love are grown
>   Cosmographers, and I their map, who lie
> Flat on this bed, that by them may be shown
>   That this is my south-west discovery,
>   *Per fretum febris*, by these straits to die;
> I joy, that in these straits I see my west;

> For, though their currents yield return to none,
> What shall my west hurt me? As west and east
>   In all flat maps (and I am one) are one,
>   So death doth touch the resurrection.

The hymn is as daring as anything Donne ever wrote. And it requires some work by the reader to follow the complex lines of thought. The conceits are packed in together, like sardines in a tin. His death will be a voyage of exploration; he will join the great sea-going voyagers on this last journey of his life. His physicians – soon to get to work on the autopsy – will find his dead body to be a map of where he is going, just as cosmographers discover the universe. Where is he going? West, into the cold dark night of the grave. But he has to pass through the east and the hot straits of his fatal fever (*per fretum febris*) to get there. Walton records that his friend 'was so far from fearing Death, which to others is the King of Terrors, that he longed for the day of his dissolution'. One can only hope the Almighty admires fine poetry as much as we do.

For those who find the complexity of Donne too rich a brew to swallow comfortably, there is simpler poetry to be found in the work of his fellow Metaphysical, George Herbert (1593–1633). Like Donne, Herbert was a clergyman – but not a high dignitary of the church. He was a country parson, and wrote a manual on how such lowly clergymen should carry out their duties. He also wrote exquisitely 'plain' verse. The following is the opening verse from his poem 'Virtue':

> Sweet day, so cool, so calm, so bright,
> The bridall of the earth and skie:
> The dew shall weep thy fall to night;
>   For thou must die.

The 'conceit', or central idea, here is that nightfall is a forecast of our death. The secondary idea, that night is the 'child' or offspring of the earth and sky (in the dark, they meet, seamlessly, at the horizon to produce it), is beautifully original. But look at how simple the language is – every word is a monosyllable, apart from 'bridall' (a pun: it means bridle, as in what joins two horses in harness, and bridal, as in marriage).

Has complex verse ever been made out of simpler – and in Donne's case, 'low' – materials? Eliot was right. This is poetry that breaks all the rules – and is the greater for it.

CHAPTER 10

Nations Rise
MILTON AND SPENSER

During the forty-five years of the reign of Queen Elizabeth I –
'good Queen Bess' – there is a new 'feel' to literature: a growth
of national pride and bursting confidence. England felt a certain
'greatness' in itself – a greatness, daring spirits might think, equal
to that of ancient Rome. It expressed itself through literature in two
ways: writing about England and writing in English, appropriating,
where required, the literary forms of other supremely great nations
and their literatures. Put another way, nationalism takes centre-
stage.

The first great English poem about England is Edmund Spenser's
The Faerie Queene of 1590–96. It was composed during Elizabeth's
mature years and is dedicated to her. Spenser was a courtier, a
soldier, and a high-stakes political player, as well as a poet. He was
not a *professional* writer. His pen was never Spenser's main source of
income (although it could win him patrons who would bring him
money) and it was not his main ambition in life to be a great figure in
English literature. Ironically, that is precisely what he was destined
to become.

Edmund Spenser (*c.* 1552–99) was born the son of prosperous cloth maker, in the rising middle classes, and educated at Cambridge University. His early career was as a colonial administrator in Ireland where his principal duty was to enforce martial law, root out troublemakers, and put down rebellion. He did this efficiently and often brutally. As a reward the Queen gave him an Irish estate.

Spenser was an ambitious man. He wanted more than Elizabeth had given him. And it was to further his ambitions, and to flatter her, that he conceived *The Faerie Queene*. The poem was prefaced by a letter to Sir Walter Raleigh who was pleasing their monarch in a different way, by making Britannia ruler of the waves.

The Faerie Queene won Spenser a small pension but not, alas, the great favours he craved. Subsequently his life was marked by disappointment. His castle was burned down by Irish rebels in 1597 and it is thought that he lost members of his family in the attack. He moved back to London where he died in distressed circumstances, in his mid-forties. We don't know why he ended his life penniless.

Spenser's career as a politician had been less than successful but his achievement as a poet was outstanding. Appropriately, his tomb lies alongside that of his 'master' Geoffrey Chaucer in Poets' Corner, Westminster Abbey. At his death the notable writers of the time (including Shakespeare, reportedly) threw commemorative verses into his grave. It was not just his passing but the dawning greatness of English literature that they were celebrating.

The subject of *The Faerie Queene* is England itself – glory, and Gloriana (the name of the queen of the faerie court, and also as Elizabeth was known). An epic poem, it was originally intended to run to twelve books, but Spenser completed only six. It nonetheless remains one of the longest poems in the language and not one of the easiest. The half of *The Faerie Queene* which Spenser completed addresses itself to six moral virtues necessary to the establishment of a nation, one virtue in each book. These virtues are: Holiness, Temperance, Chastity, Friendship, Justice and Courtesy. Each is embodied as a different kind of knightly hero, five men and a woman, all in armour and embarked on quests to set the world to rights and bring to civilisation to a pagan and primitive world. Given the title and origins of the poem, we are particularly interested in the female knight, Britomart, in Book III. Like the Virgin Queen, whom the book overtly compliments, Britomart is the embodiment of militant chastity. No man can dominate or 'own' her. If Elizabeth had a favourite part of the poem, this, surely, was it.

Spenser's poem is made up of rhymed verses, which we now call 'Spenserian stanzas' – complicated rhyming verses, extraordinarily hard to master. It is written in what is called 'poetic diction' – a 'heightened' language. With *The Faerie Queene* begins the convention that the language of English poetry is never the language of the day, nor of everyday discourse. The main poetic device in *The Faerie Queene* is allegory: saying one thing in terms of another, apparently quite different, thing. Let's look at the first lines of the poem's first stanza, which are a prime example of poetic diction and allegory:

> A Gentle Knight was pricking on the plaine,
> Y cladd in mightie armes and siluer shielde,
> Wherein old dints of deepe wounds did remaine,
> The cruell markes of many' a bloudy fielde;
> Yet armes till that time did he neuer wield:

No one, even in the sixteenth century, actually spoke in this pseudo-antique way. ('Pricking', by the way, means the knight is driving his spurs into the horse to make it gallop.) But it creates exactly what Spenser wanted – an otherworldly ('faerie') effect. And the verse is rich with meaning as regards 'holiness' (this first book's particular virtue). Why, for example, is the knight encased in *battered* armour? The detail points to the fact that the great battles of Christianity have been won for us already by our ancestors. We shall not be required to become martyrs, or be burned at the stake, to prove our holiness. Virtually every stanza of the poem is packed in this way with allegorical meaning and is rich in its 'Spenserian' artificial language.

English poetry took another important step forward a hundred years later, with the works of John Milton (1608–74). England, since the death of Elizabeth, had endured religious conflicts, in which Milton had played an active part on the side of the Commonwealth. The country was still in the process of defining itself. But the national confidence, so prominent in *The Faerie Queene*, is just as evident in Milton's *Paradise Lost*, which he began writing during the period of the Commonwealth and which was printed in 1667 during the reign of Charles II. Milton frankly acknowledged Spenser (as Spenser had acknowledged Chaucer) as his literary predecessor and a main influence. English literature now has a great 'tradition'. These three poets are connected, like links in a chain.

In *Paradise Lost* Milton set out to do something dauntingly ambitious. To write an epic – something to rival Virgil's *Aeneid* or Homer's *Odyssey* – and use that epic to 'justify the ways of God to man', as he put it. He would, in other words, re-tell the opening books of the Bible in a way that would make clearer some of the theological difficulties it poses. For instance, is it really wrong to eat 'the apple of knowledge'? Is Eden a place where no work of any kind is done by Adam and Eve? Are they 'married'? Milton grapples with these issues in the poem. It's the same kind of mission we saw in the mystery plays (now long gone from the great towns which gave them birth). But what Milton came up with was anything but literature of the streets. *Paradise Lost* is a poem that presupposes a highly educated reader – ideally one who knows some Latin.

Milton's composition of *Paradise Lost*, which he conceived as his life's work and which, incredibly, he wrote after being stricken with blindness, began with two dilemmas. The first was, what language should he write in? Milton was a scholar. The languages of scholarship, over the centuries, were Ancient Greek and Latin. Milton was fluent in both. He had written much poetry in Latin. If his poem was going to be truly Virgilian, or Homeric, should he not use their language? He decided on English, but an English so flavoured with the ancient language that it sounds more like Latin.

The other dilemma he faced was what 'form' he should write it in. He was steeped, as a scholar, in Aristotle's *Poetics*, and he recalled that the Greek critic had called tragedy the noblest literature. Milton toyed for some time with the idea of writing his great work as a tragedy, along the lines of Sophocles' *Oedipus Rex*. He went so far as to write a plan for this tragedy called 'Adam Unparadised'. In the event he went for the epic – a looser narrative form. A main reason for this was that, like Virgil, he resolved to create a work of literature that would celebrate the growth of a great nation. Milton believed that England was now a great nation, and that is a major assumption underlying *Paradise Lost* and the two choices Milton made.

Whether Milton succeeded in his great mission is debatable. In his telling of the serpent's seduction of Adam and Eve – and more particularly, Satan's war with God narrated in the first books of the poem – he comes close, as the poet William Blake put it, to 'being of the devil's party and not knowing it'. Milton doesn't quite know whose side he is on. Satan is a rebel and, in his own life, the poet was a rebel too; he had risked his life by opposing Charles I. Better to 'reign in hell than serve in heaven', says Satan. In context it sounds heroic. Also, Milton was clearly unsure whether he, personally, would not have eaten an 'apple of knowledge', whatever the consequences, or remained for all time in a state of innocent, guiltless, 'blank' ignorance. And Milton's view of the relationship of man and woman rubs many modern readers up the wrong way. This is how Adam and Eve are first pictured:

> Two of far nobler shape erect and tall,
> Godlike erect, with native honour clad
> In naked majesty seemed lords of all.
> For contemplation he and valour formed,
> For softness she and sweet attractive grace;
> He for God only, she for God in him.
> His fair large front and eye sublime declar'd
> Absolute rule …

'He for God only, she for God in him' is the line modern readers most often gag on. Illustrators have followed Milton's cue and traditionally show the couple (with the obligatory fig leaves) with Adam looking up, reverently, to heaven, and Eve gazing, adoringly, at his face as he does so. But later in the poem Eve rebels against this 'absolute' wifely submission. She insists on going off on her own to tend the Garden in Eden. Her domestic rebellion renders her vulnerable, of course, to the seductions of wily Satan (now in the form of a serpent) who persuades her, as a further act of independence, to eat the forbidden fruit of the Tree of Knowledge.

Another bone of contention is the 'English' that Milton created for his poem. It is heavily, at times overpoweringly, 'Latinised' – it's almost as if he never could shake off the intention of writing the poem in the antique language. The following, from Book VII, describing Eden's vegetation, is a good example of Miltonic diction:

> ... up stood the corny reed
> Embattled in her field: and the humble shrub,
> And bush with frizzled hair implicit: last
> Rose as in dance the stately trees, and spread
> Their branches hung with copious fruit; or gemmed
> Their blossoms ...

This is not the terminology of *Gardener's Question Time*.

There are those, like the poet T.S. Eliot, who believe that Milton's Latinism in *Paradise Lost* throws up an off-putting 'Chinese Wall' around literature. Literary language should be closer to what the Romantic poet Wordsworth called 'the language of men', not the language of pedants and scholars who are thinking in Latin and translating their thought into English – as, one suspects, Milton sometimes did. But what really matters, for his poem and for English poetry generally, is that, by his choice, Milton established that the English language in the hands of a great poet like himself could create epic poetry to rival that of the ancients.

There are many other problems raised by *Paradise Lost*. Can a poem, for example, really explain the Bible better than it can explain itself? No easy answers are possible. Great literature never makes things simpler – it gives no easy answers to difficult questions. What it does is to help us see how infinitely un-simple things are for us.

Milton confidently declares in the first book of his twelve-book poem that his purpose is to make his readers better Christians, or, at least, better-informed Christians. Who knows? He may have succeeded with some readers in his uplifting religious mission. But the central achievement of *Paradise Lost* has been very different, and wholly literary. It pointed to ways in which literature in English, and poets writing in English, could develop. It laid a foundation. And that foundation was a literature which, henceforth, would be independently English. English in subject and English in expression.

CHAPTER 11

Who 'Owns' Literature?
PRINTING, PUBLISHING AND COPYRIGHT

The book you are holding in your hand at the moment is not a work of literature, but let's take it as a handy example. I wrote it. My name is there on the title page, and in the copyright line. So it's 'my' (John Sutherland's) book. Does that mean, though, that I 'own' the book in your hand? No, it doesn't – the physical copies are not mine. If you bought it, it's yours. But suppose someone broke into my house while I was writing this book, stole my computer, found the text of what I was writing and published it under their own name. What would happen? Provided I could prove that the original work was mine, I could sue the thief for infringement of copyright – for copying my original work without my permission and passing it off as his own (an offence known as 'plagiarism').

From its beginning in the eighteenth century, modern copyright law has developed alongside the increasing availability of literary works in new formats. It has continually had to adapt to keep up with new technologies, including film adaptations in the twentieth century (Chapter 32) and, today, the challenge of e-books and the internet (Chapter 40). But in essence, *copyright* has always meant just that: 'the right to copy'. As the copyright owner of what you are reading right now, I have granted Yale University Press the exclusive right to publish it in the form of this book.

We talk about a 'work of literature' because it is the result – in very real terms – of the author's toil. Then, publishers talk about each of the works in their catalogue as a 'title': the word 'title' means ownership. Finally, when the books have been produced for sale, they are individual 'copies': you have in your hand a copy of my work. Each party 'owns' the work in a different way. Imagine a party of book-lovers. The host, pointing to his groaning shelves, proudly exclaims, 'Look at *my* books!' An author, scanning the shelves, says jubilantly, 'I see you've got one of *my* books – did you enjoy it?' A publisher, also inspecting the books, says 'I'm very glad to see you've got so many of *our* books on the shelf'. They are all right, in a sense: the host owns the physical objects, the publisher the particular format, and the author the original words. And it points to the many different people and processes involved in getting a book written, published and sold nowadays.

This little book's life began when I signed a contract with Yale University Press, granting them the right to publish my text as a book. Once my manuscript was delivered to them satisfactorily, they paid to have it edited, designed, typeset, printed, bound between hard covers, and stored, prior to sale, in a warehouse. The publishers paid for all those individual processes, and they now own the physical books. Next, the books are distributed, principally to various retailers – physical shops and electronic sellers – and libraries. The physical books now belong to them. Finally, you, the customer, bought this *Little History of Literature* and took it home. (Or if you borrowed it from the library you will have to return it there.) Today, the publishing of books is usually carried out by a company quite separate from the printers and the booksellers. But up until the nineteenth century, publishing and printing was mainly arranged by booksellers.

From the earliest period of known history, it took thousands of years, and an awful lot of literature, before any laws were devised to regulate what went on, and to protect the various parties' interests. And it was only when those laws came into being that a coherent industry – with machinery and ways of commercially distributing literary products – could be developed and that 'literature' – as opposed to a miscellaneous bundle of texts, oral tales and ballads – could be fully and properly developed.

The framework of laws and commerce within which literature is now created depended on a number of earlier things happening. Writing, literacy and educational institutions were necessary to create a market. Another necessary prior event was the shift from scrolls – which great ancient libraries such as the one at Alexandria contained – to what is called the 'codex', a book with cut, numbered pages, like the one you're reading. (*Caudex* is Latin for a block of wood; the plural is *codices*.)

The manuscript, or handwritten codex, originated in classical Rome, like the word itself. It's thought that it was invented because persecuted Christians, whose faith (unlike that of the pagan Romans) had a sacred book – the gospels – at its centre, needed texts they could keep hidden from prying eyes. A codex was smaller and easier to secrete than a large scroll.

Creating an early manuscript codex required huge manual labour – taking years, in some cases, if it was illustrated, or illuminated, or handsomely bound – by highly skilled copyists who were often artists rather than craftsmen. Many of those codices which have survived in our great libraries were manufactured as single luxury items, commissioned by a rich owner or institution (the monarch, the church, monasteries, noblemen). The workshops in which they were produced were called scriptoria, writing factories. It's estimated that the total number of works of literature that were readily available to the educated bookworm up to the fifteenth century, was less than a thousand or two. Chaucer's Clerk in *The Canterbury Tales*, for example, is regarded by his fellow pilgrims as phenomenally well read, yet he owns only half a dozen books.

This book scarcity meant that many more people had books read to them than they read, or possessed, themselves. A famous nineteenth-century painting shows Chaucer, fifty years before the arrival of the printing press, reading his great poem to an audience from a lectern, or 'reading stand'. (The lectern still survives in university lecture halls – originally they were designed for reading aloud from a text of which there was only one copy. The word 'lecture' is derived from the Latin word *lector*, a reader.)

One of the other preconditions for the production of books for a mass market was the discovery, introduced to England from the East around the thirteenth century, of the process for making paper. Before this, writing of any importance was done on parchment or vellum (cleaned and dried animal skin), or was carved on wood. Cheap paper laid the way for the major revolution in the late fifteenth century: printing.

We think of printing as a European thing, with its famous pioneers Johannes Gutenberg in Germany, William Caxton in England, and Aldus Manutius in Italy (inventor of 'italic' type). In fact it had long been practised in China. But the Chinese had a huge problem. The Chinese written language was based on thousands of pictorial 'characters'. Each of them was inscribed on a block the size of a small brick. The short paragraph you are reading would require sixty of them, and be the size of a small wall.

The Western phonetic alphabet ('phonetic' means being based on sound, not image) was a mere twenty-six letters and a dozen or so punctuation symbols. It was wonderfully convenient for the printer. You could create the necessary 'type' by pouring molten lead into what were called 'fonts' and store it when cooled in 'cases'. (Capitals were stored in the upper case – we still use the term.) Many of the pioneer printers were goldsmiths, like Gutenberg, and so used to working with hot metal. The type could be set in lines, in a page-shaped 'form' and inked. The 'press' could then be pulled down to run off as many copies of the page that were required. The press itself could be quite small – about twice the size of a modern trouser press (which worked on the same principle) if smallness were a consideration.

The first printed books looked very like manuscript codices, with elaborately styled letters. If this was a fifteenth-century Gutenberg

Bible in your hand you would be hard put to say whether it was written or printed. The difference was that Gutenberg's workshop, in Mainz, Germany, could turn out a thousand bibles in the time it took a scriptorium to produce one.

It was a breakthrough but it brought with it a new set of problems – the most urgent being our old friend, ownership. One of the first books printed in England was Caxton's 1476 edition of Chaucer's *Canterbury Tales* (good choice) which he sold from his little stall outside St Paul's Cathedral. The great poet was no longer around to give his permission, but even if he had still been alive, Caxton would not have had to pay Geoffrey Chaucer a penny out of the profits of his printing enterprise.

For the next 200 years it was copycat heaven in the book trade. Some legal mechanism to control the 'right to copy' was required, particularly in London which was swelling with large numbers of consumers: a 'reading public'. It was the London booksellers (as mentioned above, they also often doubled as publishers, with printing machinery in the back of the shop) who brought pressure to bear on Parliament to frame laws that would regulate the book business.

In 1710 Parliament came up with a wonderfully sophisticated piece of legislation – known as the 'Statute of Anne' – which had the clear intention of 'the Encouragement of Learning'. The preamble reads:

> Whereas Printers, Booksellers, and other Persons have of late frequently taken the Liberty of Printing, Reprinting, and Publishing or causing to be Printed, Reprinted, and Published Books, and other Writings, without the Consent of the Authors or Proprietors of such Books and Writings, to their very great Detriment, and too often to the Ruin of them and their families: for Preventing therefore such Practices for the future, and for the Encouragement of Learned Men to Compose and write useful Books ...

For the first time, it acknowledged that an author composes something original – the author's 'own intellectual creation', in the modern phrase – and that it has value. As soon as that original creation has been written down (typed or word-processed, these days), the author owns the copyright – the written work is what we would now call 'intellectual property'. It can be 'materialised' – as a printed book, or nowadays an e-book, or adapted into a stage play or a film. But crucially, from 1710 onward, under copyright law the original creation remains the author's and other people can only use it under the author's licence.

This first copyright statute foresaw the danger of 'perpetual ownership'. The creator of a work, or whomever they had sold it to, could own the right to copy it only for a limited period of time. After that it would enter what is called 'the public domain', and would be everybody's and nobody's. In 1710 the period of copyright protection was fairly short; it has been extended over the years and in Europe is currently seventy years after the death of the creator.

Another careful element in the Queen Anne Act was to decree that there is 'no copyright in ideas'. This makes the law very different from, for example, patent law, which does protect ideas. Let's explain it this way. If I write a detective novel in which, on the last page, it is revealed that 'the butler did it' and you later write a detective novel in which – hey presto – there is the same last-page revelation, you are free to do so. What you may not do is copy my form of words. It is the *expression*, not the thoughts behind the words, that is protected.

The author's licence to 'reap where you have not sown' is one the great, controlled freedoms that have enabled literature (notably narrative literature) to bloom. There is a network of other laws that control freedom. Libel laws make it illegal to write malicious untruths about living persons. Censorship has made it, over the centuries, illegal to publish what is considered (at any particular time) pornographic or blasphemous. More recent legislation controls the publishing of material thought to be racially provocative or an incitement to violence. But the basic freedoms, and disciplines, which make literature what it is today were created by those wise parliamentarians 300 years ago.

British copyright law was adopted further abroad, and other countries formed their own conventions. It took some time to happen. America did not sign up to international copyright until 1891, which meant the USA was free to plunder British and other nations' literary work. It famously infuriated Dickens, who never did forgive those damned Yankee pirates. Chapter 37 continues the international story.

The printed book has lasted for over 500 years. Caxton would recognise the copies of Chaucer in our high-street bookshops as a modern version of his own. But is the book at the end of its life in the twenty-first century? Will the e-book take over, as the codex took over from the papyrus scroll? No one knows for certain. But some kind of co-existence seems likely. There is something wonderfully physical about the old vehicle. You use your legs to walk to the shelf, your arms to take the volume down, your opposable thumb and index finger to turn the page. It's a bodily engagement you don't feel with a Kindle or iPad. My guess is that the 'feel' (the touch, and even smell) of the printed book will continue to give it a lasting place – if not necessarily first place – in the world of literature for some time to come.

CHAPTER 12

The House of Fiction

Human beings are storytelling animals. That goes as far back as we can trace our species. If you think of fiction, do you think of novels? Well, we did not start writing and reading novels until a fairly precise moment in literary history, in the eighteenth century. We will come to that in the next chapter. Before that moment, fiction took different forms. If we dig, we can find what we might call some 'proto-novels' in literature before, in some cases long before, what we think of as the first novel. Five European works of literature will make the point clearer. They are not novels, but we feel a novel trying to get out in their narratives:

The Decameron (Giovanni Boccaccio, 1351, Italy)
Gargantua and Pantagruel (François Rabelais, 1532–64, France)
Don Quixote (Miguel de Cervantes, 1605–15, Spain)
The Pilgrim's Progress (John Bunyan, 1678–84, England)
Oroonoko (Aphra Behn, 1688, England)

The Decameron of Giovanni Boccaccio (1313–75) became hugely popular and influential across Europe (inspiring Chaucer, for instance), particularly after it was printed in 1470. Its bundle of stories resurface everywhere in literature thereafter. The frame story of *The Decameron* is simple and gripping. The Black Death is ravaging Florence, as it routinely did in the fourteenth century. (In Wakefield, which we looked at in Chapter 6, the disease wiped out a third of the town's population.) You couldn't cure it, all you could do was run away from it and hope it didn't catch you. Ten young people of wealth and breeding – three men and seven women – take refuge in a villa in the countryside for ten days (hence the title – *deca* is 'ten' in Greek) until the plague burns out. To pass the time this *brigata* ('brigade', as the author calls them) each tell one story every day, so that the book contains 100 stories. Boccaccio, the most famous Italian man of letters of his day, used an interesting word for these stories: *novella* – Italian for 'some new little thing'. These tales are told in the warmth of the evening, under the olive trees, to the soft chirp of cicadas, with refreshment to hand.

The subjects range from the fabulous (verging on the fairy story) and neo-classical (drawing on the literature of the ancients) to the bawdy and the knockabout comic, with a stress on the infinite variety of life as it is lived. The stories are cunningly plotted and overwhelmingly subversive in tone. Many of them satirise the Church and ruling establishments – this is young persons' literature. And this 'new thing', the novella, is a literary genre that wilfully breaks literary rules and flouts convention. That is part of its newness.

Rabelais's *Gargantua and Pantagruel*, originally published as five separate books, has less of a framework than *The Decameron*. It loosely clumps a huge number of disconnected anecdotes and running jokes around two highly unlikely giants, father (from whom we get the adjective 'gargantuan') and son. It is even more mischievous – or 'licentious' – than *The Decameron* and has been, over the centuries, a book much banned. The epithet 'Rabelaisian' has become shorthand for literature which is just this side of publishable; sometimes, when the moral climate is harsh, it has been unpublishable and, occasionally, burnable.

Despite the long history of banning it suffered, there is nothing squalid in *Gargantua and Pantagruel*'s joyous naughtiness. It overflows with what the French call *esprit* – for which there is no exact English translation, although 'wit' comes near. It differs from *The Decameron* in drawing its energy from the streets, bawdy folk tales and vernacular, or common, speech. All these will be ingredients in the novel to come two centuries later. François Rabelais (*c.* 1494– *c.* 1553) was not himself of the streets. He was a formidably well-read one-time monk who, in his sprawling fantasia, takes the whole of classical and 'respectable' literature and turns it into his personal playground. To cause laughter, he proclaims in his preface, is the mission of literature. He succeeds magnificently in that mission.

Don Quixote, the third of our proto-novels, is a work whose story everyone knows but which too few nowadays read cover to cover. Miguel de Cervantes (1547–1616) was a diplomat's assistant and soldier who lived an unusually eventful life. He is supposed to have had the idea for his great work as a bored prisoner in Spain. It was written for an age in which people had more time than we do. The plot is simple – in fact there is no plot as such. *Don Quixote* popularised the variety of fiction known as 'picaresque': narratives that wander all over the place. The protagonist (more anti-hero than hero) is Alonso Quijano, a middle-aged gentleman living in quiet retirement in La Mancha. It is not, however, a serene retirement. His brain has been poisoned by ancient romances – tales of chivalry and knight errantry. He hallucinates himself into the role of a knight – 'Don Quixote de la Mancha' – and sets out, with a homemade cardboard helmet, on a 'quest'. As his squire he recruits a fat peasant called Sancho Panza. A broken-down nag, Rocinante, is his 'charger'.

There ensue a series of comic adventures, or 'sallies', the most famous of which is his battle with the windmills, which in his madness the Don thinks are giants. After a series of similar disasters he returns home, dejected but, at last, sane. Once again he is Alonso Quijano. On his deathbed he draws up his will and repudiates all the romances that have poisoned his mind and ruined his life.

Nonetheless, there is something touching – admirable even – in that rickety, deluded, old man, his nag and his fat cowardly 'squire' bravely taking on the windmills. Like all the best fiction, *Don Quixote* leaves us in two minds. Fool or lovable idealist? That uncertainty is wrapped up in the word we have taken for general use from the story: 'quixotic'.

Ever since *The Pilgrim's Progress*, our fourth proto-novel, was published over three centuries ago, it has been a runaway bestseller, and hugely influential on later English fiction. Its writer, John Bunyan (1628–88) was a son of the working classes, entirely self-educated, and he wrote much of it in jail after being sentenced for preaching 'heretical' (i.e. unofficial) religious doctrine. Bunyan's father had been a pedlar, tramping wearily across the country, a pack on his back, a staff in his hand. That, for the son, was an image of life. John was driven, however, by another vision – that of eternal bliss for the righteous, as promised in the Bible. But his view of righteousness was not that of the authorities. Hence the prison and hence – fortunately for us – *The Pilgrim's Progress*.

Like Cervantes, Bunyan sees life as a lifelong quest. In Bunyan's case it is a quest *towards* something – the gleaming city on the hill. Salvation. And what we have to conquer on the way are not foes, but the obstacles that afflict the religious mind: depression ('the Slough of Despond'), doubt ('Doubting Castle'), compromise ('Mr Facing Both Ways') and, most dangerous of all, the seductive temptations of the city – 'Vanity Fair'.

The story opens dramatically. The hero, Christian, is reading a book (the Bible, we can deduce – and, significantly, in English: see Chapter 8). What he has just been reading raises a terrible question in his mind: what shall he do to be saved? Suddenly he runs off shouting 'Life, life, eternal life'. He knows what he has to do. His wife and children try to stop him, but he puts his fingers in his ears and runs on, leaving them behind. Why this heartlessness? Because everyone must save themselves, a key tenet of the Puritan doctrine. As the next chapter explains, individualism was to become a key element in the novel as a form, which is why so many of them have names for titles: *The History of Tom Jones, Emma, Silas Marner*, and so on.

There are a number of other aspects in *The Pilgrim's Progress* that feed into the novel of later centuries. The twentieth-century writer D.H. Lawrence called the novel 'the bright book of life' – a modern Bible for an age that had outlived the traditional holy text. The kind of novel that Lawrence wrote (as did Jane Austen, George Eliot, Joseph Conrad and many others) is about how to do the right things in life to find fulfilment – what Bunyan called 'salvation' – as the historical and personal circumstances define it. This has been called 'the great tradition' of English fiction and that great tradition begins with *The Pilgrim's Progress*.

The last of these proto-novels has an added interest in that it is by a woman, the gloriously named Aphra Behn (1640–89). Women would have to wait more than 200 years before they could claim full social equality with men. That fact alone would make this author of interest. But what is still more fascinating about Behn is how cunningly she adapted her literary talents, which were great, to the turbulent historical period in which she found herself, the Restoration.

Some background history helps us understand Mistress Behn's extraordinary achievement. After the Civil War and the execution of Charles I, the victorious Oliver Cromwell went on to overrule Parliament and set up a republic known as the Commonwealth. He also imposed on the country an iron Puritan dictatorship, backed by the formidable ('Roundhead') army of the Protectorate. During these years of war and republic, King Charles's son, who would later come to the throne as Charles II, took refuge with his court in various locations in mainland Europe, particularly enjoying France's sophisticated pleasures.

Cromwell and his regime were ferociously moralistic. Many taverns were closed, along with the racecourses, cock-fighting pits, houses of ill-repute, and, most damagingly, the country's theatres. The printed word was rigorously censored. It was a difficult time for literature. An impossible time for drama.

Eventually pressure from below for more liberty (and 'cakes and ale', as Shakespeare's Sir Toby Belch calls the fun part of life) brought about the restoration of the monarchy. Prince Charles returned from the Netherlands in 1660 and was crowned the following year. A compromise was reached on the question of religious tolerance and Cromwell's corpse was exhumed from Westminster Abbey and torn into fragments. The theatres, houses of ill-repute and taverns opened again, now under noble patronage and toleration. Charles II particularly loved the stage (not least the women around it – famously Nell Gwynn, an orange-seller) and patronised it, royally.

Eaffrey (self-renamed 'Aphra') Johnson grew up during the civil war. She accompanied her father, a barber who had powerful clients, when he was appointed in 1663 Governor of Surinam, a British colonial possession in South America. Sugar was grown there on plantations worked by slaves who were brutally ill-treated. After her father's death Aphra made her way back to England, with her head packed full of impressions of Surinam, the cruel hardships endured by the slaves and the hypocrisy of their Christian masters. Married and soon widowed, in the early 1670s she took up writing plays for the theatre – the first woman to do so. But her fictional story, *Oroonoko, or the History of the Royal Slave*, published in 1688, is rightly judged her masterpiece. Aphra Behn is buried in Westminster Cathedral, the first woman author to be so honoured. On her tomb, instructs Virginia Woolf, 'all women together ought to let flowers fall ... for it was she who earned them the right to speak for themselves'.

The 'True Story', as the title proclaims itself, is the manifestly untrue story of an African prince, Oroonoko, along with his wife Imoinda, transported to Surinam to labour in the plantations. His history is 'set down' by an anonymous young Englishwoman, the daughter of the newly appointed deputy governor, who has just died. Oroonoko kills two tigers and has a closely described battle with an electric ('benumbing') eel. He organises an uprising, and is cheated into surrendering on the point of victory. He is captured and executed, sadistically, for the delectation of a white rabble. *Oroonoko* is short (about eighty pages, or 28,000 words) and lacks the technical sophistication and masterful suspense that so excited readers when they first read Daniel Defoe's *Robinson Crusoe* some thirty years later. But it is an extraordinary effort, and qualifies the author as a pioneer writer of fiction which is almost, but not quite, a novel.

Henry James called the novel a 'house of fiction'. That house stands on the foundation work of these five writers. And it would rise as itself with the work that is the subject of the next chapter, *Robinson Crusoe*.

CHAPTER 13

Travellers' Tall Tales
Defoe, Swift and the Rise of the Novel

The previous chapter explored the roots of the modern novel. Now we come to what may be called the plant's first ripe fruit. Daniel Defoe (1660–1731), the author of *Robinson Crusoe*, is the generally agreed starting point of the genre in England. In the early and middle years of the eighteenth century, with Defoe and other writers like Samuel Richardson, Henry Fielding, Jonathan Swift and Laurence Sterne, we can see the modern novel emerging from the primal soup of the many kinds of tale-telling that humanity has always gone in for.

A trigger for all this was needed. Why did what we (but not they) call the 'novel', the 'new thing', emerge at this particular time and in this particular place (London)? The answer is that the rise of the novel took place at the same time and in the same place as the rise of capitalism. Different as these two things may seem, they are intimately connected.

Put it this way. Robinson Crusoe, marooned on his island, making his fortune by his own efforts, is a new (novel) kind of man for a new (novel) kind of economic system. Economists have frequently used him as what they call '*homo economicus*': economic man. Defoe's novel, if we look at it thoughtfully, mirrors what was going on financially at the same period in the City of London – in the counting houses, banks, shops, warehouses, offices and docks on the Thames. It was the age of merchant adventurers, capitalism and entrepreneurship. You made your own way in life and, like Dick Whittington, you might arrive in the city penniless and find the streets paved with gold. Or not. In the medieval world no peasant could hope to become a knight. Social mobility is central to capitalism in this complicated system of human affairs. The lowest clerk in the city could hope to become a captain of industry. Or, like Dick, the Lord Mayor of London.

The story of Robinson Crusoe and his island will probably be familiar even to those who have never read the actual novel. This, briefly, is how it goes. A young man falls out with his merchant father and runs away to sea without a penny to his name. He becomes, after various adventures, a trader. Among the goods he trades are slaves, coffee and other things worth transporting between the Old and New Worlds. Crusoe is very much a 'new man', a man for his time.

On one of his trading voyages from Brazil, Crusoe's merchant ship is wrecked by a terrible storm. All the crew perish and he finds himself marooned on a desert island for twenty-eight years. He colonises the island and – having made it to shore with nothing but the clothes he stood up in – leaves the island a rich man. How did he do this? By entrepreneurship: by (literally) making his fortune, exploiting the island's natural resources. And throughout all this ordeal he never loses his faith in God. In fact, he believes that his Maker has done this to him, and approves of what he – Robinson – has done on the island. It is God's work as well as his.

We can get a hint of how the novel – as a 'genre' or distinct style of literature – works by examining the title page of *The Life and strange and surprising Adventures of Robinson Crusoe* as it was first published (in the environs of the City of London, appropriately). When the book's first buyers looked at this page in 1719, they saw the name of Robinson Crusoe and the line 'Written by himself'. Defoe's name doesn't appear. The book claimed to be an

authentic tale of travel and adventure. Inevitably many first readers were duped into thinking there was a real Robinson Crusoe
who had spent twenty-eight years in total isolation on an island off
the mouth of the Oronoque River in South America and made his
fortune there.

With *Robinson Crusoe* we come face to face, for the first time,
with the full-blown narrative convention known as 'realism' –
meaning not the real thing, but something so much like the real
thing that you have to look twice to tell the difference. In the case
of Defoe's novel the confusion about whether it was 'real' or merely
'realistic' was compounded by the fact that four years before the
book appeared, a very similar account of a sailor marooned on an
island had become a bestseller (as did Defoe's book). Defoe clearly
read it and used it. As it happened, that other marooned man did
not make himself rich and had a very miserable time of it. But that
was life, not fiction. The gullible reader in 1719, looking at Defoe's
title page, would have had no way of knowing that *Robinson Crusoe*
wasn't another 'true' traveller's tale.

To the uninformed eye the straightforward opening paragraph
of *Robinson Crusoe* doesn't offer any clues that we are not reading
an authentic autobiography. Read it, and imagine how you would
know you weren't being told God's honest truth:

> I was born in the year 1632, in the city of York, of a good
> family, though not of that country, my father being a foreigner
> of Bremen, who settled first at Hull. He got a good estate by
> merchandise, and leaving off his trade, lived afterwards at York,
> from whence he had married my mother, whose relations were
> named Robinson, a very good family in that country, and from
> whom I was called Robinson Kreutznaer; but, by the usual
> corruption of words in England, we are now called – nay we call
> ourselves and write our name – Crusoe; and so my companions
> always called me.

It reads like 'the real thing'. The story of a man called Crusoe, formerly Kreutzner.

As the story progresses, Crusoe has a series of thrilling adventures – one of the reasons young readers have always loved this novel. He's almost drowned; he's captured by pirates; he's enslaved by Arabs; and he wins through all adversity to become a wealthy plantation- (and slave-) owner in South America. But while taking a voyage to make even more money he finds himself alone on an island, having lost everything. On the simplest of narrative levels his story is a page-turner. How will our hero survive against the elements, wild animals and cannibals without supplies or other people to help him, we wonder – secretly suspecting that he will. Below the narrative surface, however, Crusoe is *homo economicus*. Wealth and the making of wealth is what his story is all about. That is its theme – gripping as the plot and all those adventures are.

Shortly after the wreck Crusoe makes several arduous journeys back to his ship before it breaks up and its contents are lost forever. He brings back, on improvised rafts, whatever materials he hopes will be useful to him. He gives us a meticulously exact inventory of what he salvages. Among the other items, in the captain's safe he finds £36. While noting that it will not be useful on the island, and recognising that removing it will be theft, he takes it anyway. The incident is telling. What is the most important thing? Money. The incident is inserted to remind us.

Over the following twenty-eight years Crusoe uses what he has brought ashore to sustain himself and gradually he cultivates the island. Everything on it is his property. He refers to himself as the 'sovereign' (king) of his island. From this angle we see *Robinson Crusoe* as an allegory of empire, and of England, which in this period had begun the process of seizing great chunks of the globe as its imperial property.

After many years Crusoe acquires a companion, a native from a neighbouring island who has barely escaped with his life from cannibals. Crusoe renames him 'Friday' (that being the day he found him) and makes him his servant. More importantly Friday is his chattel – bluntly, his slave. Empires always need slaves.

Daniel Defoe is one of the most interesting writers in all of English literature – and one of the most versatile. Over the course of a long (for that period) life, he was a pamphleteer, a businessman, a speculator on the recently invented stock exchange, a government spy, and the acknowledged 'father of English journalism', writing hundreds of books, pamphlets and journals. He was never well off, sometimes fell foul of the law, and was wholly impoverished in his later years. But it was in those late years that he invented what we know as the English novel. If Virginia Woolf could instruct women to throw flowers on the grave of Aphra Behn, we should throw some pound coins and dollar bills on the grave of Daniel Defoe, the chronicler of *homo economicus*.

The novel was not destined to remain shackled to Defoe's rigid realism. The genre could also 'fantasise' – maintaining a realistic external structure with contents as imaginary as any fairy tale. The great pioneer of the 'fantasy novel', so to call it, is Jonathan Swift (1667–1745).

Swift, an Irishman, was born into what is called 'the Ascendancy' – the upper class of the country who were favoured by their English masters and given privileges denied the Irish population at large. He spent much of his life in his home country, and is considered the first great Irish writer. He received his higher education at Trinity College Dublin, where he excelled as a scholar. He was ambitious and travelled to England to become secretary to a nobleman, in the hopes of advancing his career. Patronage was necessary for any such advancement. This was not yet a world where you could make it on your own.

His patron introduced him at court and imbued him with the Tory (Conservative) beliefs that stayed with Swift all his life. He eventually earned a doctorate in divinity ('Dr Swift' is what he is usually called) and became an ordained priest in the (Protestant) Church of Ireland. The Revd Dr Swift was given a series of parishes and eventually the post of Dean of St Patrick's Cathedral in Dublin. But he never received the great favours he expected from the English court and government. It sharpened his anger to the level of savagery. He felt, he said, 'like a rat in a hole'.

In the 1720s, as *Robinson Crusoe* was at its best-selling height, Swift began writing the work for which he is most remembered,

Gulliver's Travels. Like Defoe's story, the book, as it was published in 1726, offered itself as an authentic 'traveller's tale' (which some deluded contemporaries, as with *Robinson Crusoe*, took it to be). It encompasses four voyages. The first is to Lilliput, where the people are tiny yet fancy themselves being of great consequence – Swift was satirising the court and cronies around Queen Anne. The second voyage takes Lemuel Gulliver to Brobdingnag. Here the inhabitants are rural giants and it is the hero himself who is now doll-sized. Brobdingnag is the most agreeable of the four countries created by Swift because it is old-fashioned and traditional, and in every sense 'unmodern'. Swift loathed progress.

That loathing is apparent in the story of the third voyage. Gulliver travels to Laputa (Spanish for 'the whore'), which is a scientific utopia. Swift despised science, which he thought unnecessary and contrary to religion. Here he pictures the advanced scientists of his age as geeks, pointlessly labouring, for instance, to extract sunbeams from cucumbers. The third book also contains the Struldbrugs, who live forever, and decay forever, suffering an eternity of pain and mental infirmity. They fall to pieces but can never die. The travels are becoming progressively more horrible.

The fourth book is the most perplexing. Gulliver travels to Houyhnhnm Land, the pronunciation of which represents the neighing of a horse. In this country the horse rules and humans are excrement-spraying, mindless filthy apes called 'yahoos'. Horses, given that they consume grain and grass, have less offensive bodily wastes – something that George Orwell suggested, plausibly, lies behind Swift's strange vision of what is bearable or unbearable in life. Of course horses have no technology, no institutions, no 'culture' and no literature. Nor do they in Houyhnhnm Land. But this, apparently, is the nearest to 'utopia' that Swift will allow us to come. He does not have a lot of hope for mankind.

Gulliver's Travels, like Robinson's travels, open the way for innumerable novels to come over the following centuries, in their innovative blendings of the real and the fantastic. For everyone they are the best place to start your own voyage of discovery into the wonderful world of fiction.

CHAPTER 14

How to Read
DR JOHNSON

The first literary critic most of us will encounter is our English teacher in the classroom. Someone, that is, who helps us understand, or better appreciate, the more difficult and finer points of literature. Literature is made by 'authors'. Literary criticism involves something connected, but different: 'authority', or 'the person who knows better than we do'.

The subject of this chapter is Samuel Johnson (1709–84). He is commonly known as 'Dr Johnson', following the example of his admiring friends and contemporaries. Why do we also choose to call him that? We don't, for example, talk about 'Mr Shakespeare' or 'Miss Jane Austen'. We call him 'Dr Johnson' for the same reason that in our schooldays we call the teacher 'Miss' or 'Sir'. They are in charge. They have the authority. They know things we don't (yet). 'Doctor', literally, means one who has knowledge. Interestingly, the first real job Dr Johnson had was schoolteaching – the chalk in one hand, the cane in the other. In a sense he never put those schoolteacherly instruments down. He was never slow to thrash bad literature, or bad thinking about literature. His pugnacity is one of the things that makes him endearing.

Literature, as we have seen, goes as far back (via epic and myth) as humanity itself. Samuel Johnson is the first great critic of English literature and he, like the 'discipline' he represents, came much later in the day when the machineries of literary production had reached an advanced historical stage. Dr Johnson is very much a product of the eighteenth century – an age which prided itself on its social sophistication and 'polish'. Literary people of that century liked to see themselves as 'Augustans' – named after the high-point of classical Roman culture under the 'golden age' of the Emperor Augustus, whose achievements they aimed to copy. It was in the eighteenth century that our great institutions (Parliament, the monarchy, the universities, business, the press) took on their modern form. And, among all that, what we now call the 'book world' came into being. Johnson would, in his glory years, rule over that book world. One of his other names was 'the Great Cham' (cham being another word for 'khan', or 'king').

We know Johnson very well as a person. He was the subject of a biography (itself a fine work of literature) written by his young friend and disciple, James Boswell (1740–95). From Boswell's pages an endearing and vivid portrait emerges. Consider, for example, Boswell's recollection of his first meeting with the great man, tucking into his dinner like a wild animal:

> His looks seemed riveted to his plate; nor would he, unless when in very high company, say one word, or even pay the least attention to what was said by others, till he had satisfied his appetite, which was so fierce, and indulged with such intenseness, that while in the act of eating, the veins of his forehead swelled, and generally a strong perspiration was visible.

The two men went on consume two bottles of port wine at their first meeting. Lifelong friendship proceeded from that merry point.

Samuel Johnson was born in a small provincial town, Lichfield, the child of a bookseller (of rather advanced years for the trials of fatherhood). As a boy he suffered from a disease called scrofula,

which destroyed much of his eyesight. But he could read phenomenally well, even though he had to lean so close to the light that he
sometimes burned his hair on the candle he was reading by.

Largely self-educated, Sam was reciting the New Testament at
three and translating from the classics at six. At nine years old, he
picked up a volume of *Hamlet* from his father's shelves while sitting
in the family's basement kitchen. The words on the page induced
a hallucinatory vision of Elsinore and ghosts. It terrified him. He
threw down the book, and rushed into the street outside, 'that he
might see people about him'. His long love-affair with literature had
begun. It would, thereafter, be the most important thing in his life.

During his childhood his family teetered on the brink of
bankruptcy. But an unexpected bequest allowed Samuel to go
to Oxford University. The money, however, ran out and he was
obliged to leave without a degree (his doctorate would come, fifty
years later, as a mark of public esteem). On his return to Lichfield
Samuel married an elderly widow with money. He was, in the
circumstances, a good husband and his wife Tetty's wealth enabled
him to set up a school. It attracted only three pupils. On his wife's
death he took off with one of those pupils (later to be the famous
actor, David Garrick) on what he liked to call the 'best road' in
life – that leading to London. He went on to establish himself in
the literary world, commonly known as 'Grub Street' after a street
in the poor London district of Moorfields, inhabited by 'maggot-
like' hacks who earned their living by their pen. Johnson too made
his way without benefit of patrons (whom he despised) or private
income. He was a professional writer, proudly independent. He
paid his own way.

Johnson wrote fine poetry, in a neo-classical manner; he was
a great prose stylist; he wrote a novel, *Rasselas*, which was dashed
off in a few days to earn the money to provide a decent funeral for
his mother. (It's surprisingly good, given the sad circumstances.)
Johnson's views on the human condition were always profoundly
pessimistic. It was, he believed, a situation 'in which much is to be
endured, and little enjoyed'. His gloom is magnificently expressed
in his long poem, *The Vanity of Human Wishes* (the title says it

all). But, despite his depressed view of things, he believed that life should be lived with courage, as he lived his.

For all his many achievements, it is as a literary critic that Johnson is most revered. As a critic he brought two things to the understanding and appreciation of literature. One is 'order', the other 'common sense'. His common sense is legendary. It is vividly depicted in a conversation which he had with Boswell, while walking, on the then fashionable view (put into circulation by the philosopher Bishop Berkeley) that matter does not exist and that everything in the universe is 'merely ideal'. Imaginary. Boswell observed that, logically, the theory could not be refuted. Johnson responded by violently kicking a large stone which stood in their way and exclaiming, equally violently, 'I refute it thus!'

He adopted the same common-sense attitude in his literary judgements. He loved, said Johnson, to 'concur with the common reader'. It is not the least attractive thing about him that he never talks down to us. It's also interesting to note that – an unusual thing among literary critics – he had great respect for young minds. In another conversation, Boswell asked what Johnson (the former schoolmaster) thought were the best subjects for children to learn first. Johnson's reply was that it did not matter: 'Sir, while you are considering which of two things you should teach your child first, another boy has learnt them both.'

Johnson's most enduring achievement is the order and manageable shape he brought to the appreciation of literature. It took the form of two vast monumental works: his *Dictionary* and his *Lives of the Most Eminent English Poets*. Approached by a group of booksellers, he embarked on the research for his *Dictionary* in 1745 – still unaided by any patron, and single-handed. It would take him ten years to complete and would ruin what was left of his eyesight. On its completion he was awarded a government pension of £300 a year – appropriately, since the dictionary was a service to the English nation and people.

When it was published the two-volume *Dictionary* was the size of a small coffee table. It is famous for the eccentricity and wit of many of its definitions (for example: '*Patron*. Commonly a wretch who supports with insolence, and is paid with flattery'). But the underlying principle was more ambitious, something indicated by the full description given on the title page:

> A Dictionary of the English Language: In which the Words are deduced from their Originals, and Illustrated in their Different Significations by Examples from the best Writers. To which are prefixed A History of the Language, and An English Grammar. By Samuel Johnson, A.M.

Johnson did not merely offer 'definitions', he traced how the meanings of words evolved over time and how they contain within themselves all sorts of ambiguities and multiple meanings according to where, when and how they were used. He demonstrated this complexity with some 150,000 historical examples.

Take an example from the very 'best' writer of all, and the text that so struck the nine-year-old Samuel. In *Hamlet*, as the drowned Ophelia is being buried, Gertrude throws something into the open grave, with the comment 'Sweets to the sweet. Farewell!' But what is she throwing? Chocolates? Biscuits? Sugar cubes? No, fresh flowers. For the Elizabethans, the adjective 'sweet' primarily indicated what one could smell with the nose, not what one could taste with the tongue, which is how we generally use it now. This earlier usage, among others, is the kind of thing recorded by Johnson. The major point Johnson makes in the *Dictionary* is that language – particularly the language writers use – cannot be set in stone. It is a living, organic, ever-changing thing.

Johnson's other *magnum opus* (great work) is his *Lives of the Most Eminent English Poets*, published in 1779–81. Again, the title page is illuminating:

> The Lives of the Most Eminent English Poets, with Critical Observations on their Works by Samuel Johnson.

The point he makes with his selection of fifty-two 'most eminent poets' is that an appreciation of literature requires a separation of the worthwhile from the less than worthwhile. There are, in the vaults of Britain's and America's great national libraries, many millions of books which classify as 'Literature'. How, in the limited time available to us in a human lifetime, should we choose what is worth reading? Critical assistance can supply a 'curriculum' (what is prescribed for us to read at school) and a 'canon' – the best of the best.

But does this mean that we should always agree with literary critics – submit, meekly, to their authority? Certainly not. Imagine a classroom of thirty students tackling an algebra equation. However difficult the sum there will be one correct answer. Imagine, however, an English lesson being asked 'What is *Hamlet*, the play, about?' There should be a whole range of different answers, from 'The best way to appoint a king' to 'In what circumstances is suicide a proper decision?' It would be a disaster if every member of the class simply parroted what someone else had said or thought.

There is a complicated line from taking literary criticism on board, weighing it, and then going on to form your own opinions. Johnson understood that. Literary works, he once said, must be batted about like shuttlecocks in a game of badminton. The last thing one wants is consensus. We can even disagree with Johnson himself. He revered Shakespeare and edited the plays (editing is one of the most useful things a literary critic can do). Johnson believed that Shakespeare was a genius. It was Johnson's admiration, expressed everywhere in his edition of and commentary on Shakespeare, which established him as the greatest of the nation's writers. But he also believed that the author of *Hamlet* often lacked sophistication and polish – he was sometimes 'untutored', even primitive. He lacked something that Johnson and his contemporaries valued above all things: 'decorum'. Shakespeare's work was the result of the uncultivated age in which he lived. Most of us would strongly disagree. That is a privilege that Johnson, the most generous and open-minded of literary critics, allows us. He gives us the tools to make up our own minds.

CHAPTER 15

Romantic Revolutionaries

Literary lives do not generally make interesting films. There is nothing dramatic in scribbling – which is what most writers do most of the working day. John Keats (1795–1821) is an exception. His short life was the subject of a fine film in 2010, *Bright Star*. The title was taken from one of Keats's sonnets – 'Bright star, would I were steadfast as thou art' – addressed in 1819 to the woman he loved, Fanny Brawne. In it the poet longs to be

> Pillow'd upon my fair love's ripening breast,
> To feel for ever its soft swell and fall,
> Awake for ever in a sweet unrest,
> Still, still to hear her tender-taken breath,
> And so live ever – or else swoon to death.

Sad to say, he would never be so happily 'pillow'd'. Fanny's mother considered her too young to marry (Keats was twenty-five, Fanny nineteen). She was a class or two higher than John and would have to marry 'below herself' if she took the plunge. He was poor – the son of a stable-hand, a failed medical student, not yet famous, and, most worryingly, a poet with 'radical' friends of dangerous political opinions. Fanny's widowed mother urged caution. It was further advisable since John was 'consumptive' – he had symptoms of tuberculosis. His brother Tom had recently died of the disease and his mother before that. Keats went to Rome with hopes of repairing his lungs, but – as predicted in the poem – 'swooned to death' in the eternal city, ever faithful to the woman he loved. Why did Keats weave his love for Fanny around a 'bright star' (Polaris)? He was alluding to the 'star-crossed lovers', Romeo and Juliet. He had somehow anticipated a similarly tragic end to his own love.

I've summarised Keats's life because it's a wonderfully *romantic* story, and makes a romantic film. It can still move us. But when we call Keats, Wordsworth, Byron, Coleridge or Shelley 'Romantic' poets (the capital 'R' is important here), we think of something other than their love lives (most of which were tangled to the point of chaos). We allude to a school of poetry that has very distinctive properties and which represents an evolutionary moment in Western literature.

At its simplest, 'Romantic' is simply a convenient date-range for literature written, roughly, between 1789 and 1832. It's common, for example, to find Jane Austen lumped together with other writers of the Romantic Period despite the fact that, in terms of what she wrote, the author of *Pride and Prejudice* is on a different literary planet from, say, Shelley, who deserted a pregnant wife (who later committed suicide) to elope with the sixteen-year-old Mary Shelley who would, a couple of years later, write *Frankenstein*.

Why take 1789 as a starting point? Because Romanticism coincided with a world historical event: the French Revolution. Romanticism was the first literary movement to have, at its core, 'ideology' – the set of beliefs by which people, and peoples, live their lives. There had always been literature which was political: John Dryden's poems on 'affairs of state', for example, or Jonathan Swift's sniping at the Whigs in *Gulliver's Travels*. Shakespeare's *Coriolanus* can be read as a political play. Politics is concerned with running the state (it originates in the Ancient Greek word for 'city'). Ideology aims to change the world. Romanticism has that impulse at its heart.

What's meant by 'ideological', as opposed to 'political', can be neatly demonstrated by the deaths in war of two great poets, Sir Philip Sidney and Lord Byron. Sidney died in 1586 of wounds incurred fighting the Spanish in Holland. While dying he is famously supposed to have passed the water bottle offered him to another wounded man with the words, 'Thy need is greater than mine'. The act has become legendary. He was thirty-two years old. What was Sir Philip dying for so gallantly and so young? 'Queen and Country,' he would have responded. 'England.'

Lord Byron (1788–1824) died at Missolonghi in Greece, having volunteered to fight for the Greeks in their war of independence against their Turkish occupiers. He was thirty-six years old. What was Byron dying for? A 'cause'. That cause was 'liberty'. He was not giving up his life in the service of his country – which in Byron's view was woefully unliberated. Liberty was what the Americans were fighting for when they made their Declaration of Independence in 1776, it was what the Parisian masses had risen up against the Bastille for in 1789, it was what the Greeks were fighting for in 1824. And that is what Byron gave his life for.

Byron did not, like Sidney, 'die for England'. The poet was an exile from a country that found his doctrines of sexual liberty, as celebrated in his longest and finest poem, *Don Juan*, wholly scandalous. In Byron's analysis Juan is not the sexual predator of legend (and of Mozart's opera *Don Giovanni*) but a sexually liberated man – as Byron believed himself to be. A hero in Greece (there is no city that does not have a street named after him and a statue), England would have a 'Byron problem' for over a century. It was not until 1969 that the authorities saw fit to lay a stone to his memory in Westminster Abbey's Poets' Corner. The poet himself, one fancies, would rather have liked the swinging sixties.

Put at its simplest, Sidney's sacrifice was patriotically motivated, Byron's sacrifice was ideologically motivated. When we read him and other Romantics we must tune in to the ideological positions (the 'cause') they are adopting, advocating, probing, opposing or questioning. Where, as the current idiom puts it, is their work coming from?

The leading Scottish Romantics, for example, were Robert Burns (1759–96) and Sir Walter Scott (1771–1832). One of Burns's best-known poems is 'To a Mouse'. It opens:

> Wee, sleekit, cow'rin, tim'rous beastie,
> O, what panic's in thy breastie!

Burns, a farmer, had cut into a field-mouse's nest with his plough. Looking down on the life he has wrecked he reflects:

> I'm truly sorry Man's dominion
> Has broken Nature's social union ...

The 'beastie' is not just a little rodent, but, like Burns himself, a fellow victim of 'social' injustice – 'me, thy poor, earth-born companion /An' fellow-mortal!' And Burns's use of Lowland Scottish dialect makes the added point that the language of the people, not the 'King's English', represents the heart of the Scottish nation.

Walter Scott's first and most influential novel is *Waverley* (1814). At its centre is the 1745 uprising in which an army of Highland rebels, under the 'Young Pretender', Charles Edward Stuart, swept down victoriously through Scotland into the north of England, intent on reclaiming the British throne. If they had succeeded, they would have wholly changed the history of the United Kingdom. Scott himself was staunchly Unionist, believing in the partnership of Scotland and England, and he had mixed feelings about 'Bonnie Prince Charlie'. He was, the novelist said, in his head a Hanoverian (a supporter of the English king, George II) and in his heart a Jacobite (a supporter of the Scottish Pretender). But what is significant in *Waverley* is that Scott portrayed 'the '45' as less a war of failed conquest – between two powers of more or less equal standing – than a failed revolution. Or, put another way, a clash of ideologies.

The most powerful revolutionary statement among the British Romantics is Wordsworth and Coleridge's *Lyrical Ballads*

(1798) with the long argumentative preface later added by Wordsworth. In it he proclaims:

> The principal object, then, proposed in these Poems was to choose incidents and situations from common life, and to relate or describe them, throughout, as far as was possible in a selection of language really used by men.

The contents were called 'ballads' in honour of those poems that are passed down orally by communities, not individual writers. The traditional ballad represents a kind of literary togetherness – although Wordsworth would have used the word 'radicalism' (in the literal sense of going back to roots) or, if pushed, the French slogan 'fraternity'.

Samuel Taylor Coleridge (1772–1834) made a majestic contribution to the project in the form of his long ballad, in pseudo-medieval diction, *The Rime of the Ancyent Marinere*. In it he sets out to demonstrate that the complex issues of life and death – the meaning of it all – can be expressed in a literary form as simple as a tum-te-tum nursery rhyme. A ballad.

It wasn't all ideology. The Romantics were fascinated by human psychology and the emotions that condition our lives. Wordsworth loved, as he said, to be 'surprised by joy' – and joy is an important word in all his major poetry. But at the same time the Romantics were fascinated by joy's opposite emotion, 'melancholy'. Keats wrote one of his great odes to it. Other Romantics, famously Coleridge and Thomas De Quincey (author of *Confessions of an English Opium Eater*), investigated emotional states with the aid of drugs. Opium and its derivatives (for poets later on, morphine) allowed a voyage of exploration into the self as daring as any undertaken by the Ancient Mariner. The drugs themselves needed no great exploration to come by. They were on sale, for pennies, in every apothecary's shop and even in some bookshops. You could buy a pint of laudanum (morphine dissolved in alcohol, and used as a painkiller) together with your copy of *Lyrical Ballads*.

The danger was that if you followed that route (as, most

dramatically, did De Quincey), you entered the realm of what has been called 'Romantic agony'. The writers who experimented with opium took huge risks with their creativity and lives. Coleridge wrote, it is generally agreed, three wonderful poems. Two of them are tantalisingly unfinished. Most frustrating is what promised to be his great work, 'Kubla Khan'. The whole poem was being inscribed on his mind, as he tells us, in an opium-induced dream. Then there came a knock at the door. He woke up. The poem was lost – only a tiny fragment remains.

William Wordsworth (1770–1850) thought a lot about how the poet should cultivate himself. He had a lot of time to do so. Unlike the other leading Romantic poets he lived a long, abstemious, well-regulated life in the Lake District, and was the movement's most eminent author. Some would say he sold out in his later years, when he became Queen Victoria's poet laureate (see Chapter 22). By general agreement he wrote his best works early in life. As a young man he had been in France at the time of the Revolution. Looking back, he wrote of those turbulent months, in *The Prelude*:

Bliss was it in that dawn to be alive,
But to be young was very heaven!

There is something inherently 'glamorous' about the young Romantics. It is only at this period of life, it is suggested, that a person really lives. Shelley died, aged twenty-nine, sailing in a sudden storm, whipped up by the same wind he had adressed in his famous 'Ode to the West Wind' of 1819. Before Keats died in Rome, aged only twenty-five, he instructed that his name should not be on his tombstone – only the description 'A young English poet'. 'An old Romantic' is something of a contradiction in terms. Like sportsmen, the best of them had a short career – or wrote their greatest work while young.

We talk about the Romantics as if they were somehow a group, allied in a collective literary endeavour. They weren't. There were, of course, alliances. But Byron, for instance, despised and satirised the 'Lakers', as he called Wordsworth, Coleridge, Southey and their disciples. Not for him mooning over the damp northern English hills. Scott, and his Edinburgh clique, hated the 'Cockney Poet' Keats and his patron, Leigh Hunt. None of the poets of the time seem to have registered the existence of (as we now think) one of the greatest of their number, William Blake (1757–1827). Some of Blake's magnificently illustrated volumes – made and written by himself – sold barely in double figures in his lifetime. His *Songs of Innocence and of Experience*, infused as they are with his idiosyncratic views on life and religion, are now everywhere read, studied and enjoyed. No other writer, of any period, so effectively combined the visual with the textual. Blake's poems (like 'The Tyger') are things we 'look at' as much as read.

Despite these personal differences, rivalries and blind spots, the Romantics joined their creative force in a massive redefinition of what literature was and what it could do outside its merely literary environment – how it could change society and even, as the more optimistic of the Romantics thought, the world. 'Revolution' is not an overstatement. The movement burned too hot to last long. Effectively it was burned out in Britain by the time of Scott's death in 1832 and the country's own 'quiet' political revolution, the First Reform Bill. But Romanticism changed, forever, the ways in which literature was written and read. It bequeathed to the writers who came after, and who cared to use it, a new power. Not bright stars, but burning stars.

CHAPTER 16

The Sharpest Mind
JANE AUSTEN

It has taken a long time for us to realise that Jane Austen (1775–1817) is one of the great English-language novelists. One of the reasons we can overlook her is that the world of her fiction is (there is no other word) small. And, to the superficial eye, the big question posed in each of her six novels – 'Who will the heroine marry?' – looks, if not similarly small, something less than earth-shatteringly important. We are not, it is clear, in the same league as Tolstoy's *War and Peace* (even though virtually all of Austen's fiction was actually written in wartime – the longest war that modern Britain had ever fought).

In a letter written in 1816, Austen likened her novels, with her characteristic irony, to miniature paintings: 'the little bit (two inches wide) of ivory on which I work with so fine a brush'. Charlotte Brontë took up the same image, but much more critically:

There is a Chinese fidelity, a miniature delicacy, in the painting. She ruffles her reader by nothing vehement, disturbs him with nothing profound. The passions are perfectly unknown to her:

she rejects even a speaking acquaintance with that stormy sister-hood.

Hard words, but it's a common criticism. Austen, implies the author of *Jane Eyre* (who wrote her fiction from behind a male pseudonym), is not a writer who can hold her own in the man's world. And she is too tame – 'un-stormy' is Brontë's term – even for the more demanding woman reader.

Can literary greatness find room for itself on those two inches of Austen ivory, restricting itself, as her novels do, to such a limited range of largely female, exclusively middle-class experience? The answer, modern readers would reply, is 'Yes indeed'. Explaining why is trickier. But a firm yes is the right place to start from.

Jane Austen was born the daughter of a country parson, moderately prosperous and wholly respectable. She was brought up in a happy family environment with brothers and a sister, Cassandra, to whom she was particularly close – so close that for many years they shared a bed. After her sadly early death, it is from her favourite brother Henry's fond recollection of her, and the surviving letters to Cassandra (most of which were deliberately destroyed), that we know what little we do know of Jane Austen's life. What one can safely suppose is that there was little high drama in it.

Austen's novels were written in the first instance for her own amusement. There is a pleasant recollection of her hiding her work-in-progress under the blotter of her *escritoire* when the creaking door warned that someone was coming into the room. She insisted the door mustn't be mended. They might not peep, but they could listen when she was ready, as her stories were tried out first on her family. They it was who heard their clever young Jane read 'First Impressions', the early version of the novel published years later, in 1813, as *Pride and Prejudice*. (The action is set fifteen years before its publication date.) One would give a lot to know what the Revd George Austen and Mrs Austen made of Mr and Mrs Bennet – characters depicted in a not entirely sympathetic light in their daughter's narrative. Probably they chuckled, if a little nervously.

Austen travelled very little in her life. Nor do her heroines travel much. The family spent some time in Bath, the Regency spa-town and marriage market, a place Austen seems to have disliked. She visited London but never lived there, and it figures little in her writing; usually, as in *Sense and Sensibility*, as a place it's good to get away from. The 'home counties' – principally Hampshire – were her home ground. It's quaint to be told that she had a strong loyalty to the local cricket team, the 'Gentlemen of Hampshire'.

An attractive woman, one gathers (no reliable portrait of her survives), she is known to have had an offer of marriage. She accepted, but then withdrew her consent the next morning. She never did marry, although all her novels are centrally concerned with her heroines' courtship problems. Austen's motives for remaining single can only be guessed at. Whatever those motives might have been, lovers of her work may be grateful that she changed her mind on that fateful night in 1802. A wife and mother would have had less time to produce the six novels on which her reputation rests. She died that most pitied object in her fiction: an old maid.

Old, though, is the wrong word. Austen was only forty-one at the time of her death. As with so much in her life, we don't know what disease killed her. But it was not sudden, and her last novels were composed in growing physical weakness through her final illness. An understandable darkness tinges her last complete work, *Persuasion*. In the ending to that novel, one can almost feel the pen drooping with exhaustion on the paper. She did not live to revise it to her satisfaction.

The Austen heroine invariably has both a suitable and an un-suitable suitor. Will Emma Woodhouse marry Frank Churchill or consent to become the wife of the older, duller Mr Knightley? Will Elizabeth Bennet mend her family's fortunes by accepting the offer of the Revd Mr Collins, or stick to her guns and (after some heavy counter-fire from Lady Catherine de Bourgh) become Mrs Darcy? Will Marianne succumb to the Byronic Willoughby or discover the attractions of the dull, but worthy, Colonel Brandon with his flannel waistcoat (he is middle-aged and feels the cold)? All the novels end with a peal of church bells, the right choice having been made.

Famously Jane Austen never goes beyond what a 'lady' would decently know. ('By a Lady' is the description under the title of her anonymously published first novel, *Sense and Sensibility*.) There are many men in her novels but she never depicts males in conversation together without a lady present and listening. There are few truly grand aristocrats – exceptions are Sir Thomas Bertram in *Mansfield Park* and Sir Walter Elliot in *Persuasion*, but neither of them stands high in the register of peers of the realm. Equally, there are no working-class characters in the foreground of her novels. Shabby-genteel is as far down the social scale as we go in Jane Austen's world. There are, of course, servants everywhere. Some of their names (James the coachman in *Emma*, for example) we know. But life below stairs is another, unvisited world in Austen's fiction.

Occasionally we get glimpses of a harder world than the novels choose to dwell on. In *Emma* Jane Fairfax finds herself in a cruel dilemma. Penniless, but talented, she must make her own way in the world. Marriage would be a solution but the man she loves (and who may have taken cruel advantage of her) seems more interested in rich Emma Woodhouse. The only means by which Jane can support herself is by becoming a governess – earning barely enough to live on and enduring the humiliating household status of 'upper servant'. She describes applying for such positions as being like a slave on the auction block. Charlotte Brontë would make a novel, *Jane Eyre*, out of this scenario. For Jane Austen it is a sideline to the main plot, which she chooses not to go too far into, other than to draw the reader's attention to Jane's plight.

One can rack up any number of things that Jane Austen's novels don't do. She lived and wrote through some of the greatest historical upheavals the world had known – the American and French revolutions and the Napoleonic Wars. Sailors (she had brothers in the Navy) and military men (Colonel Brandon in *Sense and Sensibility*, for example, and the naval hero Frederick Wentworth in *Persuasion*) make an appearance in her narratives, but only as eligible or ineligible suitors for the heroines. If Horatio Nelson himself appeared in an Austen novel one suspects the novel's only interest in him would be whether he was 'Mr Right' for the heroine.

A grand estate such as Mansfield Park supports itself, financially, by its sugar plantations in the West Indies, worked by slaves. The fact is alluded to – but not examined or dwelled on. Nor, perish the thought, is the reader given a glimpse of what is going on in those West Indian plantations. Austen's political and religious views are those of her class, although in her later novels they seem to have hardened somewhat. She was a devout Anglican, and clergymen figure prominently in her fiction. But not once do her novels take us inside a church, or venture into theological matters. That was reserved for Sundays, not fiction.

The feminist movement that took off in the 1960s has stoutly championed Austen's fiction. Her own view on these latter-day champions might have been doubtful. Her novels never question the status of men as the superior sex. We don't know whether she resented the fact that her publishing contracts had to be negotiated by her father or brother – women having no property rights, even in the fruits of their own brains. The richest of her heroines is Emma, possessed, when she reaches twenty-one, of some £30,000 (a vastly huger amount in modern value). When she marries Mr Knightley, it will become his. The novel accepts that, serenely.

Austen's views on literature were as conservative as her social beliefs. Although she coincided, historically, with the Romantic movement – and is often classified as a Romantic – she belonged to an earlier, more stable age, whose values her novels collectively endorse. Much contemporary fiction – particularly the 'tale of terror' – offended her sense of literary propriety. *Northanger Abbey* has a heroine, Catherine Morland, who is morally poisoned by her addiction to modern novels – temporarily, thank heavens.

All the above would seem to make the point that Jane Austen was a writer of very limited range. Insignificant, even. What then do the novels do that makes them so supremely good? Two things. The first is Austen's technical mastery of her novel's form, particularly in her use of irony. The second is her moral seriousness – her ability to articulate, in all its complications, how one should live one's life. We could also cite her wit, her tolerant observation of human foibles, and her sympathy.

There are few more artful plot-wrights than Austen. It is hard for her fans to remember their first readings of the novels, because they know them so well. 'Janeites', as her devout followers are called, take it on themselves to re-read the six novels every year like holy writ. But for first-time readers especially, her novels are page-turners, masterly in their winding up of suspense. Will Emma (or Elizabeth, or Catherine, or Elinor) do the right thing? The reader is on tenterhooks until almost the last chapter.

No writer uses her prose instrument more skilfully than Austen. Moreover she has the knack of making us, her readers, use our own skill-set to the limits of our ability, and beyond what we normally trouble to do. Take, as an example, the opening of *Emma*:

> Emma Woodhouse, handsome, clever, and rich, with a comfortable home and happy disposition, seemed to unite some of the best blessings of existence; and had lived nearly twenty-one years in the world with very little to distress or vex her.

Two words grate interestingly in this sentence. 'Handsome': is that not a word more applicable to a man? Would not 'pretty', or 'beautiful' be more appropriate? 'Emma Woodhouse' (no 'Miss', you note) may, we suspect, be her own woman, and not necessarily conformist. The other reverberating word in the sentence is 'seemed'. That confidence about 'the best blessings of existence' will, we are warned, be tested: as indeed it is, almost to destruction, in the pages that follow. And the word 'vex' (not 'upset'): it suggests a haughtiness, a pride waiting for its fall. This one sentence bristles with irony and suggestion.

Austen's command of prose style and narrative technique is combined with a high moral seriousness. Her novels are much more than a maiden's fraught progress to the marriage altar after a few mistakes en route. Her heroines invariably start life as good young women determined to do the right thing. Inexperience and innocence – sometimes exacerbated by thoughtlessness or obstinacy – lead them into life's difficulties and dangers. Put another way, they make mistakes which they pay for. Out of the resulting stress and suffering they emerge as 'adult', morally mature. What Austen's novels tell us is that in order to live properly, you have first to have lived. Life is an education for life. Here again (as with the skills mentioned above) Austen has been seen as the pioneer in what is called the 'Great Tradition' of English fiction – a line that runs through George Eliot, the Brontës (despite Charlotte's moans), Dickens, Henry James and D.H. Lawrence. All take their starting point from the modest lady writing in a rectory in Hampshire who understood the world more than the world gave her credit for.

Austen's fiction demonstrates, supremely well, that a literary work need not be large to be great. And what can two inches of ivory contain? Everything worth writing about, if the brush and the surface are in the hands of a genius.

CHAPTER 17

Books for You
The Changing Reading Public

Reading has always been an intensely private act. Even in a reading group, members will bring their private responses to the meeting and 'share them'. They do not share the act of reading itself. Nonetheless what readers buy, beg, borrow or steal *en masse* is a crucial element in the long evolution of literature. The market determines the product. And, in the largest sense, that market (made up of millions of individual readers) constitutes what we can call the 'reading public'. It is no more predictable in its choices than the voting public, but, like them, it calls the shots. As in any branch of business the customer (reader) is always right. Readers create a demand and authors – along with producers and distributors – respond and supply. Anyone in the book business who doesn't respond to demand will quickly go bust.

The reading public emerges as a force in and on literature in the eighteenth century, with urbanisation and growing prosperity. At the same time, an interesting characteristic developed: the emergence of new, smaller reading publics within the whole. There was in this period an ever-growing mass of middle-class, leisured women who could read, even if they could not write proficiently, or were not encouraged to – there were few opportunities for them to exercise their skills in the outside world. They represented a reading public relatively unexploited until this date. Attractive reading matter for the woman reader of the time arrived in the form of fiction. Samuel Richardson's *Pamela* (1740) and *Clarissa* (1747–48) – runaway bestsellers in the mid-eighteenth century – were clearly targeted at women like the heroines themselves: young, decent, middle-class, virtuous, waiting for marriage, or already married. Richardson's great adversary, and the satiriser of his fiction, Henry Fielding, just as clearly targeted young men with the bawdy tale of *Tom Jones* (1749). Young men were another section of the diversifying reading public, with its own particular tastes and preferences.

Fiction for women, by women, about women took root in this period. It was significant in all sorts of ways. The modern critic Elaine Showalter calls the novels written at this time and later 'a literature of their own': a way in which women could converse at a time when their access to the outside world, and their opportunities to assemble (other than in church, and in church-related activities), were limited. The novel was one of the foundation stones of what would later evolve as feminism. (Chapter 29 takes up this point.)

There was, however, a major drawback: the educational deficit. To rise above the levels of literacy prescribed for most of their sex, women needed an unusually well-stocked library of books in the house, and parents or guardians interested in their intellect. The Brontës (Chapter 19) and Jane Austen (Chapter 16) had that good luck, as did a few women readers of literature. Most did not. Even in the twentieth century, Virginia Woolf's tract for the intellectual liberation of women, *A Room of One's Own* (1929), opens with the description of her being denied entrance to a library at the University of Cambridge. She is not, a Fellow informs her, a fellow. It's a symbolic scene. She does not belong in the reading world of men ('yet', one should add). The first two women's colleges at Cambridge were opened in the late nineteenth century and it was not until well after Woolf's death that the college on whose steps she was standing admitted women students.

George Eliot (real name Mary Anne Evans) was allowed, as a little girl, the free run of the library of a nearby country house, where her father was a land agent. She had no more than a sound school education. By a heroic course of self-instruction, and with the help of friends, she taught herself German and began her writing career as a translator of complicated works of theology and philosophy. She became one of the first women 'higher journalists' of her time. Few, of either sex, ranked higher. When, in her late thirties, she turned to fiction (using a male pseudonym) with *Adam Bede* (1859), she was already a self-made woman – an 'autodidact' and a 'blue stocking', as women who dared to educate themselves were called. Few could do what she did. Eliot saw the kind of fiction that the bulk of her sex consumed and did not like it one bit: 'silly novels by lady novelists', she called it. There were, of course, silly novels for men as well. But men's access to the treasure house of very un-silly literature was less restricted than women's. The situation changed, slowly. In modern times, Iris Murdoch, Margaret Atwood, Joyce Carol Oates, Toni Morrison and A.S. Byatt, have all been university teachers, the cleverest going. Their reading public tends to be well educated, and with as many, or more, women readers as men. In this respect, the reading public has evened out.

At any point in history, and from whatever angle we look at it, however, the 'reading public' is not monolithic like a football crowd. In our own day, it is more like a kind of mosaic – a lot of small reading publics, loosely strung together. This point can be illustrated by dropping into any large bookshop. Wander through and you will find different 'category areas' (genres) with different kinds of books. Customers know what they like, and whether they want to choose within Teen Fiction or Classic Fiction or Gay and Erotic Fiction or Romantic Fiction or Horror or Crime Fiction or Children's Literature.

Somewhere – usually in some unfrequented corner – there will be a section devoted to Poetry. It will not, for a certainty, attract the same potential consumers as are sniffing interestedly around the bestsellers heaped mountainously on front-of-shop display tables. Poetry has always been literature's poor sister. 'Fit audience though few', was Milton's description of his reading public. So little interested was he in sales that he parted with the manuscript of *Paradise Lost* for £10; a pittance, even in the seventeenth century. Ironically – and thanks to higher education – Milton now has a vast readership. *Paradise Lost* is a year-in, year-out bestseller and will be as long as it is a studied text. Oscar Wilde sensibly moved from writing verse, his first love, to hugely popular stage comedy. He followed the money. 'Why should I write for posterity?' he is said to have quipped. 'What has posterity ever done for me?' Many poets stick with their 'fit audience though few'. Bestselling poetry is a contradiction in terms, unless we count balladeers such as Bob Dylan and David Bowie.

The book industry undertakes rigorous and expensive market research to know as much as it can about 'reader preferences'. As a general rule, science fiction is consumed by young college-educated males, who buy large numbers of books and are 'brand-addicted'. They keep in touch with their genre, and with fellow genre followers, through web fanzines.

A slightly different type of reader will congregate around graphic fiction (a modern form of comic books), although its constituency too will be overwhelmingly young(ish). On the fantasy fringe of science fiction – where zombies and vampires roam – women readers enjoy new authors such as Stephenie Meyer. Horror, another fringe territory, has some reader overlap with science fiction and graphic novels, although its followers are predominantly older. Male action novels (in the past, westerns, now more often war stories) appeal to men who are usually past the age of military service and have never ridden a horse. Crime too attracts the older reader both male and female, with queens of crime such as Agatha Christie nowadays superseded by harder-boiled practitioners such as Patricia Cornwell.

Romance is largely consumed by women in midlife and later years. Oddly, the recent boom in e-books was led by this particular reading public. Reasons suggest themselves. Mothers, for example, tend to be more housebound and bookshops (unlike supermarkets) are unfriendly to prams.

Nowadays bookstores have EPoS systems – Electric Point of Sales devices – from which buying data is analysed and feeds back as stock delivery. If customers are buying a particular book fast, more copies will be supplied to fill the empty spaces on the shelves. The glove is fashioned to fit the hand. Even your particular hand, if you use electronic bookshops. Buy or browse regularly on Amazon, and it will profile you. Advertisements to suit your taste will pop up on your screen. We all have different preferences, as we have different fingerprints. The reading public is now 'profiled' by the book industry in more detail, and more accurately, than at any time in literary history. That, however, does not mean that it can predict what readers will want – merely that their wants, once expressed, can be met more rapidly and efficiently.

Taken as a whole, the reading public has always wanted more reading matter than it can comfortably afford. Over most of its history, literature, in book form, was an expensive luxury. Two innovations brought literature within reach of ordinary people, making it more affordable and giving the public access to vastly more of it.

The first was the library system. Jane Austen's two voracious readers, Catherine Morland and Isabella Thorpe (in *Northanger Abbey*, 1818), get their 'horrid' gothic novels from the local 'circulating library' in Bath, where one book could circulate among many customers. Librarians today estimate that a hardback novel is good for 150 loans. Lending fees could be reduced equivalently. In the mid-nineteenth century there emerged large metropolitan commercial libraries (called 'leviathans') serving the Victorian reading public. In the first half of the twentieth century every town and city also had cornershop 'tuppenny' libraries, where popular novels would sit alongside cigarettes, sweets and newspapers. In the 1950s, in the UK, every municipal council was obliged, by law, to supply books to the local population via a 'comprehensive' public library service. It was free.

The other innovation was the cheap book, a result of mechanical improvements in the printing press and, in the nineteenth century, the manufacture of low-cost, vegetable-based paper. Most influential in modern times has been the paperback revolution, which took off in the USA in the 1960s. In the twenty-first century we have electronic supply (e-books), and every internet-connected screen opens the door to an Aladdin's Cave.

If, today, the reading public gets far more to choose from, and gets much more of what it wants, is that a good thing? Not everyone thinks so. Some have claimed that 'more means worse'. There are those – I am one – who think that out of quantity comes quality. The larger the reading public, the healthier. And the bigger the pudding, the more plentiful the plums within it.

CHAPTER 18

The Giant
DICKENS

Few people would disagree with the idea that Charles Dickens (1812–70) is the finest British novelist ever to have put pen to paper. 'A no-brainer', we might say. 'The Inimitable', as he nicknamed himself (even *he* thought he was peerlessly superb), would have flashed an angry look at the impertinence of even thinking, let alone asking, such a question.

What other novelist has had his image on both a banknote and a postage stamp? What other novelist has had his work so often adapted for large and small screen? What other Victorian novelist still sells a million copies of his works every year? In the 2012 celebration of the 200th anniversary of his birth, both the Prime Minister and the Archbishop of Canterbury declared that Dickens was a writer of Shakespearean stature. Who will argue with them?

But what precisely is it in Dickens's novels which merits the supreme and universal praise he receives? It's a tricky question, requiring a whole range of answers. And over the years those answers have changed. If, for example, you had asked one of

Dickens's contemporaries, who had just finished reading *The Pickwick Papers*, 'Why do you think "Boz" (Dickens's pen-name in his early fiction) is great?' he or she might well have said, 'He makes me laugh more than any other writer I have ever come across'. If, eight years later, you had asked one of Dickens's contemporaries, 'What is there in *The Old Curiosity Shop* that makes the author so great?' they might well have replied – thinking of the famously sad death of Little Nell – 'Because I have never wept so much at a novel. Dickens moves me as no other writer has done'.

Readers in the nineteenth century reacted, by and large, rather differently from us. They did not feel any obligation to hold back their emotions. We like to think we are made of sterner stuff, or that we are more sophisticated readers of literature. Hence Oscar Wilde's much recycled wisecrack, 'One would need a heart of stone not to laugh at the death of Little Nell'. Perhaps we chuckle at the funnier scenes in Dickens's fiction (describing Mr Micawber's perennial struggle with the debt collector, for example); our eyes may moisten a little at the sadder scenes (the long-lingering death of Paul Dombey, for example); but we generally keep a tight control on our emotions. It makes us more objective and rational in our literary judgements. Does it make us better readers? Arguably not.

We are not Victorians, but there are five good arguments why modern readers should also see that Dickens is the greatest ever novelist.

First is that Dickens was, over the course of his long writing career, uniquely inventive. While still in his early twenties, he had a huge success with his first novel, *The Pickwick Papers*. Like all his novels, it first appeared in instalments; monthly episodes started appearing in April 1836 under the title *The Posthumous Papers of the Pickwick Club*. Lesser writers would have written a string of novels along the same Pickwickian lines, but Dickens, the most restless of writers, immediately moved on to a very different kind of novel with *Oliver Twist* (1837–38). This is a dark, angry and politically-engaged work, quite different from the comic adventures of Mr Samuel Pickwick. Its anger is directed as much towards the British government as the British reading public. This tale of a workhouse boy turned pickpocket turned burglar, is the first of his 'social problem' novels in which he attacked abuses of the day. In the fiction that followed, Dickens carved out other new kinds of novel. The first detective in English fiction, for instance, is found in *Bleak House*, and with him the detective novel was born.

Dickens pioneered the 'autobiographical novel', in which the novelist takes himself as subject, with *David Copperfield* (1849–50) and *Great Expectations* (1860–61). We learn more about Dickens the man in those two novels than we do from any of the eighty-or-so biographies that have been written about him.

As he moved from novel to novel we can see him perfecting his work technically, particularly in his mastery over plot. The serialist's motto (as Dickens's fellow novelist Wilkie Collins put it) was: 'Make 'em laugh. Make 'em cry. Make 'em *wait*.' By the middle of his career, when he was taking immense pains over the construction of his novels, Dickens had become a master of suspense. He knew exactly how to keep the reader waiting, eagerly purchasing the next weekly or monthly issue to find out what happened next. In a late novel, such as *Little Dorrit* (1855–57), Dickens 'plays' the reader expertly, and we enjoy being played with. Dock-workers in the New York harbour, we are told, yelled out to the ship bringing early copies of *The Old Curiosity Shop*, 'Is she [Little Nell] dead?'

Dickens's fiction moves through many authorial moods over the years, generally becoming less comic, something about which his contemporaries complained – they wanted more Pickwick jollities. But as his fiction darkened, Dickens became increasingly fascinated by the power of symbolism, and his work became more 'poetic' in that respect. In the late novel *Our Mutual Friend* (1864–65), for example, the River Thames is the dominant symbol. (All the later novels have one.) It baptises London with its incoming tide and carries away the city's filth (implying its sin) with the outgoing tide. The hero of the novel is drowned and 'reborn' (with a different identity) in the river. This poetic dimension in the late novels enriches Dickens's texts but, more importantly, it opened ways for other novelists to follow and explore. Like all the great writers of literature, Dickens did not just write great fiction, he made great fiction, by other hands, possible.

A second reason for Dickens's greatness is that he was the first novelist not merely to make children the heroes and heroines of his fiction (as in *Oliver Twist*) but also to make his reader appreciate how vulnerable and easily bruised the child is, and how unlike an adult's is the child's-eye view of the world. When he was still a young man, anticipating that his would not be a long life (it wasn't), he chose his close friend John Forster to be his biographer. To Forster Dickens entrusted a few sheets of paper describing what he called 'the secret agony of my soul'. These described Dickens's own acute sufferings as a child. His father, an admiralty clerk, could never manage money and ended up in the Marshalsea, a debtors' prison. This was the setting of *Little Dorrit*, a location familiar to Dickens as an eleven-year-old boy. While his father languished behind bars, he was put to work sticking labels on jars of boot-blacking in a rat-infested factory on the Thames, for just six shillings a week. It was brutal but, more than anything, it was the shame that scorched him. The scars never healed. The cleverest of boys, Dickens never got the education his cleverness deserved. His schooling was grossly disturbed and it finished when he was fifteen. That shame too was a burden. He was routinely dismissed as 'low' and 'vulgar' by contemporaries, even in his obituary in *The Times*. Underlying Dickens's central concern with children is the belief that they are not merely little adults but have something that all adults should aspire to repossess. Dickens (who wrote a *Life of Christ* for his own children) was a firm believer in Jesus's dictum, 'Except ye become as children ye shall not enter the kingdom of heaven'.

In fact, Dickens's early life was a heroic feat of self-education and self-improvement. He got work as an office clerk, learned shorthand, and was taken on as a journalist reporting on House of Commons debates. He was to become a mirror of his changing age – the third reason we consider him a great writer. No novelist has been more sensitive to his own times than Dickens. Historically his was a period of explosive growth in London. The city was doubling in population every ten years, creating both huge leaps forward and huge municipal crises. Thirteen of Dickens's fourteen major novels are set or largely set in London. The one that isn't – *Hard Times* (1854) – is a story of strike and strife in the area around Manchester ('the workshop of the world', as it was called). Dickens had his finger firmly on the pulse of England. He realised the huge change that the railway network would bring as it spread across the country in the 1840s, replacing the old (and, for Dickens, romantic) stagecoach. *Dombey and Son* (1848) deals centrally with the horribly disruptive yet wonderfully interconnected new world that the railway brought with it.

Our fourth point. It was not simply the fact that Dickens's fiction *reflected* social change. He was the first novelist to appreciate that fiction itself could *change* the world. It could enlighten, it could expose, it could advocate. A rather surprising example of Dickens the reformer can be found in the preface to *Martin Chuzzlewit*, where he says that in all his fiction he has tried to show the need to 'improve public sanitation'. It seems an odd thing to say to readers about to embark on a novel like, say, *Bleak House*. But look for a moment at the famous opening to that novel:

> LONDON. Michaelmas Term lately over, and the Lord Chancellor sitting in Lincoln's Inn Hall. Implacable November weather. As much mud in the streets, as if the waters had but newly retired from the face of the earth, and it would not be wonderful to meet a Megalosaurus, forty feet long or so, waddling like an elephantine lizard up Holborn Hill. Smoke lowering down from chimney-pots, making a soft black drizzle, with flakes of soot in it as big as full-grown snow-flakes – gone into mourning, one might imagine, for the death of the sun.

In a word, 'filth' everywhere. (That 'mud' in the street is largely horse droppings and human waste.) So much filth in the air that it has blocked out the sun. And filth's inevitable companion is sickness. There is disease everywhere in the novel – it kills poor little Jo the child street-sweeper, and disfigures the heroine. The first instalments of *Bleak House* appeared in 1852. Six years later, the engineer Joseph Bazalgette began construction of the sewer system under the London streets. That 'mud' would disappear. It's not far-fetched to say that Dickens, although he never dug a spade into the London soil, or lifted a flagstone, or soldered a metal pipe, helped in the great Victorian sanitary reform. We still read *Bleak House*. Every London bookstore will have copies on sale. And city dwellers still walk – most of them wholly unconsciously – over the same sewer system that our Victorian predecessors laid under our feet.

Lastly, and most importantly, one of the things that gives Dickens's novels their everlasting appeal is his honest belief in the essential goodness of people. Us, that is. There are villains (it would be hard to mount a defence for murderous Bill Sikes in *Oliver Twist*) but in general Dickens has huge faith in humanity – he always felt that people were good at heart. This faith in human goodness is the central feature in his most famous work, *A Christmas Carol* (1843). Ebenezer Scrooge is a hard-hearted skinflint who simply does not care if poor people die in the street outside his door. Are there no workhouses, he asks? But even Scrooge, when his heart is touched, can become a benevolent person – a second father to crippled Tiny Tim and a generous employer of Tim's father, Bob Cratchit. This 'change of heart' is an all-important moment in most of Dickens's narratives. And – if you'd asked him and he'd felt able to give a straightforward answer – Dickens would probably have said that the aim of all his writing, both his fiction and his journalism, was to change or, at least, 'soften' hearts. More than most writers, he succeeds. Even today.

Charles Dickens would have been the first to admit that he was not, in every respect, a perfect man. Although most of his novels end with happy marriage, he himself was not the best of husbands or fathers. After his wife of twenty years had borne him ten children he got rid of her and took up with someone twenty years his junior, who suited him better. Even by Victorian standards Dickens was a man who was occasionally wrongheaded in his social views, attitudes and prejudices. But this wrongheadedness is more than outweighed by his wholly admirable beliefs in progress and the human race's ability to make a better world – if their 'hearts' are in it. Our world is what it is, a better place than what it was, thanks, in part, to Charles Dickens. That, ultimately, is why his novels are great. 'Quite so', as the Inimitable would say (probably grumpily, if you had ever dared to think otherwise).

CHAPTER 19

Life in Literature
THE BRONTËS

The lives of the Brontë sisters – Charlotte (1816–55), Emily (1818–48) and Anne (1820–49) – could themselves serve as the plot of a sensational novel. They were the daughters of a remarkable self-made man, born Patrick Prunty, one of ten children of a dirt-poor Irish farmer. By dint of native cleverness, work and a lot of good luck, Patrick got himself to Cambridge University. On graduation he was ordained into the Church of England and prudently changed his name to Brontë, one of the titles of Lord Nelson. Not everyone liked the Irish at the time – there were regular uprisings and bloodshed. The Revd Brontë married well, and in 1820 got himself a living (as religious postings were called) in Yorkshire, on the Pennine Moors not far from Keighley, a mill town producing textiles. The family lived with wild nature on one side, the Industrial Revolution on the other.

The 'living' was misnamed. The handsome parsonage at Haworth was a place of death. Patrick's wife, worn out by six pregnancies, died in her mid-thirties, when Anne was a baby. The two eldest daughters died in childhood. Of the three sisters who survived, none reached forty – Charlotte lived longest, to just short of her thirty-ninth birthday. The son, and great hope of the family, Branwell, went to the bad, took to drink and drugs, and died, raving, aged thirty-one. All the children either died, or were fatally weakened, by 'consumption' (as tuberculosis was called at the time). Ironically their father, poor man, outlived them all. Was it for this he had dragged himself up by his bootstraps?

Had the Brontë family been as healthy, happy, prosperous and long-lived as that other famous parson's daughter, Jane Austen (who was forty-one when she died), how different would their un-written fiction have been, in that unlived decade? Very. That, at least, would seem undeniable. They were all of them developing as artists at phenomenal speed, almost up to the last moments of their short lives.

Haworth – the parsonage, church, and adjoining graveyard – forms the climate and the small world of the sisters' fiction. None of the three broke free and they all spent virtually their whole lives within the boundaries of their father's parish. The fact they saw so little of the larger world is evident enough in their novels. In Emily Brontë's *Wuthering Heights* (1847), for example, all the action takes place within a ten-mile radius of the ancient house that gives the novel its title. This tiny territorial reach leaves holes in the narrative. At the beginning of the story Mr Earnshaw has just walked to Liverpool and back ('Sixty miles each way') bringing with him a foundling – the infant Heathcliff, destined to over-throw the house he is fostered in. Other novelists would have dredged up some 'back story' for this strange child, or, at least, have given us the scene in which Earnshaw found the waif, as he claims (unconvincingly), in the Liverpool gutter. Is he an unac-knowledged bastard, with some gipsy mother? Emily offers no explanatory scene. Why not?

The most plausible reason is that she did not know Liverpool, and did not want to take her story to a place she did not know. The largest such hole in the *Wuthering Heights* plot concerns Heathcliff's 'missing years'. On overhearing Cathy tell Nelly (another of the novel's many narrators) that she intends to marry

Linton, Heathcliff runs away without so much as packing a bag, and with not a penny in his pocket. He comes back, three years later, rich, well-groomed and cultivated – a 'gentleman'. How did that happen? Where has he been that this change could happen? The novel does not say.

These 'holes in the plot', as I've called them, can be seen as touches of art, deliberately there as features of the novel's design. But they also witness the fact that the author was a provincial, unworldly woman who simply had no experience of the places and situations in which an ignorant country boy, like the runaway Heathcliff, could return so strangely different.

Anne went to London, for a couple of days, only once in her life (to prove that she was the author of her first novel). Her two novels (which are traditionally underrated) frugally use her very limited life experience to the full. Drawing on the two years she spent as a governess with a family near York, in *Agnes Grey* (1847) she created the finest work of Victorian fiction to delineate the humiliations and frustrations of that 'upper servant' station in the middle-class household. The other thing she knew more than most women about was alcoholism. Because she was asthmatic, she spent more time at home and was more biddable than her sisters (as a child she won a medal for 'good conduct'; it's hard to imagine Charlotte or Emily winning one). So it was Anne who had to look after Branwell in his wild bouts of drunkenness and dreadful withdrawals. It forms the plot of Anne's novel *The Tenant of Wildfell Hall* (1848), the most painfully accurate depiction of 'dipsomania', as alcoholism was then called, in Victorian literature.

A fact often forgotten is that the Brontës were a clergyman's daughters. It is woven into the fabric of their writing – sometimes invisibly. Most readers of *Jane Eyre* (1847) will remember the first line ('There was no possibility of taking a walk that day') and the horrors of the 'red room' and the odious Mrs Reed. But readers are often stumped to remember the last words of the novel: 'Amen; even so come, Lord Jesus!'

It is important to remember, when reading their novels, that the sisters had virtually no institutional education. Their brief experience of Cowan Bridge Clergy Daughters' School proved disastrous, and led to the eldest sisters' deaths. Charlotte immortalised the awful place, vengefully, as Lowood in *Jane Eyre*. After fifteen years, she still felt the physical pangs that sadistic school had inflicted on her and her sisters:

> we had no boots, the snow got into our shoes and melted there; our ungloved hands became numbed and covered with chilblains, as were our feet: I remember well the distracting irritation I endured from this cause every evening, when my feet inflamed; and the torture of thrusting the swelled, raw and stiff toes into my shoes in the morning.

After typhoid swept through the school, closing it, their father took over his three surviving daughters' education and tutored them at home, exceptionally well. For these five years – probably the happiest years of their lives – the sisters were free to rummage at will throughout the well-stocked parsonage library. They were stimulated by the books they found – Scott's romances and Byron's poems, notably.

Around 1826, the three young sisters, together with Branwell, began secretly to write long serials, in tiny, almost illegible script, about imaginary worlds. This 'web of childhood' was initially inspired by games with Branwell's toy soldiers. The narratives ranged as far abroad as Africa, featuring Napoleonic and Wellingtonian heroes. The super-heroism of the characters in the imaginary Angria and Gondal filtered through in the later novels to such characters as Edward Rochester and, most glamorously, Heathcliff, that hero composed – as was his name (forename or surname?) – of the two hardest, least human elements in Emily's beloved moorland landscape.

Once grown up, what should unusually clever young women like the Brontë sisters do? Marry, of course. When their father died they would be penniless. The few portraits and a single photograph (of Charlotte) that survive confirm they were physically attractive. There were young, eligible clergyman in plenty for them to choose from. But the sisters wanted more than marriage. Charlotte, for example, is known to have turned down early offers. They could, they resolved, pass on the home schooling their father had passed on to them. All three girls became governesses: Emily and Charlotte briefly and unhappily, Anne for longer and more long-sufferingly.

In 1842, Emily and Charlotte went off to Brussels, to work, as student teachers, in an exclusive boarding school for girls, with the aim of mastering French. It would help them, they believed, set up a school of their own one day. In Brussels, Emily was chronically unhappy away from Yorkshire and the moors. She, like Heathcliff and Cathy, loved 'wilderness'. One of the fascinating moments in *Wuthering Heights* is when the young Cathy and Heathcliff compare their favourite summer days. For her it is when the clouds scud across the sky, driven by the wind, and the land is dappled. For him it is still, sultry, cloudless days. That is not an episode we would find in Charlotte's fiction.

Emily left Brussels to return to Haworth as soon as she decently could. The foreign place held nothing for her. Charlotte stayed another year. Disastrously for herself, but happily for literature, she fell madly in love with the principal of the school, Constantin Héger. He behaved well. She, consumed by passion, behaved, if not quite badly, then rather recklessly. Héger was the great love of her life. It was not to be, but nonetheless that wretched experience forms the stuff of the novels to come – Rochester's teasing, cat-and-mouse games with his governess, for example, in *Jane Eyre*. In *Villette* (1853), Héger appears, more realistically, as the man Lucy Snowe loves while working as a student teacher in a Brussels boarding school. The autobiographical element is heightened by both novels being written by the heroines in first-person narrative ('I' narrative) form. Rarely has an unhappy love affair produced greater fiction. And knowing what lay behind these novels helps us as readers to appreciate that greatness.

After Brussels the three women found themselves reunited at Haworth. They were now in their twenties. Neither governessing nor Belgium had worked. But apparently they were still unwilling to put themselves on the marriage market and collectively resolved to earn their own income – never easy for women of the early Victorian period.

They decided that they would write. On the profit their books made they would, one day, set up a school. To break into the world of authorship, dominated as it was by men both as authors and publishers, they adopted male pseudonyms (Currer, Ellis and Acton Bell). They paid for a volume of their verse to be printed under their pen-names, loosed it on the world, and waited expectantly. It sold two copies. Posterity has made some amends by recognising Emily, particularly, as a major poet.

One wonderful year, 1847, saw the publication of all three of the great Brontë novels. But they were not all immediately successful. *Wuthering Heights* and *Agnes Grey* – Emily's and Anne's first novels (again published under their male pen-names) – were accepted by the most dishonest publisher in London. Under his mistreatment they sank without trace or payment. Long after the women's deaths, these novels would go on to be recognised as masterworks of Victorian fiction. Too late, though, for their authors.

Charlotte fared better. Her first novel was rejected by the publisher she sent it to, but with the comment that the firm would be very interested to see her next work. She duly dashed off *Jane Eyre* in a few weeks. It became a bestseller and 'Currer Bell' (she did not keep the pseudonym going for long) found herself the novelist of the day. The novelist William Makepeace Thackeray, like many others, stayed awake to read the story of the plain little governess who takes on the world and wins the man she loves, after he has conveniently disposed of the madwoman (his first wife) in the attic, and been 'tamed', Samson-like, by losing his sight and a hand.

Emily died a few months later, barely thirty, without finishing the second novel which she is thought to have been working on. Anne died, aged twenty-eight, five months after her sister. Her second novel, *The Tenant of Wildfell Hall*, was, like the first, shamefully mishandled by her publisher. Both sisters died of consumption.

Charlotte lived on for another six years. She was also the only child of the family to marry, having accepted the proposal of her father's curate. Not long after the marriage, she died too, aged thirty-eight, from the complications of pregnancy. She was buried in the family vault at Haworth, one of three sisters who left behind them a body of fiction that will live forever.

CHAPTER 20

Under the Blankets
LITERATURE AND CHILDREN

Let's play some literary hide and seek. Where is the child hiding in *Hamlet*? Where are the little ones in *Beowulf*? *Pride and Prejudice* was, in 2012, voted the most influential novel in the English language. Where are the children in Austen's story about the Bennet family? Come out, come out, wherever you are! You'll seek in vain.

If, for the traditional parent, the ideal child was 'seen and not heard', in the long history of literature the child was, for centuries, neither seen nor heard. They are, of course, *there*, but they are invisible.

Children's literature – in the double sense of books *for* children, and books *about* children – emerged as a distinct category of fiction in the nineteenth century. The new interest in 'the child' as something worth writing about and for can be credited to two leading spirits of the Romantic movement: Jean-Jacques Rousseau and William Wordsworth. In Rousseau's *Émile* (1762) – a manual for the ideal education of the child – and Wordsworth's long autobiographical poem *The Prelude* in the following century, childhood is the period of life which 'makes' us. As Wordsworth put it: 'The child is father of the man'. Not on the sidelines, but at the centre of the human condition.

Wordsworth's cult of the child had two sides to it. One was that childhood experience was 'formative' (it could also be traumatic – 'deformative'). In *The Prelude* (and childhood is a prelude to adulthood) he argues that it is in childhood that our relationship with the world around us is established. In the poet's own case it was in childhood that his intimate relationship with nature was forged.

The other aspect was Wordsworth's religious belief that the child, having been most recently in the company of God, was a 'purer' being than the grown-up person. This belief is proclaimed in his poem, 'Ode: Intimations of Immortality'. We come into the world, the poem asserts, 'trailing clouds of glory', which are gradually dispersed as the years pass. Conventionally the term 'growing up' suggests addition: we become stronger, more knowledgeable, more skilled. It is not (in Britain or America) until we reach a certain age, when we are 'mature' enough, that we can see some films, drink alcohol, drive a car, marry or vote in public elections. Wordsworth saw it differently. Growing up was not *gaining* something, but *losing* something much more important.

As we saw in Chapter 18, Wordsworth's heir in terms of a shared belief in childhood's primacy in human existence is – who else? – Charles Dickens. In his second novel, *Oliver Twist* (written in his mid-twenties, in 1837–38), he attacks new legislation, recently introduced, which made it more painful for the poor to rely on public aid – in order to motivate the 'idle' members of society to find useful employment and get off the municipal payroll. It's one of the recurrent swings in political thinking about the 'welfare state'.

How, though, does Dickens frame his critique of cruel Britain? By following the 'progress' of a young child from orphan to 'workhouse boy', to under-age chimney sweep, and – finally – to apprentice criminal. You want to know why your society is as it is? Look at how you treat your children. 'As the twig is bent, so the tree is shaped', as they would have said. Dickens believed that his own character as a man and an artist had been formed by what had happened to him before he was thirteen years old and instructed his biographer to make that clear.

After *Oliver Twist*, Wordsworth's theme that children's experiences shape them for life can be followed through Charlotte Brontë (notably *Jane Eyre*, 1847), Thomas Hardy (especially *Jude the Obscure*, 1895), D.H. Lawrence (see *Sons and Lovers*, 1913), all the way to works such as William Golding's *Lord of the Flies* (1954) and Lionel Shriver's *We Need to Talk About Kevin* (2003).

Literature, in short, 'found' the child in the nineteenth century and has never lost its interest in him and her.

So far, we've covered books by adults, for adults, about children. There is, however, a category of books that works equally well for child readers and older readers, even if they were not initially targeted at the latter. For example, Lewis Carroll's *Alice's Adventures in Wonderland* (1865), Mark Twain's *Huckleberry Finn* (1884) and J.R.R. Tolkien's *The Lord of the Rings* (1954–55). These works can be read to, or by, young readers. And it's worth reminding ourselves, at this stage, that 'child' is a very broad definition. The reading, listening and understanding of a five-year-old is very different from that of an early teen, and bookshops have separate sections for them. But however many candles on our birthday cake, there is, of course, a child in all of us and these three works satisfy readers (or listeners) from seven to seventy.

Lewis Carroll, an Oxford University professor and philologist, wrote his 'Alice books' for the clever daughters of a colleague. The story he span to entertain the youngsters on a summer afternoon's punt down the river, tells of a girl who follows a white rabbit down a hole in the ground. In the curious underground hall in which she finds herself, she drinks a potion that makes her shrink, and eats a cake that makes her gigantic, then journeys through a world full of mysterious and sometimes violent adults. Carroll's story is clearly a fable about the trials and tribulations of 'growing up' and it has always fascinated young readers going through that process. But embedded within it are innumerable things to amuse and interest Carroll's university colleagues – parodies of poems, for example (including one hilarious spoof of Robert Southey on the subject of growing old), and a range of other philosophical conundrums.

Mark Twain's *Huckleberry Finn* is the most admired and written-about American book for, and about, the child. It has a simple story. Huck, Tom Sawyer's friend in an earlier story, goes on the run with an escaped African-American slave, Jim. They ride an improvised raft down the Mississippi to where, it is hoped, Jim will find freedom. They have adventures, and Huck learns to respect Jim as an equal. Tom Sawyer appears in the last, highly comic chapters. Mark Twain got sackfuls of letters about 'Tom and Huck' from young readers, some as young as nine, most around twelve. They loved the lads' scrapes. *Huckleberry Finn* was so popular with young readers, in fact, that it was banned in American libraries in case 'the young' imitated Huck's ungrammatical way of speaking and love of 'stretchers' (lies). But, particularly over the years since the Civil Rights Act of 1964, adult readers have been fascinated by Twain's subtle depiction of the relationship between Huck and the African-American Jim, and the way in which the young hero's racist prejudices are gradually corrected. This is an adult theme. Yet it co-exists with the pleasures the story can give readers of all ages.

The Lord of the Rings ponders the perpetual conflict of good and evil – as do the more recent works of Philip Pullman and Terry Pratchett. The latter have their adult readership. But Tolkien's narrative of the epic struggle between the dark Lord Sauron, in his quest to take over Middle-earth, and its elvish, dwarf and human populations, has an added dimension. Tolkien was the most respected literary critic of Old and Middle English of his time, and an expert on *Beowulf* (see Chapter 3). *The Lord of the Rings* is a novel that has kept children awake until well past lights out, night after night, but it also teased the minds of Tolkien's fellow scholars. It was with a group of them, in the pleasant surroundings of an Oxford pub, that he first discussed his project.

Digging down into what is meant by 'children's literature' raises some fascinating questions. Let's look at three of them. The first is: How do we, as children, come by the basic skills required to 'take in' literature? We are not born literate. Typically our first experience of literature is through the ear, aged two(ish), with bedtime stories and nursery rhymes: *Jack and the Beanstalk* and 'Three Blind Mice', for example. Illustrations draw the child's attention to the page. The tales and ditties become more complex, and the illustration less central, with the passing months. Roald Dahl becomes the bedtime favourite. Dr Seuss takes over from the nursery rhymes.

Many of us learn to read and love literature at home – the bedtime story is one of the treats of the day. Children go on to read 'with' their parent (or sometimes an older sibling) rather than being read 'to' by their parent. For many children, as they progress, there is a third stage – reading by themselves under the blankets, with a torch, after lights out. The books we have read as a child tend to be our dearest literary companions through life.

There is another aspect of children's literature that makes it distinct from the adult kind. Books are expensive and children have little cash to spend. A new novel has over the last hundred years cost a sizeable chunk of the average person's weekly income. Historically children have had empty pockets. So children's literature has tended to be bought for them, not by them. The Victorians were particularly fond of what were called 'Rewards' – gift-books for good conduct (often given by the Sunday School). Children's literature, because of their minimal financial clout, has always been subject to adult control and censorship in the interest of instilling that same 'good conduct'.

Children by nature prefer sweets to medicine. When he could scrape together enough of his meagre pocket-money, the six-year-old Charles Dickens splurged on 'penny bloods', as they were called – grisly illustrated stories of crime and violence. One, about rats, haunted him all his life.

All of which brings us to the most interesting phenomenon in recent children's literature – J.K. Rowling. Rowling's *Harry Potter* books sold, by the time the seven-part saga concluded, getting on for half a billion copies. Part of the reason for her success lies in the fact that Rowling has refused to fence herself in. She titled herself 'J.K. Rowling' to avoid being 'branded' as a boys' or a girls' author

– and the series is as much about Hermione as it is about Harry. As the years have passed she has also cunningly avoided the 'age group' trap. In the first volume, *Harry Potter and the Philosopher's Stone* (1997), the hero is a bullied eleven-year-old cowering in a cupboard under the stairs. In the seventh and last of the series, *Harry Potter and the Deathly Hallows*, the hero and his Hogwarts comrades are on the verge of seventeen. Fleur gives him an 'enchanted razor' ('eet will give you ze smoothest shave you 'ave ever 'ad', the worldly Fleur tells him). That razor represents Harry's entry into the adult world as symbolically as his first broomstick represented his entry into the world of wizardry.

Children's literature – a non-existent thing 150 years ago – is now, as Rowling supremely demonstrates, not merely a vast money-making enterprise but where many of the most interesting things, for readers of all ages, are happening. It is evolving, excitingly. Keep reading.

CHAPTER 21

Flowers of Decadence
Wilde, Baudelaire, Proust and Whitman

Towards the end of the nineteenth century a new image of the writer begins to take centre-stage in Britain and France: 'the author as dandy'. Suddenly writers were not just writers but 'celebrities'. Their modes of dress and demeanour were closely studied and imitated, their *bon mots* recycled. Their persons were admired as much as their writings. The authors, on their part, played up to their celebrity. As Wilde quipped in his novel, *The Picture of Dorian Gray*, 'there is only one thing in the world worse than being talked about, and that is not being talked about'.

Historically one can see Lord Byron ('mad, bad and dangerous to know' – Chapter 15), with his hallmark shirt-collars and *hauteur*, as the first author to be as notorious for his lifestyle and image as he was revered for his poems. Byronism took on new life in the *fin de siècle* ('end of century') period as the Victorian era was winding down and new literary, cultural and artistic influences – notably those from France – were eroding middle-class English certainties.

In end-of-century Britain the cult of literary dandyism was epitomised by one writer above all others, Oscar Fingal O'Flahertie

Wills Wilde (1854–1900). Wilde's career was spectacular. As a celebrity, no author promoted himself more successfully. But where it eventually took him demonstrates the dangers for writers whose lifestyles were too flagrantly different from what was felt to be 'respectable' at the time. Dandyism, decadence and degeneracy were easily run together in the public mind. Wilde crossed the line – but not before he blazed magnificently.

Wilde's literary achievements, viewed objectively, are not overwhelmingly impressive. He has one undisputed masterpiece to his credit, the play *The Importance of Being Earnest* (1895). He published a gothic novel, *The Picture of Dorian Gray* (1891), sensational in its own time, interesting today largely because of its floridly gay subtext. It chronicles a 'Faustian pact' with the devil by which the hero Dorian (*d'or* – French for 'made of gold') remains for eternity a 'golden youth' while a portrait of him in the attic (his 'grey' self) withers and degenerates. Other writers have handled the theme better, but none more provocatively than Wilde.

Wilde was born in Dublin into a highly cultivated world. His father was a distinguished surgeon; his mother herself a woman of letters. Socially the family belonged to the Anglo-Irish 'Ascendancy' – the Protestant colonist class. (Always religiously ambivalent, Wilde would convert to Catholicism on his deathbed.) After reading Classics at Trinity College in Dublin, he completed his education at Magdalen College, Oxford, where he came under the influence of the high-priest of aestheticism (the 'cult of beauty'), Walter Pater, whose instruction to his young pupils was that they should 'burn always with this hard, gem-like flame'. None burned more gem-like than young Mr Wilde. Pater's doctrine of 'art for art's sake' was given an extreme expression in one of Wilde's later witticisms: 'All that I desire to point out is the general principle that Life imitates Art far more than Art imitates Life.'

Even religion was secondary to art: 'I would number Jesus Christ among the *poets*', Wilde asserted – not a remark to please strait-laced Christians. Elsewhere, and even more provocatively, Wilde proclaimed that 'The final revelation is that Lying, the telling of beautiful untrue things, is the proper aim of Art' – not a remark to please lawyers. In these daring statements Wilde came close to the philosophical theory later to be called 'phenomenology' – a simpler doctrine than it sounds. It is through the forms of art, phenomenology suggests, that we shape and understand the formlessness of the world around us. In Wilde's frivolity there is always a kernel of what Matthew Arnold (a poet he admired greatly) called 'high seriousness'. He played the dandy, but never the fool.

Wilde left Oxford formidably well read and deeply cultured. He wore his learning (like his exquisitely tailored clothes) lightly and with panache. He threw himself into the London literary world and was feted in Paris and New York when he went there. Everyone wanted to see Oscar, and hear what his latest provocative quip was – for example, on seeing Niagara Falls, a favourite honeymoon location, 'It must be the second greatest disappointment for American brides'.

Above all he threw himself into the world of publicity, gossip sheets, newspapers and photography. His image was as famous to his age as Queen Victoria's. (She was not, one suspects, one of his admirers – Alfred, Lord Tennyson was more to the monarch's taste.) The 'unnatural' green carnation in the buttonhole, the 'effeminate' velvet jackets, the flowing hair, the cosmetics were all justified by Wilde as neo-Hellenism – the age of ancient Athens and Platonic love which he, and Pater, revered. He was the incarnation of Narcissus and 'gilded youth' and, as he drew on in years, became the patron of gilded youth.

The years following *The Picture of Dorian Gray* represented the zenith of Wilde's career, when he was writing plays for the London stage. Drama was the perfect vehicle for Wildean wit. His last play, *The Importance of Being Earnest*, is, as the sly title indicates, a delicious satire on Victorian morality. (The play led to the name 'Ernest' becoming temporarily unfashionable.) It has a masterfully farcical plot and almost every scene contains dazzling paradoxes such as:

I hope you have not been leading a double life, pretending to be wicked and being really good all the time. That would be hypocrisy.

As his play was packing out the Haymarket Theatre in London, Wilde fell like Lucifer. He was accused by the father of his young lover, Lord Alfred Douglas, of being a 'sodomite'. Wilde filed a slander suit, which he lost, and was immediately prosecuted for 'offences against public decency'. He was found guilty and imprisoned for two years' hard labour, becoming prisoner C.3.3. After his release, Wilde wrote 'The Ballad of Reading Gaol' (1898). There is nothing remotely dandyish in the poem, which ends bleakly, with bitter criticism of the lover who had betrayed him:

> And all men kill the thing they love,
> By all let this be heard,
> Some do it with a bitter look,
> Some with a flattering word,
> The coward does it with a kiss,
> The brave man with a sword!

In prison Wilde wrote an apology for his life, *De Profundis* ('from the depths'). A version was published in 1905, but the full text, details of it being considered scandalous, was not published until the 1960s.

On his release Wilde took refuge in France, without his wife and children, who had never figured much in his public life. He died in 1900, as the Victorian era, which he had done so much to offend and make fun of, was winding down. Near the end of his life, he said: 'To live is the rarest thing in the world. Most people exist, that is all.' Oscar Wilde survives in literary history as a writer who indeed made his life a fine work of art and left some literature that was equally worth our attention. A petition in 2012 to have him pardoned posthumously has, as I write, received no response from the government.

'Dandyism' in France was elevated into a manifesto by the poet Charles Baudelaire (1821–67), in an essay in his collection *The Painter of Modern Life* (1863). (Interestingly, Baudelaire was the first writer to define 'modernism', the subject of Chapter 28.)

Dandyism, claims Baudelaire, is 'a kind of religion' – aestheticism, art in all things. He too would see Jesus Christ as a poet. It goes well beyond fashionable attire:

> Contrary to what a lot of thoughtless people seem to believe, dandyism is not even an excessive delight in clothes and material elegance. For the perfect dandy, these things are no more than the symbol of the aristocratic superiority of his mind.

There is, Baudelaire discerned, a core of sadness in the 'superior' mind of the dandy:

> Dandyism is a setting sun; like the declining star, it is magnificent, without heat and full of melancholy.

Melancholy, because dandyism 'flowers' when things are coming to an end, 'decaying'. We are living in a 'corpse time', but even in decay beauty can be found; poetry can be made. The cult of 'decadence' was picked up by many other writers in France. But as with Baudelaire, it meant a life of great risk: early death from various kinds of overindulgence, prosecution by authorities, poverty. Excess was the only way, even if it led to self-destruction. 'Get drunk!' instructed Baudelaire: 'So as not to be the martyred slaves of Time, get drunk; get drunk without stopping! On wine, on poetry, or on virtue, as you wish.'

The pose ('default setting', as we would say) that Baudelaire advocated for the poet was 'ennui'. The English 'boredom' does not catch the flavour of the word precisely. The poet, Baudelaire elsewhere instructed, should be a *flâneur*. That term too is not easily translated into English. A 'saunterer', watching the life of the streets as it flows past, is as close as we can come. Baudelaire characterised the *flâneur* as a 'passionate spectator':

> The crowd is his element, as the air is that of birds and water of fishes. His passion and his profession are to become one flesh with the crowd.

The American writer of this period who most perfectly fits Baudelaire's description of the modern poet is Walt Whitman (1819–92). The title of one of his poems, 'Manhattan Streets I Saunter'd, Pondering', could, with a change of metropolis, be one of Baudelaire's own. In his 'sauntering', writes Whitman, he ponders 'on time, space, reality'. The meaning of these great abstractions are to be found in the buzzing maelstrom of the city streets. Whitman and Baudelaire did not know each other or each other's work. But they are clearly collaborators in the same literary movement – a movement that was shifting literature out of the nineteenth and into the twentieth century, and into full-blown modernism (Chapter 28).

Whitman called his poems 'songs of myself'. It fits neatly with Wilde's belief that his life was his most perfect work of art. The writer who pursued this idea to the most artistic of conclusions was Marcel Proust (1871–1922), in his massive autobiographical novel *À la recherche du temps perdu* (1913–27; published in English from 1922 as *Remembrance of Things Past*). Proust starts from the view that life is lived forward but understood backward; and at some point in our lives, what is behind is more interesting than what is in front. The novel, which took fifteen years and seven volumes to complete, is of all things triggered by the taste of a madeleine cake. 'One day in winter', the narrator (manifestly Proust) writes,

> my mother, seeing that I was cold, offered me some tea, a thing I did not ordinarily take. I declined at first, and then, for no particular reason, changed my mind. She sent for one of those squat, plump little cakes called 'petites madeleines', which look as though they had been moulded in the fluted valve of a scallop shell. And soon, mechanically, dispirited after a dreary day with the prospect of a depressing morrow, I raised to my lips a spoonful of the tea in which I had soaked a morsel of the cake. No sooner had the warm liquid mixed with the crumbs touched my palate than a shudder ran through me and I stopped, intent upon the extraordinary thing that was happening to me.

What had happened was that, stimulated by that taste, the whole of his life was flooding back into his mind. All that mattered now was to get it on paper.

Proust's novel is a life's work. Nothing of great moment happens in the life it records (as the above passage implies) but Proust's art creates out of 'himself' one of the great monuments of world literature. Proust and Wilde knew each other and in his exile the French author went out of his way to be kind to his disgraced fellow author. *Remembrance of Things Past* is the kind of novel Wilde might himself have written (and comes close to sketching in *De Profundis*) had he been spared prison and given years in which to continue as 'Oscar' rather than Prisoner C.3.3. The Decadent movement came and went, and left behind it flowers as well as decay.

CHAPTER 22

Poets Laureate
TENNYSON

The poet. What images does the little word call up? Like me, perhaps, your mind's eye pictures a man with blazing eyes, a far-away look, flowing hair, clad in loose garb. Or a woman, standing on a rock, or some other eminence, gazing into the far distance. Cloud, sea, wind and storm are in the air. Both figures are solitary. 'Lonely' as Wordsworth put it, 'as a cloud'.

There may be an aura of madness – the Romans called it '*furor poeticus*'. Many of our greatest poets (John Clare and Ezra Pound, to take two of the very greatest) actually spent portions of their lives in mental institutions. Many contemporary writers spend more time on the psychoanalyst's couch than in the literary agent's office.

The critic Edmund Wilson borrowed an image from antiquity to describe the poet. He was, said Wilson, like Philoctetes in the *Iliad*. Philoctetes was the greatest archer in the world. His bow could win wars. Things were going badly for the Greeks at the siege of Troy. They needed Philoctetes. But they had banished him to an island. Why? Because he had a wound that stank so much no one could bear to be around him. Ulysses was sent to bring him to besieged Troy. But if the Greeks wanted the bow, they also had to put up with the stench. That, thinks Wilson, is the image of the poet – necessary, but impossible to live with.

We tend to think of a poet as not just lonely but – essentially – an outsider. A voice in the wilderness. The poet, said the philosopher John Stuart Mill (whose life had been transformed by his reading of Wordsworth's poetry) is not 'heard', but 'overheard'. The poet's most important relationship is not with us, the reader, but with their 'muse'. The muse is a mean employer. She showers the poet with inspiration (the word suggests 'sacred breath'), but no cash. None can expect poverty as confidently as the maker of verses – hence the expression, 'poet's garret' (a garret is a dingy attic). Who talks about 'the doctor's garret', or 'the lawyer's garret'?

The poet Philip Larkin once said that the poet sings most sweetly when, like the legendary thrush, the thorn is pressed most sharply against its bosom. But it's not a question of giving poets more money, or removing the many thorns from their bosom. Another image, this time George Orwell's, makes the point graphically. Orwell liked to picture society as a whale. It was the nature of this monster to want to swallow up human beings – as, in the Bible, the whale swallows the living Jonah. Jonah is not chewed up and eaten by the leviathan, he is imprisoned 'in the belly of the beast'. It was the duty of the artist to remain 'outside the whale' as Orwell put it: close enough to see it (or 'harpoon' it with satires like his own *Animal Farm*), but not, like Jonah, to be swallowed up by it. The poet is the artist for whom it is most necessary to keep their distance from things.

Poetry long pre-dates any written or printed literature. Every society we know of – historically and geographically – has its poets. Whatever one calls them – bard, skald, minstrel, singer, rhymer – the poet has always had the same difficult 'outsider-insider' relationship with society.

In feudal society, nobles liked to have their personal minstrels (along with their court jesters) to entertain them and their guests. Sir Walter Scott wrote his finest poem, *The Lay of the Last*

Minstrel (1805) about it. Since the seventeenth century England has had its poet laureate, the monarch's appointed verse-maker and a member of the royal household. More recently the USA has begun appointing its poet laureates, too. Before 1986 they were called, awkwardly, 'Consultant in Poetry to the Library of Congress'. The term 'laureate' refers back to ancient Greece and Rome, and means 'crowned with laurel leaves'. The laureate won his (always his) leafy crown by verbal gladiatorial combat with other poets. (Rappers, the bards of our day, still do this in freestyle battles.) The first official poet laureate in England was John Dryden, who held the post under Charles II from 1668 to 1689, although he seems not to have been overly conscientious about his responsibilities. Thereafter the poet laureate was, for centuries, something of a joke. One who held the post, for example, was Henry Pye (laureate 1790–1813). The study of literature has been my profession for more years than I care to remember, but I could not come up with a single line from memory of Henry James Pye's verse. I'm not ashamed.

All too often, mockery was what the poet laureate could expect, along with the dubious honour of the title and the paltry payment that came with it (traditionally a few gold coins and a 'pipe', or barrel, of port). When Robert Southey (laureate 1813–43) wrote a poem on the recently deceased King George III being welcomed into Heaven by a toadyish St Peter, called *A Vision of Judgement* (1821), Byron tore into him with *The Vision of Judgment* (spot the – very slight – difference?), regarded as one of the greatest satires in the language. When he wrote it, Byron was an exile in Italy, having been hounded out of England for supposed immorality. Which poet is remembered today? The insider, or the outsider? Sir Walter Scott (see Chapter 15) declined the honour of the laureateship (in favour of Southey) because, as he put it, the post would adhere to his fingers like sticky tape, preventing him from writing freely. Scott wanted his poetic freedom.

The poet who succeeded in the post and the role of the 'institutional poet' – the poet wholly inside Orwell's whale – but who despite that wrote great poetry, was Alfred Tennyson (1809–92).

Unusual for his times, Tennyson lived to over eighty, two decades longer than Dickens, five decades longer than Keats. What might they have done with those Tennysonian years?

Tennyson published his first volume of poems when he was just twenty-two. It contained what are still many of his best-known lyrics, such as 'Mariana'. Alfred regarded himself at this period as very much a Romantic poet – the heir to Keats. But Romanticism, as a vital literary movement, had faded by the 1830s. No one wanted warmed-over Keats. There ensued a long fallow period in his career – the 'lost decade', critics call it. It was a period in the wilderness. He broke out of this paralysis and in 1850, aged forty-one, produced the most famous poem of the Victorian period – *In Memoriam A.H.H.* It was inspired by the death of his best friend, Arthur Henry Hallam, with whom, it is speculated, his relationship was so intense it might have been sexual. It probably wasn't, but intense, in the kind of 'manly' way approved by Victorians, it certainly was.

The poem is made up of short lyrics, chronicling seventeen years of bereavement. The Victorians mourned the death of a loved one for a full year – in dark clothes, and with black edged note-paper; women wore veils and specially sombre personal jewellery. In this mournful poem Tennyson meditated on the problems that most tormented his age. Religious doubt afflicted the second half of the nineteenth century like a moral disease. Tennyson was afflicted even more than most. If there was a heaven, why did we not rejoice when someone dear to us died and went there? They were going to a better place. But *In Memoriam* remains essentially a poem about personal grief. And finally, the poem concludes, despite all the pain, ' 'Tis better to have loved and lost /Than never to have loved at all'. Who, having lost a loved one, would wish they had never existed?

Queen Victoria lost her beloved consort, Albert, to typhoid, in 1861. She wore 'widow's weeds' until the end of her life forty years later. She confided that she found great consolation in Mr Tennyson's elegy for his dead friend, and on the strength of it the two, poet and queen, became mutual admirers. Tennyson was not just a Victorian poet – he was *Victoria's* poet. Appointed her poet laureate in 1850, he would hold the post until his death, forty-two years later.

The great enterprise of his later years was a massive poem on the nature of ideal English monarchy, *Idylls of the King*, a chronicle in verse of the reign of Arthur and the Knights of the Round Table. It was, clearly, an indirect tribute to the English monarchy. Tennyson wrote, as all poet laureates do (even the dynamic Ted Hughes when he held the post from 1984), some very dull stuff. But he also wrote, as poet laureate, some of the finest public poems in English literature, most notably 'The Charge of the Light Brigade' (1854), commemorating a bloody and absolutely hopeless assault by some 600 British cavalry on Russian artillery guns, during the Crimean War. The casualties were huge. A French general watching said, 'It is magnificent, but it is not war'. Tennyson, who read the account of the engagement in *The Times*, came up with a poem, written at great speed, which catches the thundering hooves, the blood, and the 'magnificent madness' of it all:

> Cannon to right of them,
> Cannon to left of them,
> Cannon behind them
>   Volley'd and thunder'd;
> Storm'd at with shot and shell,
> While horse and hero fell,
> They that had fought so well
> Came thro' the jaws of Death
> Back from the mouth of Hell,
> All that was left of them,
>   Left of six hundred.

In his later years, Tennyson played the part of poet majestically, with flowing hair, a luxurious beard and moustache, and a Spanish cape and hat. But beneath the costume and the pose, Tennyson was the most businesslike of authors, as keen as the next man for money and status. He rose to the top of the slipperiest of literary poles to die Alfred, Lord Tennyson, and richer, from his verse, than any poet in the annals of English literature.

Did he sell out, or was it a finely judged balancing act? Many who care about poetry see a Victorian contemporary, Gerard Manley Hopkins (1844–89), as a 'truer' kind of poet. Hopkins was a Jesuit priest who wrote poetry in what little spare time he had. It has been said that his only connection with Victorian England was that he drew breath in it. Hopkins admired Tennyson, but he felt his poetry was what he called 'Parnassian' (Parnassus being the poets' mountain in ancient Greece). Bluntly, he felt that Tennyson had surrendered too much by 'going public'. Hopkins himself would rather have died than publish a poem like *In Memoriam* for any man or woman in the street to pore over his grief.

Hopkins burned many of his highly experimental poems. His so-called 'terrible sonnets', in which he struggled with religious doubt, are intensely private. He probably never intended anyone other than his closest friend, Robert Bridges, to see them. Bridges (destined, ironically, to become poet laureate himself in 1913) decided, almost thirty years later, to publish the poems Hopkins had entrusted to him. They are regarded as pioneer works of what would, a few years after his death, be called modernism, and change the course of English poetry.

So who, then, was the truer poet, 'public' Tennyson or 'private' Hopkins? Poetry has always been able to find room for both kinds.

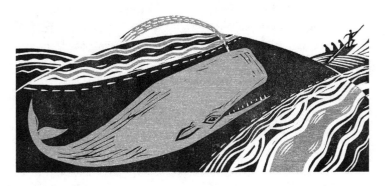

CHAPTER 23

New Lands
AMERICA AND THE AMERICAN VOICE

One of the insults that used to be directed at American literature by outsiders was that it didn't exist – there was only English literature written in America. It's ignorant as well as insulting and, not to waste words, plain wrong. George Bernard Shaw commented that 'England and America are two nations divided by a common language'. It is true of the literature of all different English-speaking nations, but especially true in this case. There is, whatever the fuzzy edges, an American literature as rich and great as any literature anywhere, or that there has ever been in any period in recorded history. It helps to characterise the nature of that literature by looking at its long history and considering some of its masterpieces.

The starting point of American literature is Anne Bradstreet (1612–72). Every anthology bears witness to the fact. All American literature, said the modern poet John Berryman, pays 'homage to Mistress Bradstreet'. It marks a difference between British and American literature that in the New World the founding figure is a woman. No one ever said English literature started with Aphra Behn.

Mistress Bradstreet was born and educated in England. Her family was part of the Puritan 'Great Migration' – under religious persecution – to the place they called 'New England', the Eastern seaboard of America. Anne was sixteen when she married, and undertook the voyage two years later, never to return. Both her father and her husband would go on to be governors of Massachusetts. While the men of the family were off governing, Anne was charged with running the family farm. She evidently did it well. But she was much more than a competent farmer's wife and the mother of their many children.

The enlightened Puritans believed that daughters should be as well educated as sons. Anne was intelligent, extraordinarily well read (her contemporary Metaphysicals were of particular interest – see Chapter 9), and was herself an ambitious writer, something which was not frowned upon by her Puritan community, as it might perhaps have been in England. She wrote vast amounts of poetry, but as a spiritual exercise, an act of devotion, rather than for any fame, current or posthumous. Her best poems are short; her life was too busy for long works. Her brother, recognising her genius and the originality of her mind, made heroic efforts to get her verse published in England. There was, as yet, no 'book world' in the American colonies.

Despite their self-imposed exile, the Puritans felt an unbreakable bond with the Old Country – hence placenames like 'New' England or 'New' York, but there was also a strong sense of permanent spiritual separation. Anne Bradstreet's poems are quintessentially of the New World, as the Puritans saw America and their place in it. Take, for example, her poignant 'Verses upon the Burning of Our House July 10th, 1666':

> I blest His name that gave and took,
> That laid my goods now in the dust.
> Yea, so it was, and so 'twas just.
> It was His own, it was not mine ...

The poem concludes, poignantly,

The world no longer let me love,
My hope and treasure lies above.

It's a traditional Puritan sentiment – this world is of no real consequence: what matters is the world to come. But what we hear in
the verse is an entirely new voice – an American voice, moreover
the voice of an American 'making' the new country. Anne and her
husband had built that house that now lay in ashes. They would, of
course rebuild. America is a country constantly rebuilding itself.

Puritanism is a foundation stone of American literature. It
flowered as literature in the work of the so-called Transcendentalists
of New England in the nineteenth century – writers such as Herman
Melville, Nathaniel Hawthorne, Henry David Thoreau and Ralph
Waldo Emerson. Transcendentalism is a big word for what was
essentially the faith of the early colonials – that the truths of life
are 'above' things as they appear in the everyday world. Melville's
Moby-Dick (1851), chronicling Captain Ahab's hunt for the great
white whale, is routinely cited as an archetypally American novel.
What makes it that? The sense of endless quest, the pacification
(even if it means the destruction) of nature, and the voracious
appetite for natural resources to fuel this ever growing, ever self-
renewing new nation. Why were whales hunted? Not for sport.
Not for food. They were hunted to the point of extinction for the
oil extracted from their blubber for lighting, machinery and any
number of manufacturing activities.

Walt Whitman (Chapter 21), the self-declared disciple of
Emerson, embodies another aspect of the Transcendentalist
tradition – its sense that 'freedom', in all its many facets, is the essence
of all American ideology, including poetic ideology. In Whitman's
case it took the form of 'free verse' – poetry unshackled from rhyme,
just as the country itself had thrown off the shackles of colonialism
in its War of Independence against the British in 1775–83.

Freedom, in America, presupposes literacy. It has always been
a more literate country than Britain. The country's forging of its
identity began with a document, the Declaration of Independence.
In the nineteenth century America could boast the most literate

reading public in the world. But the literature that originated in the United States was somewhat stunted by the country's refusal (in the name of 'free trade') to sign up to international copyright regulation until 1891. Before that date, works published in Britain could be published in America, without any payment to the author. Writers like Sir Walter Scott and Dickens were 'pirated' in huge quantity and at budget prices. It fostered American literacy but it handicapped the local product. Why pay for some promising young writer when you could get *Pickwick Papers* free? (American plundering of his work drove Dickens to apoplectic rage – he got his own back in the American chapters of his novel *Martin Chuzzlewit*.)

This is not to say that there was no homegrown American literature at this time. The 'great war', according to no less an admirer than Abraham Lincoln himself, was started by Harriet Beecher Stowe with her anti-slavery novel, *Uncle Tom's Cabin* (1852). It sold by the million in the troubled mid-nineteenth century and, if it is not true that it started a war, it did change the public mind.

A powerful, unique and self-defining impulse in American literature of the nineteenth and twentieth centuries is the 'frontier thesis' – the idea that the essential quality and worth of Americanness is most clearly demonstrated in the struggle to push civilisation westward, from 'shining sea to shining sea'. James Fenimore Cooper, author of *The Last of the Mohicans* (1826), is one of the early writers who chronicled the great push west. Virtually every cowboy novel and film springs from the same 'frontier thesis' root. Where civilisation meets savagery (at it crudest, paleface meeting redskin) is where true American grit is displayed. Or so the myth goes.

The western is one of the few genres one cannot credit to the author Edgar Allan Poe, father of science fiction, 'horror' and the detective story, notably 'The Murders in the Rue Morgue' (the orang-utan did it). Along with the idea of 'genre' it was in America that, in 1891, the first bestseller list was established. Eight of the top ten bestsellers on the first all-fiction list were novels by English hands. It settled down, with an ever more prominent American content, after the literary world came to terms with international copyright regulation.

'*E pluribus unum*', says the inscription on US coinage: 'out of many, comes unity'. It's as true of literature as demography. America is a tapestry of regional and distinctively different urban literatures. There is Southern literature (such as William Faulkner and Katherine Anne Porter), New York Jewish fiction (think Philip Roth and Bernard Malamud) and West Coast literature (the Beats). Reading widely in American literature is like a road trip across that immense continent.

'Make it new', Ezra Pound instructed his fellow American poets. They have done just that, embracing modernism and post-modernism more enthusiastically and adventurously than their British counterparts. Any anthology demonstrates the point, from Pound himself, through Robert Lowell's *Life Studies* (Chapter 34) to the L=A=N=G=U=A=G=E school of poetry, whose poets, as their name indicates, open up language like an orange into its many segments. This obsession with the new can be seen, from another angle, as an impatience with the old. America, as any frequent visitor will observe, is a country that tears down its skyscrapers to build even newer ones. So too in literature.

Ezra Pound (1885–1972) was, among all else, an Anglophile, and one of the things that American writers have made new, in a small but important way, is the literature of the 'old country'. Writers born and brought up American – such as Henry James, T.S. Eliot and Sylvia Plath – who lived, worked and died in Britain, injected into its literature new, vital and essentially 'American' ways of writing and seeing the world. James, 'the master' as he came to be called, 'corrected' English fiction, which he believed had become formless and (his word) 'baggy'. He was a stern master. T.S. Eliot established Modernism as the principal voice of British poetry. Plath's poems, with their controlled emotional violence, smashed what one critic called 'the gentility principle' which was strangling English verse. British literature gave much to American literature, and has received a lot in return.

Had he been addressing American writers of fiction, Pound might have rephrased his instruction, 'Make it *big*'. There are a whole host of candidates, more of them every year, for the title of

'Great American Novel'. Big themes have always attracted American writers, more so, one could plausibly argue, than their British counterparts, for many of whom Jane Austen's 'two inches of ivory' will suffice.

There is also an energy, verging on aggression, in American literature, which can be seen as different and distinctly of that country. Few novels, for example, have been angrier – or more effectively angry in terms of bringing about social change – than John Steinbeck's *The Grapes of Wrath* (1939). It tells the story of the Joad family in the great 'Dust Bowl' disaster of the 1930s who, when their farm parches up, leave Oklahoma and take to the road towards the promised land, California, only to discover, when they get there, that it is a false Eden. In the lush farms and orchards of the West they find themselves as exploited as were the slaves transported to America from Africa 200 years earlier. The family breaks up under the strain.

Steinbeck's novel, which is still widely read and admired although the circumstances that gave it birth have long passed, is not merely social protest at the ruthless exploitation of farm workers. Running through *The Grapes of Wrath* is the sense that what happens to the Joad family is a betrayal of what America stands for, the principles on which it was founded – the better life that, centuries before, people like Anne Bradstreet came to the New World to find and make. There are, of course, angry novels to be found in all literatures (Émile Zola in France, for example, and Dickens, of course). But it is a peculiarly American kind of anger one finds in *The Grapes of Wrath*.

So, to sum up. What makes American literature peculiarly American? Is it the Puritan heritage, the constant battle to extend the 'frontier', the geographical and ethnic diversity, the aspiration for 'newness' and 'greatness', the constant innovation, the belief in America which underlies even denunciations of America, like Steinbeck's?

Yes; all of these things. But there is something else, even more important. Ernest Hemingway (1899–1961) put his finger on it when he proclaimed, 'All modern American Literature comes from one book by Mark Twain called *Huckleberry Finn*'. What is definitive, Hemingway contended, is 'voice' and what Twain himself called 'dialect'. You hear it in Huck's first sentence:

> You don't know about me without you have read a book by the name of *The Adventures of Tom Sawyer*, but that ain't no matter.

There is an American idiom that only American literature fully captures. It carries with it the sense of something more in 'the American grain' (as the poet William Carlos Williams called it) than 'accent'. The detective-story writer, Raymond Chandler, who gave great thought to the subject, called it 'cadence'. Hemingway's own fiction bears out his point about the American idiom but the novel which, for me, most perfectly encapsulates the wholly distinctive modern American voice is J.D. Salinger's *The Catcher in the Rye* (1951). Read (and 'hear') its first wonderful sentence, with its if-you-really-want-to-know challenge, and see if you don't agree.

CHAPTER 24

The Great Pessimist
HARDY

Imagine you could create something called the 'Literary Happiness Scale', with the most optimistic authors basking in sunshine at the top and the most pessimistic authors sunk in gloom at the bottom. Where, to name names, would you put Shakespeare, Dr Johnson, George Eliot, Chaucer and Dickens?

Chaucer projects the happiest vision of life, most would agree. The band of pilgrims riding to Canterbury are a merry crew, and the tone of their tales is comic. Chaucer would surely top the scale. Shakespeare is also pretty upbeat – with the exception of a handful of tragedies (especially *King Lear*) which seem to have been written in the terrible aftermath of losing his only son, little Hamnet. A critic who undertook a census of good versus bad characters in his drama came up with a 70/30 ratio on the plus side. Shakespeare's world is not, on the whole, a bad place to live in. Seven out of ten people would be good to know.

George Eliot, as her novels reflect, believed in a world that was getting better ('ameliorating' was her word) but in a very bumpy way. Human costs were paid – some of them, as with Dorothea in *Middlemarch*, sizeable costs – but on the whole the future looked brighter, to this author, than the past. The Eliot universe is a moderately hopeful place: sunshine breaks through. All her novels have a happy ending, however glumly they start. It would, she suggested, be a long time before humanity reached the sunny uplands, but they were getting there.

Dickens is difficult to locate on our happiness scale because his earlier work (*Pickwick Papers*, for example) is so much jollier than the novels produced in what is called his 'dark period', some of which project a very gloomy view of things indeed. It's hard to close the covers of, say, *Our Mutual Friend* feeling jolly. There are, one concludes, two Dickenses, at two different points on the scale.

Dr Johnson was pessimistic but stoic. 'Human life', as he surveyed it, was 'a state in which much is to be endured, and little to be enjoyed.' But he believed life, if you were lucky, had what he called its 'sweeteners': friends, good conversation, buckets of tea, good food and, above all, the pleasures of intercourse, through the printed page, with great minds of the past. (He did not much enjoy the theatre and his eyes were not good enough to appreciate fine art.) The sunshine glimmers between the clouds in the Johnson universe.

At the very bottom of the happiness scale, indeed arguably below its zero point, would be Thomas Hardy (1840–1928). Hardy liked to tell the story of his birth on the kitchen table in a little cottage in rural Dorset (the county he would later immortalise as his invented region of 'Wessex'). When he popped out into the world the doctor took one look at the shrivelled little thing and declared him to be stillborn – dead before he lived. He was put on one side for Christian disposal. Then he cried. It saved his life and, arguably, for the rest of that life Thomas Hardy never stopped crying.

The reader can, like Little Jack Horner, stick a thumb anywhere in Hardy's mass of fiction and poetry and pull out a pessimistic plum. Take, for example, his poem 'Ah, Are You Digging on My Grave?' The question is asked by the corpse of a woman, lying buried in her coffin. Not a cheerful scenario, you may think, but it gets even less cheerful. She hears a scrabbling in the dirt above her. Her lover? No, it's her little dog. A dog's fidelity, she thinks, is so much nobler than a human's. And then the dog explains:

'Mistress, I dug upon your grave
  To bury a bone, in case
I should be hungry near this spot
When passing on my daily trot.
I am sorry, but I quite forgot
  It was your resting place.'

The summaries of any of Hardy's major novels are chronicles of depressiveness. Someone once said every novel of his should have a cut-throat razor attached. One thinks, for example, of *Tess of the d'Urbervilles* (1891), and its noble young woman, lying on the sacrificial slab at Stonehenge, waiting for the police to arrest her, the court to declare her guilty, the hangman to execute her, and the gravedigger to throw her body in quicklime and an unmarked grave. Who would not shake their fist at the heavens, thinking of the fate of Tess, whose only fault was loving unwisely?

Should we see Hardy's pessimism, as expressed in his poems and novels, as merely the reflection of his own peculiarly unhappy feelings about life, or something more serious? If it were merely a lifelong grump, who would bother reading him? And why, in spite of his glum view of things, do we rank him as one of the giants of English literature?

There is a simple answer to those questions. What Hardy expresses in his work is not just the personal opinion of Thomas Hardy but a 'world-view' (literary critics often use the German term for it, '*Weltanschauung*', which sounds more philosophical). The dominant world-view into which Hardy was born was that things were 'progressing'. Life was getting better. A young Victorian born in 1840 could confidently expect a better life than his parents and grandparents. For most people born in this period, that was indeed their life experience. Hardy's father was a stonemason, and a self-made man. His mother was a great reader. Both wanted more for their only child than they had had, only a generation or two away from being peasants. And, indeed, Hardy soared far above the social level into which he was born. He died an honoured 'Grand Old Man' of English literature, his ashes laid alongside the greats in Poets' Corner in Westminster Abbey. His heart was buried separately, in his beloved Dorset, alongside the graves of the peasants he wrote about.

Even those whose careers were not as starry as Hardy's could expect to rise, and to enjoy a more comfortable life than their parents. The mid-Victorian, when Hardy was growing up, had clean water, macadamised (tarred) roads, a network of new railway lines and a better school education, culminating in the Education Acts of the 1870s, which ensured schooling for every child to the age of twelve, or thirteen in Scotland. There was social mobility. Dickens's career, for instance, is one of rags to riches and eternal fame. He could not have done it a hundred years earlier. He would have died, unknown to posterity, in rags.

But there were flies in the Victorian ointment. The southwestern counties of Hardy's 'Wessex' were still, in the early 1800s, the 'bread basket' of England and the region prospered on the cereals it supplied to the nation. Then in 1846 came the repeal of the so-called Corn Laws. What that meant was international free trade. Wheat and other cereal crops could now be imported more cheaply from abroad. The region Hardy was born in, and loved, entered a long economic depression from which it has never entirely recovered. That depression infected Hardy and every word he wrote.

There were other flies in the ointment. Hardy felt the stuffing had been knocked out of 'his' world by a book published when he was nineteen years old: Darwin's *On the Origin of Species* (1859), with its closely-argued case for evolution. The British had always believed that theirs was 'a nation under God' but what if there was no God up there? Or it was not the benevolent God described in Genesis but a mysterious 'life force' with no particular interest in the human race? What if the system of belief on which the whole of life used to be based was simply not true?

Hardy was persuaded by Darwin, but it hurt him. He pictured his hurt beautifully. An architect by early training, he loved old churches but he saw himself having to listen to the hymns (which he also loved) from outside the church walls. He could not enter, in good faith, because Darwin had destroyed that faith. He was, as he put it, like a bird singing forever outside, unable to join the 'bright believing band' inside the comforting church walls.

For Victorians, the Darwinian contradiction of what most of them had so profoundly believed was painful in ways that we, who have lived with it for 150 years, find hard to imagine. Hardy's literature (and the world-view which sustains it) is an expression of that Victorian pain, beautifully crafted into prose and verse.

Hardy also had his doubts about 'progress', particularly the advances brought about by the Industrial Revolution. Did the railways, roads and (after the 1840s) telegraph – the 'networking' of Britain – mean everything was better in every region? Hardy doubted that optimistic view of history. The character of the wonderfully diverse regions of the British Isles, with their individual accents, rituals, myths and customs – everything that makes 'a way of life' – was being merged into a bland national unity. His term 'Wessex' (Anglo-Saxon in origin) is a kind of protest. He would not call the region where he was brought up 'south-west England'. Wessex was distinct – its own kingdom.

Hardy's first Wessex novel, *Under the Greenwood Tree* (1872), is a critique of what was commonly thought of as 'improvement'. The novel describes the replacement of the church orchestras, in which local parishioners played instruments (you can still see the galleries in old places of worship). The orchestras were replaced by harmoniums – vulgar instruments, but new-fangled. Progress. But was it?

The downside of industrial progress is given its most vivid description in *Tess of the d'Urbervilles*. In the early sections of the novel the milkmaid heroine is as much part of the natural order of things as the grass that grows in the fields. Then comes the steam-powered combine harvester. Tess, working as it chuffs its way through the harvest fields, is no more than a human cog in the machine. 'Progress', Hardy argues, can destroy. As the novel shows, Tess is progressively uprooted and displaced by the forces that are, on the face of it, making the world a better place and dragging Wessex into the nineteenth century.

The Industrial Revolution was indeed a wonderful thing. But, Hardy believed, mankind should not be too complacent about it. Nature might well take her revenge. This warning is given in the poem 'The Convergence of the Twain'. (Hardy loved grand words, but 'The Crunch of the Two' would probably not have had the same titular punch.) As we saw in Chapter 2, the *Titanic* ocean liner was one of the proudest industrial achievements, and greatest disasters, of the century. As the poem puts it:

> And as the smart ship grew
> In stature, grace, and hue,
> In shadowy silent distance grew the Iceberg too.

Reading the poem, one wonders what icebergs are growing for us, in our world. Were he alive today Hardy would, for a certainty, direct his 'pessimistic' gaze at climate change, overpopulation, the clash of civilisations – those things which, in our constitutional optimism, we prefer not to think about.

What Hardy's 'pessimism' tells us is that we should indeed look at things from all angles. Nor should we flinch from what may seem frightening – our salvation may depend on it. He put this very well in one of his poems:

> If way to the better there be
> It exacts a full look at the worst.

There may be a better world to come. But we shall never get there unless we make an honest assessment (however painful) of where we are. Pessimistic? No. Realistic? Yes.

What we think of as progress may not be progress. What we think of as a more efficient world may be a world headed for self-destruction. Hardy's is a pessimistic world view which instructs us to think again about our own world view. And that, very simply, is why we value him as the great writer he is. That and the fact that he writes so well, packaging his pessimism so wonderfully.

CHAPTER 25

Dangerous Books
LITERATURE AND THE CENSOR

Authorities, everywhere and at every period of history, are always nervous about books, regarding them as naturally subversive and potential dangers to the state. Plato, famously, establishes the security of his ideal Republic by kicking out all the poets.

And so on through the ages. At the creative edge, where great writers work, there is always the professional hazard of incurring the wrath of those currently in power. We can draw up an impressive list of martyrs to the literary cause. As we saw in Chapter 12, John Bunyan wrote most of his great work, *The Pilgrim's Progress*, in Bedford prison; earlier, Cervantes too had hit on the idea for *Don Quixote* while languishing in prison. Daniel Defoe (Chapter 13) stood in the stocks for a satirical poem he wrote (legend has it sympathetic onlookers threw flowers, rather than rotten eggs). In our own time, Salman Rushdie (Chapter 36) spent a decade in safe houses for a satirical novel he dared to write. Alexander Solzhenitsysn composed great works in his head while rotting for eight years in the Soviet Gulag after his arrest in 1945.

After the 1660 Restoration, John Milton (Chapter 10) had to go on the run, and his writings were ordered to be burned. It was, of course, Milton who, in his great work on freedom of expression, *Areopagitica* (1644), proclaimed:

> As good almost kill a man as kill a good book: who kills a man kills a reasonable creature, God's image; but he who destroys a good book, kills reason itself ...

This is commonly paraphrased as, 'Where books are burned, men are burned'.

Different societies come down in different ways on 'dangerous' books, as a comparison of France, Russia, the USA, Germany and Britain will illustrate. Each has made war on literature, or imposed restrictions on its freedom, in its own unique way.

The French way is conditioned by the defining event in the country's history, the Revolution of 1789. The pre-revolutionary government (the *Ancient Régime*) maintained an iron grip on publication: every book required a 'privilege' – state permission – to exist. Unprivileged, 'under-the-cloak' works, such as Voltaire's *Candide* (1759), served the revolutionaries as weapons. More so if they were written abroad by Enlightenment (that is, 'free-thinking') writers and, as was *Candide*, lobbed over the border into France like ideological hand grenades. The novel, whose full title was translated in English as *Candide: or, All for the Best*, tells the story of a naïve youth who has been brought up to believe everything he is told – exactly the kind of citizen the authorities like to have. Voltaire thought otherwise.

With the Revolution in France, freedom of expression, and the right to hold any opinion – rights which had so helped the cause – were proclaimed in the Declaration of the Rights of Man and of the Citizen (1789). Following Napoleon's takeover France became more restrictive, but always less so than its neighbour and great foe, England.

In 1857 two works were published in France, their authors being being immediately prosecuted in trials that were to have huge consequences for world literature. Gustave Flaubert's novel *Madame Bovary* and Charles Baudelaire's verse collection *Les Fleurs du mal* ('The Flowers of Evil') were accused of 'outraging public decency'. In Flaubert's case the alleged outrage was that his novel endorsed adultery. The offence in Baudelaire's case is summed up in the provocative title, which of course is exactly what the poet intended. The French phrase is '*épater le bourgeois*' – 'scandalise the middle classes'. Flaubert was acquitted. Baudelaire incurred a small fine and six of his poems were banned – otherwise, the book survived.

The trial of these works (now high classics of French literature) created an open zone for the literature of their country. Writers such as Émile Zola – translations of whose novels were ferociously suppressed in the English-speaking world with punishments of prison sentences – were free to take literature to new places. They did.

It was freedom for not just French writers. Many British and American authors (D.H. Lawrence, Ernest Hemingway, Gertrude Stein) published works in Paris, between the two world wars, which were wholly unpublishable in their home countries. James Joyce's *Ulysses* is a prime example. The novel was first published in book form in Paris in 1922 and, after a trial, eleven years later in the USA (on the perverse legal conclusion that it was 'emetic', not 'erotic'). Britain lifted its ban on *Ulysses* a few years later, in 1936. It was never actually banned in Ireland. It simply was never available.

During the Second World War, great French writers such as Jean-Paul Sartre, Albert Camus, Simone de Beauvoir and Jean Genet contrived to produce works allegorically attacking the Germans occupying their country – notably Camus's *L'Étranger* (1942; published in English as *The Outsider*) and Sartre's *Huis Clos* (1945; *No Exit*). Camus's novel, with its title meaning 'the stranger' or 'the foreigner', can be seen as reflecting the hated foreigners who had taken over his country. Sartre's play has three characters, after death, imprisoned with each other for eternity. Hell, they discover, is 'other people'. It was written in a different kind of prison: German occupation.

Traditional Gallic freedoms established themselves after the Second World War. Ironically the liberations in the English-speaking world followed trials, in 1959 and 1960, of a novel that had been published, without protest or scandal, in Paris thirty years earlier – *Lady Chatterley's Lover*.

Revolution was late coming to Russia. Nonetheless some of world literature's greatest works were conceived and published under the bureaucratic oppression of the Tsar's censors. Paradoxically – a paradox frequently observed in the history of literature – authors raised their game to evade their bumbling inspectors (a character slyly lampooned in Nikolai Gogol's play *The Inspector-General* of 1836). Subtlety and indirectness – artfulness, in a word – were employed in their critiques of society. In Fyodor Dostoevsky's novel *The Brothers Karamazov* (1880), for example, three brothers conspire to murder their obnoxious father. What was the Tsar known as to his people? 'Little Father'. Anton Chekhov's plays similarly, if more nostalgically, chronicle the inner decay of the ruling class. In *The Cherry Orchard* (1904), the orchards are a symbol of beautiful futility, and they are being felled, making way not for something better, but for a new, uglier world. Chekhov is a master of literary 'pathos'. Yes, of course things must change: history demands it. But must it be change for the worse?

With a few textual ammendments, Chekhov's seditious comedies slipped past the Tsar's censors onto the stage. But soon after the Revolution in 1917, for Russian (now 'Soviet') authors one censorship was replaced by another, far more oppressive – that of Stalin. It persisted, more or less intensely and with the occasional 'thaw', until 1989. Using the devious skills of their predecessors, dissident writers like the poets Anna Akhmatova, Yevgeny Yevtushenko and novelists like Boris Pasternak and Alexander Solzhenitsyn contrived to create and (all too occasionally) publish great works under the very nose of the censors. Novels such as Solzhenitsyn's *Cancer Ward* (1968; a scathing satire on Stalinism as the tumour at the heart of Russia) were often circulated in 'samizdat' – clandestine typewritten form – much, one might recall, as early Christians in Rome kept their seditious manuscript texts under their cloaks. Pasternak and Solzhenitsyn were both awarded the Nobel Prize in Literature, in 1958 and 1970 respectively. Will Russia without such censorship produce as great a literature? It will be interesting to see. It is one of the great literary experiments happening before our eyes today.

The USA was founded by Puritans who brought with them a reverence for free expression and literacy. It was further enforced in 1787 with the Constitution whose first amendment enshrines freedom of speech in law. That freedom, however, has never been absolute and universal. Over the years the USA, a federation made up of many divergent states, wove a confused patchwork of tolerance and repression. A work of literature could be 'banned in Boston' (the phrase became proverbial) but selling like hot cakes in New York. Particularly where public libraries and local educational curricula are concerned, this patchiness ('community standards') is still a peculiarly American feature of the American literary environment.

Authors in Germany historically enjoyed a relatively liberal regime, particularly so in the Weimar Republic of 1919–33. This was when writers like the dramatist Bertolt Brecht, with works such as *The Threepenny Opera* (from which comes the still popular song 'Mack the Knife') could create a uniquely political and revolutionary form of theatre which has left a lasting mark, worldwide. With the Nazi takeover in 1933, repression was tyrannic. The burning of books was as much part of the theatre of Nazism as the Nuremberg Rallies. The aim was to control the 'mind' of the population by denying it any sustenance not approved by the Party. It worked too well. No literature of the slightest historical value was produced for a dozen years. Worse still, Hitler's regime left a poisoned bequest when it ended in 1945. After the war, writers such as the novelist Günter Grass had the literary equivalent (as Grass put it) of literary bomb-blast rubble to work with.

In Britain, until the eighteenth century the control was political, and an arm of the state. A writer who offended could find himself in the Tower of London, without due process of any law, or (like Defoe) consigned by the magistrate to the stocks. Writers were wise to be wary. Shakespeare, for example, sets none of his plays in England of the present day. Why? Because he was not merely a genius, but a careful genius.

Censorship of the stage, particularly, is a long-running feature in Britain. Why? Because audiences are 'gatherings' and can easily become 'mobs'. Censorship of the theatre remained in place until the 1960s. George Bernard Shaw was in constant battle with the Lord Chamberlain (whose office licensed all drama). Witty 'Shavian' plays such as *Mrs Warren's Profession* (1895), which mischievously portrays a house of ill repute as a legitimate commercial enterprise, had a hard time making it to the public stage. Shaw was a self-proclaimed supporter of the Norwegian dramatist, Henrik Ibsen. Attempts to stage plays such as Ibsen's *Ghosts* (which touched on the supremely dangerous topic of venereal disease) provoked scandal and inevitable bannings. Even in the 1950s, first performances of plays such as Samuel's Beckett's *Waiting for Godot* (Chapter 33) required the Lord Chamberlain's say-so. Small changes were required and duly supplied.

Britain did not formalise censorship in law until 1857 (the same year that *Madame Bovary* went on trial in Paris). The first of a series of Obscene Publications Acts that Parliament passed that year was purest British fudge. A work of literature was deemed 'obscene' if it tended to 'deprave and corrupt those whose minds are open to such immoral influences'. Dickens satirically paraphrased the offence as anything which would 'call a blush into the cheek of a young person'. Henry James called it 'the tyranny of the young reader'. Morality – whether prosecuted in court or simply 'the spirit of the age' – ruled. Thomas Hardy gave up fiction altogether when in 1895 the Bishop of Wakefield burned his novel, *Jude the Obscure* (as usual, for condoning adultery), and published only inoffensive poetry for the last thirty years of his life. The 'corrupt and deprave' rule made the kind of novel he wanted to write impossible.

Hardy's disciple, D.H. Lawrence, had the whole first edition of his novel *The Rainbow* judicially burned in 1915. It contained highly poeticised but wholly inoffensive (to our eyes) descriptions of sex, without a single four-letter word. After the war Lawrence left England, never to return. Those who stayed behind watched their step. E.M. Forster wrote and published many great novels (see Chapter 26). One novel he wrote around 1913, and circulated privately but didn't publish, was *Maurice* – a work that dealt, frankly, with his own gay sexuality. It would not see the light of print until 1971, after his death, when it had only historical interest.

Canny British writers and publishers 'self-censored', as did Forster. When George Orwell tried to get *Animal Farm* into print in 1944 he could not find a publisher willing to take on a fable that attacked Britain's wartime ally, the Soviet Union. The whole literary establishment was, Orwell concluded, 'gutless'. 'Prudent' is the word they would have used.

The climate changed radically with the *Lady Chatterley's Lover* trial, in 1960. In 1959 a new Obscene Publications Act had come in, by which an intrinsically offensive work of literature could be published if it was for the public good: 'in the interests of science, literature, art or learning'. D.H. Lawrence had died in 1930, but Penguin publishers decided to test the new Act by publishing his novel. It had been written, as Lawrence put it, to 'hygienise' literature. Why, the novel asks, cannot we use good old Anglo-Saxon words, rather than Latin euphemisms, for the most important acts of our personal lives? On their side, the prosecution adopted the same line as those French authorities that had hauled Flaubert into court: Lawrence's story of an aristocrat's wife who falls in love with a gamekeeper endorsed adultery. Various 'expert witnesses', including respected authors, testified in defence of the publication, and the defence won.

The fight against the censorshp of literature in the world continues, as every issue of the London-based journal, *Index on Censorship*, testifies. It is a constant battle. Literature, literary history demonstrates, can do great things under oppression, in chains, or in exile. It can even, like the phoenix, rise from the flames of its own destruction. It is a glorious vindication of the human spirit that it can do so.

CHAPTER 26

Empire
KIPLING, CONRAD AND FORSTER

The point was made in earlier chapters that great literatures tend to be the product of great nations. Those, that is, which have enlarged their territory by conquest, invasion or, in some cases, downright theft. No subject in literature raises thornier issues than 'empire' and 'imperialism' – most particularly the right by which one country claims to own, dominate, plunder, and in some instances destroy another country. Or, as the imperial power may argue, 'to bring civilisation'.

Literature's engagement with the subject of the rights and wrongs of empire, is complex, fraught and at times quarrelsome. The nature of that engagement has changed over the last two centuries as the global picture has changed. Literature which is relevant in one period is hopelessly dated in another. No other variety of literature requires knowledge of when it was written, and who for, than this kind of literature.

It helps to sketch out the big historical picture. During the nineteenth and twentieth centuries, Britain, a small cluster of islands off the coast of northern Europe, acquired and ruled over an empire which, at its height in the Victorian era, stretched from the meridian line at Greenwich over vast tracts of Africa, to Palestine, the Indian sub-continent, Australasia and Canada. In the eighteenth century the thirteen colonies that would become the United States of America was included in that list. Not even ancient Rome could boast about 'owning' a larger expanse of Planet Earth than Great Britain.

By the second half of the twentieth century that empire was virtually gone, with traumatic suddenness. One after another, countries claimed and won independence. The last time Britain fought to defend its overseas territories was in 1982, for a tiny set of islands in the South Atlantic, the Falklands, with its population barely larger than an English village. No epics were forthcoming.

Literature is a sensitive recorder of socio-historical change, registering both the facts of the international world and the nation's complex and fluid responses to those facts as they happen. The British frame of mind, in the high imperial and immediately post-imperial phase of the country's history, was touched – as literature reflects – by a fluctuating mixture of pride and shame.

Let's consider the famous, and in its time much admired, poem by Rudyard Kipling, 'The White Man's Burden' (1899). It opens:

> Take up the White Man's burden –
>   Send forth the best ye breed –
> Go bind your sons to exile
>   To serve your captives' need;
> To wait in heavy harness
>   On fluttered folk and wild –
> Your new-caught, sullen peoples,
>   Half devil and half child.

Rudyard Kipling (1865–1936) was British but 'The White Man's Burden' was addressed specifically to the people of the USA. (Kipling, significantly, had an American wife.) It was inspired by the US suppression of an independence uprising in the Philippines, and its acquisition, in the same period, of Puerto Rico, Guam and Cuba. The Philippines campaign was particularly bloody. Up to a quarter of a million Filipinos were estimated to have perished. The white man's burden has always been streaked with red.

The poem was an immediate hit in the USA, and its title became a proverbial phrase. One still hears it from time to time – usually ironically. As the nineteenth century ('Britain's Century') came to an end, Kipling believed the role of supreme world power would pass, as historically it did, to the USA. The twentieth century was destined to be America's. Britain, Kipling fondly anticipated, would be a partner, if a junior partner, with its great ally. The two nations, between them, would run the world as benign masters.

Kipling had been born in colonial India and his novel *Kim* (1901), reflecting his childhood in Bombay (now Mumbai), contains a much more sympathetic depiction of the relation of what he called 'East and West'. The basic idea of Kipling's poem is clear enough. Empire is the imposition of a white civilisation on peoples who are, and will always be, 'half devil and half child'. The act of empire is essentially benign. It is a 'burden' undertaken with no thought of national gain and, most poignantly, no expectation of any thanks from those inferior races lucky enough to be colonised by the white man. Today Kipling's poem is a literary embarrassment. It met with overwhelming approval in 1899. Times change.

In that same year, 1899, another work about empire and the white man's imperialism was published – *Heart of Darkness*, by Joseph Conrad (1857–1924). It is a much more thoughtful effort and, most would agree, a much greater work of literature. Conrad had been born in Ukraine, of Polish parents, as Józef Teodor Konrad Korzeniowski. His father was a patriot, a poet and a rebel against the Russian occupation of his homeland. He dedicated his life to the cause of independence. It meant the young Józef could never base himself in Poland. Exile was his destiny. He embarked on a career as a sailor, and in 1886 became a British subject and an officer in the British merchant navy, and changed his name to Joseph Conrad. Then, in his mid thirties, he left the sea for literature.

The autobiographical seed for *Heart of Darkness* was Conrad's being commissioned in 1890 to skipper a decrepit steamer up the Congo River to an inland station, run by a dying manager, called

Klein (renamed 'Kurtz' in the novel: *klein* means 'small', and *kurz* means 'short' in German). For a few months Conrad – a man of decency, if not entirely immune from the racial prejudices of his age and class – was in the service of a colonial agency that Europe should, forever, be ashamed of: the Société Anonyme Belge pour le Commerce du Haut-Congo.

The so-called Congo Free State had been founded in 1885 by Belgium, one of the smaller European imperial nations. 'Free' meant free to plunder. King Leopold II farmed out the million square miles his country 'owned' to whatever firm would pay most. What the purchaser did thereafter with their colonial leasehold was entirely up to them. The result was what has been called the first genocide of the modern era. Conrad called it 'the vilest scramble for loot that ever disfigured the history of human conscience'.

The river voyage had a profound influence on Conrad: 'Before the Congo I was a mere animal', he later said. It took eight years for the 'horror' (a key word in the novel) to settle sufficiently in his mind for him to write *Heart of Darkness*. The story is simple. Marlow (Conrad's hero-narrator in a number of his novels) enter-tains some friends, as the sun sinks over the yardarm, on his boat, the *Nellie*, bobbing sedately in the mouth of the Thames. Look-ing down towards London, in a momentary lull in conversation, he muses: 'This also has been one of the dark places of the earth.' He is thinking of the Romans and ancient Britain. Behind every empire, we apprehend, lies crime.

Marlow goes on to recall a command he had in his early thirties. He was recruited in Brussels (a 'whitened sepulchre' of a city) to go on a mission in Africa (the heart-shaped 'dark' continent) up the Congo to the heart of the Belgian colony, where a station manager, Kurtz, had gone crazy in the process of harvesting elephant ivory. (Ivory was in huge demand in Europe and America to make things like billiard balls and piano keys.) The voyage is one that takes Marlow into the dark truth of things – capitalism, human nature, himself and, most importantly, the nature of empire.

Loyal (in a sense) to his adoptive country, Conrad maintains that Belgian imperialism is crueller and more rapacious than its British counterpart. But within Marlow's remark about 'the dark places of the earth' is the implication that all empires are, at root, the same. Good empire and bad empire is a false distinction: it's all bad. *Heart of Darkness* is a profoundly unsettling novel, written by a man himself profoundly unsettled by what he saw in Africa's darkest place.

The 'jewel in the crown' of the British Empire was, proverbially, India. By general agreement the most thoughtful and masterful novel about colonial India is E.M. Forster's *A Passage to India* (1924). The idea of the work was inspired by Forster's trips to the sub-continent. He fell in love with the country and its people. He was entirely free of any Kiplingesque sense of colonial superiority. Forster was a liberal to the core – one of the free-thinking Bloomsbury Group (Chapter 29).

The odd title requires explanation. Superficially it refers to the travel ('passage') taken from England to India by ocean liner. One of the main narrative strands in the novel follows a young English woman, Adela, who has come to the country to marry a British official. Things go very wrong after she may, or may not, have been assaulted in some local caves (which have ancient religious significance) by a young Muslim doctor, Aziz. Her innocent intention was to make friends with a native. Near riots and a trial ensue in which Aziz is acquitted. Adela's 'passage to India' – and her prospective marriage – end in humiliating ruin. No one knows precisely what happened in the Marabar Caves – it is part of the 'mystery and muddle' that is colonial India.

Forster's title echoes a poem of Walt Whitman (Chapter 21) with the same title, published in 1871. Whitman's poem poses a question that goes to the heart of the imperial situation and which Forster's novel sets out to probe. Is it possible to have a fully human relationship if that relationship is complicated by colonial possession and racial difference? This is how Whitman puts it:

> Passage to India!
> Lo, soul, seest thou not God's purpose from the first?
> The earth to be spann'd, connected by network,
> The races, neighbors, to marry and be given in marriage,

The oceans to be cross'd, the distant brought near,
The lands to be welded together.

Whitman was gay, as was Forster. At the core of Forster's novel, the relationship between a male British schoolteacher and a Muslim doctor is intense, verging, the novel hints, on passionate. But, as Kipling had written: 'East is East and West is West, and never the twain shall meet.'

Forster found his novel almost impossible to finish. No ending seemed 'right'. It was not because of any writing block. What Forster was up against was the fact that fiction, by its nature, cannot 'solve' the problems of empire. *A Passage to India* ends inconclusively, but with fine artistic effect, with the two men who can never come together, becoming 'welded', as Whitman puts it. They are last seen riding horses across the monsoon-soaked Indian landscape:

> But the horses didn't want it – they swerved apart; the earth didn't want it, sending up rocks through which riders must pass single file; the temples, the tank, the jail, the palace, the birds, the carrion, the Guest House, that came into view as they issued from the gap and saw Mau beneath: they didn't want it, they said in their hundred voices, 'No, not yet,' and the sky said, 'No, not there.'

Forster's 'not yet' would be a quarter of a century coming, with Indian independence in 1947. Salman Rushdie would celebrate it in his novel *Midnight's Children*, one of the greatest of post-colonial works (more of which in Chapter 36). *A Passage to India* is anti-colonial. Written when it was, it could not be, Forster implies, anything else.

The theme of empire has inspired a whole literature in its own right, from Shakespeare's *The Tempest* to works such as Paul Scott's *The Raj Trilogy Quartet*, the novels of V.S. Naipaul, and William Golding's *Lord of the Flies* (where it is the ultra-white English public schoolboys who are 'half devil and half child'). We shall see how things look from the other side of the colonial relationship in a later chapter. But the central moral complexities of empire have never been more sensitively explored – if not 'solved' – than in Conrad's and Forster's novels. They can still be read, and enjoyed, with those strange mixtures of pride, guilt and perplexity. But make sure you know the history first.

CHAPTER 27

Doomed Anthems
THE WAR POETS

War and poetry have always gone hand in hand. The first great
work of poetry that has come down to us, the *Iliad*, is about nations
in conflict. War figures in most of Shakespeare's plays which are not
comedies (and it comes up in some of them, too). One of the most
graphic descriptions of the 'horrors of war' (as the Spanish artist
Goya called it) is to be found in *Julius Caesar*:

> Blood and destruction shall be so in use,
> And dreadful objects so familiar,
> That mothers shall but smile when they behold
> Their infants quartered with the hands of war

No war, however, has produced a greater wealth of English poetry
than the war that was called 'Great', the First World War of 1914–18.

It was the most blood-drenched war in British history. At the
Battle of Passchendaele in 1917, a quarter of a million British soldiers were lost in months of fighting in deep mud, with barely five
miles of ground won. Of those who came from Britain's public

schools (many of them straight from the classroom) to the Front, one in five never returned; instead, their names appeared on their schools' 'boards of honour'. These young men were both the 'officer class' and the 'poetry-writing class'.

In almost every village in Britain, somewhere prominent will be a monument, now often moss-covered and barely legible. It will record the flower of that community's youth, cut down in the awful 1914–18 conflict. Under the list of names, if you can read it, will be an inscription such as 'Their Name Liveth Forever More'.

The Great War was different from other wars not merely by virtue of its unprecedented scale and the lethal nature of its weapons (notably the machine gun, the aeroplane, poison gas and tank) but because it involved conflict not merely *between* nation states, but *within* nation states. Put another way, many soldiers, on both sides, were driven to ask themselves, 'Is the enemy in front of us, or behind us?' This is the question asked by the most famous novel to come out of the war, *All Quiet on the Western Front* (1929), by the German author Erich Maria Remarque. Remarque had fought and been wounded in the trenches barely a mile or so away from another famous survivor called Adolf Hitler.

The poets of those awful four years whom we most admire struggled to come to terms with the fact that their real enemy might not be the Kaiser (a first cousin of their own king, George V) and his jack-booted Huns but an English society which had somehow lost its way and blundered into a wholly meaningless slaughter of its own best and brightest, for no good reason at all.

The angriest of the poets, Siegfried Sassoon (1886–1967), was a thoroughly English 'fox-hunting' man, despite his German forename. He illustrates this sense of England-vs-England in his short poem, 'The General':

> 'Good-morning; good-morning!' the General said
> When we met him last week on our way to the line.
> Now the soldiers he smiled at are most of 'em dead,
> And we're cursing his staff for incompetent swine.

'He's a cheery old card,' grunted Harry to Jack
As they slogged up to Arras with rifle and pack.

But he did for them both by his plan of attack.

Who, then, is 'the enemy' in this poem? Let's recall Tennyson's 'The Charge of the Light Brigade' (Chapter 22). With a botched plan of attack a general in that engagement caused the death of almost half of his 600 cavalry. But Tennyson does not criticise the commander, or his country. Instead he lavishes praise on the bravery of those soldiers who rode to their death ('theirs not to reason why') into the barrels of the Russian artillery. Their deaths were 'glorious'.

Sassoon has a different and more complicated attitude. There was no such 'glory' in his view of things. 'The General' was written in 1916 and published in 1918, when the question 'Why did we fight this war?' was still white-hot. Cowardice ('the white feather', as it was called) did not come into it. Sassoon himself was a ferocious fighter, nicknamed 'Mad Jack' by his comrades (ironically 'Siegfried' means 'joy in victory' in German) but for the life of him (literally) he could not see the point of the war. When he was awarded a Military Cross for outstanding valour, he is supposed to have thrown the medal into the River Mersey.

The last surviving British 'Tommy' to have fought in the First World War, Harry Patch, who died in 2009, aged 111, agreed. On visiting Passchendaele, on the ninetieth anniversary of the battle, Patch described the war as the 'calculated and condoned slaughter of human beings. It wasn't worth one life'. By its end, in November 1918, it had cost over three-quarters of a million British lives. More than 9 million soldiers are estimated to have died, on both sides.

A better poem than Sassoon's was 'Futility' by his friend and comrade-in-arms, Wilfred Owen (1893–1918). A decorated and gallant officer, Owen contemplates the corpse of a soldier, lying in the snow, to whose family he must now write the formal letter of condolence:

Move him into the sun –
Gently its touch awoke him once,
At home, whispering of fields unsown.
Always it woke him, even in France,
Until this morning and this snow.
If anything might rouse him now
The kind old sun will know.

Think how it wakes the seeds, –
Woke, once, the clays of a cold star.
Are limbs, so dear-achieved, are sides,
Full-nerved, – still warm, – too hard to stir?
Was it for this the clay grew tall?
– O what made fatuous sunbeams toil
To break earth's sleep at all?

The poem, which shows the clear influence of Keats, has an emotional warmth bordering on the erotic. Will the sun bring this unknown warrior back to life, as it brings the seeds out of the earth in spring? No. Was his death worthwhile? No, it was futile. A total waste.

Owen is a more experimental poet than Sassoon technically and his anger is cooler. 'Futility' is an artfully constructed sonnet, with uneven lines and half rhymes (e.g. 'once' / 'France'). Invoked subtly throughout are the traditional funeral lines, 'Ashes to ashes, dust to dust'. It's generally agreed that, had he lived, Owen would have had a huge influence on the course of English poetry in the twentieth century. He died in the last week of the war. The telegram announcing his death was delivered to his family as the church bells began ringing for the declaration of peace.

By the time 'Futility' was written the war had degenerated into bloody stalemate. Lines of trenches and barbed wire stretched, like a badly stitched wound, across Europe. Neither army was able to break through and thousands died every week. This bloodbath had begun with an obscure street crime: the assassination of Emperor Franz Ferdinand in Sarajevo, in the Balkans. The Austro-Hungarian

Empire, a vast conglomeration of states, almost immediately fell apart. A succession struggle ensued and complex international alliances were called into play. The dominoes began to fall. By August 1914 (a glorious summer in England), war was inevitable.

Most people fondly thought the war would be over by Christmas. The spirit of the nation was summed up in the word 'jingoism' (it's wonderfully evoked in the 1963 musical play, *Oh, What a Lovely War!*). The most famous poem written at this jingoistic early stage of things was 'The Soldier', by Rupert Brooke (1887–1915):

> If I should die, think only this of me:
> That there's some corner of a foreign field
> That is for ever England. There shall be
> In that rich earth a richer dust concealed;
> A dust whom England bore, shaped, made aware,
> Gave, once, her flowers to love, her ways to roam,
> A body of England's, breathing English air,
> Washed by the rivers, blest by suns of home.
>
> And think, this heart, all evil shed away,
> A pulse in the eternal mind, no less
> Gives somewhere back the thoughts by England given;
> Her sights and sounds; dreams happy as her day;
> And laughter, learnt of friends; and gentleness,
> In hearts at peace, under an English heaven.

It's a noble sentiment, made all the nobler by what we know of its author. Brooke was a very handsome young man and bisexual. He was close to E.M. Forster and Virginia Woolf and other 'Bloomsberries' (Chapter 29). He was a gifted poet, but compared with Wilfred Owen he was more traditional in technique. So was his patriotism traditional. He volunteered on the outbreak of war, although somewhat overage, and died in the first year of the conflict of an infected mosquito bite, not an enemy bullet. He is indeed buried in a 'foreign field', the Greek island of Skyros.

Brooke's poem was instantly taken up by the war propaganda

machine. It was read out to the congregation in St Paul's Cathedral. Clergymen all over the country gave sermons on it. Schoolchildren had it recited to them at morning assembly, encouraging the older pupils to volunteer *en masse* to die honourably in foreign fields. It was a particular favourite of Winston Churchill, First Lord of the Admiralty. It was Churchill who wrote the glowing obituary of Brooke in *The Times*, the national 'paper of record'. But three years and all those deaths later, Brooke's anthem to patriotism rang very hollow. War was not glorious or heroic: it was, many fighting men believed, futile.

Virtually all the great war poets were upper, 'officer', class. But one of the very greatest had a quite different background. Isaac Rosenberg (1890–1918) was Jewish and from the working class. His family had recently emigrated from Russia, fleeing the Tsar's pogroms. Isaac was brought up in London's East End, then something of a Jewish ghetto. He left school at fourteen to become an apprentice engraver. From childhood on, he displayed unusual artistic and literary talent, though he was chronically ill with lung problems. He was physically tiny. Despite these handicaps – and clearly unfit – he volunteered for the military and went 'up the line to death' (as soldiers said) in 1915. He was killed in hand-to-hand combat in April 1918.

Rosenberg's best known poem, 'Break of Day in the Trenches', is what is called an *aubade* – a 'dawn poem'. Hailing the newly broken day is traditionally a joyous act, but not for a soldier in France in 1917. By military regulation soldiers 'stand to' at dawn, because this is the time of day most favoured for attacks:

The darkness crumbles away.
It is the same old druid Time as ever,
Only a live thing leaps my hand,
A queer sardonic rat,
As I pull the parapet's poppy
To stick behind my ear.
Droll rat, they would shoot you if they knew
Your cosmopolitan sympathies,

Now you have touched this English hand
You will do the same to a German
Soon, no doubt, if it be your pleasure
To cross the sleeping green between.

The rats, of course, had a 'lovely war' – feasting on the corpses of both armies.

The four poems we have looked at in this chapter are unquestionably great verse. We are lucky to have them. But were they worth three lives?

CHAPTER 28

The Year that Changed Everything
1922 AND THE MODERNISTS

Of all wonderful years in literature, 1922 qualifies as the most wonderful. It produced a bumper crop of books. But the reason for the year's wonderfulness is not the quantity or variety of what was produced but the fact that what was published in that year (and the years on either side) changed the reading public's sense of what literature could be. The 'climate', as the poet W.H. Auden later put it, was altered. A new and dominant 'style' came into play – 'modernism'.

Historically one can trace modernism's roots back to the 1890s and the 'end of century' (*fin de siècle*) decade covered in Chapter 21. Writers in that period, worldwide, seemed to have all bought into a kind of creative nonconformity, a breaking of ranks. Think of writers like Henrik Ibsen, Walt Whitman, George Bernard Shaw and Oscar Wilde. Writers, to put it at its simplest, came to see that their principal obligation was to literature itself – even if, like Wilde, it meant ending up in prison or, like Thomas Hardy, having their latest work burned by a bishop. Authority never had an easy time with modernism. It wasn't listening. It was, as we say, doing its own thing.

If it began in the 1890s and swelled in the Edwardian (pre-war) period, it was in 1922 that this new literary wave crested. One can identify a number of forces and factors that were instrumental. The traumatic effect of the First World War had broken, forever, old ways of looking at the world. Nothing in 1918 seemed the same as it had in 1914. The war could be seen as a gigantic smash-up which left the field barren, but clear for new things to come along. It was what in Latin is called a *tabula rasa*: a blank slate.

What, then, were the works that can be said to have spearheaded the innovations of this great year, 1922? James Joyce's novel *Ulysses* and T.S. Eliot's poem *The Waste Land*, both published that year, are the first that come to mind. One could also add to these Virginia Woolf's *Mrs Dalloway* (the author's most virtuosic exercise in the 'stream of consciousness' technique, more of which in Chapter 29). Woolf's novel was published in 1925, but conceived and set in 1922. Wilfred Owen's wartime poems, published posthumously in 1920, and W.B. Yeats's work, rewarded with the Nobel Prize in 1923, were accompaniments to the great year's achievements. By general agreement the greatest Irish poet, Yeats developed strikingly during his long career, from a rhapsodiser about the so-called 'Celtic Twilight' (Ireland's mythic past) to a modernist poet engaged with the present – not least the post-1916 civil disorder which was tearing his country apart. Some of his greatest work can be found in the collection *Later Poems*, published in 1922.

Before looking at a couple of the masterpieces given to the reading world in and around 1922, let's consider some general characteristics. Exhaustion and its perverse energies has been mentioned. All the literary works start from a kind of baseline zero. *Mrs Dalloway*, for example, is set against two great holocausts. One is the First World War, from which the shell-shocked hero of the novel, Septimus Smith, never recovers and whose mental torments (Post Traumatic Stress Disorder, as we would call it now) drive him to a horrible suicide, throwing himself from a high window onto spiked railings. Septimus is a post-war war casualty. The other holocaust was the influenza pandemic known as 'Spanish flu' which swept through the world in 1918–21, killing more people than the war itself. Woolf's heroine, Mrs Dalloway, is herself in recovery from the infection, which she has barely survived.

Another general characteristic of modernism is that its sources spring from outside the literary mainstream, rather than from within it. *The Waste Land* and *Ulysses* were introduced in parts to the public in 'little magazines', with tiny 'coterie' readerships. As we saw in Chapter 25, Joyce's work, in its complete form, was first published in Paris. No publisher in the two major English-speaking markets would touch it for decades – in Joyce's home country, Ireland, for half a century.

Exile and a sense of not belonging anywhere played its part. A large quantity of what we see as groundbreaking modernist litera-ture was published by what the American writer Gertrude Stein (herself a notable modernist) called the 'lost generation' – writers without roots in any 'home' market. But modernism is something other than an 'international' literary movement. It is, more prop-erly, what we could call 'supranational' – above and beyond any national origin. T.S. Eliot (1888–1965) was born, brought up and educated (at Harvard) as American as the Stars and Stripes itself. The manuscripts of *The Waste Land* reveal that early unpublished sections of the poem were set in Boston (near Harvard). Eliot was, in 1922, resident in Britain (he would later become a British citi-zen) although important parts of the poem were composed in Swit-zerland where he was recovering from a nervous breakdown. Is it a poem by an American, a Briton, or an American in Britain?

Ulysses is a similarly 'rootless' work. James Joyce (1882–1941) had left Dublin, where the novel is set, in 1912, never to return. His departure was an artistic decision. Great literature, he believed, should be published 'in silence, *exile*, and cunning'. What the novel implies is that its author could only write about Dublin if, in a sense, he was outside Dublin. Why? Joyce explained it with an image in another work. Ireland, the hero of *A Portrait of the Artist as a Young Man* affirms, is the 'old sow that eats her farrow [piglets]' – the mother that both nourishes and destroys you.

D.H. Lawrence's great work, *Women in Love*, had been published the year before, in 1921. Both it, and the novel that he published in

1922, *Aaron's Rod*, assert the need to 'get up and leave'. The great
tree of life ('Ygraddisil') was, Lawrence believed, dead in England.
He himself left the 'waste land' in which he had been born, the
child of a miner, to find what he was looking for in life elsewhere.
He was, he said, a 'savage pilgrim'.

Now let's consider the two 1922 masterpieces after which, truly,
literature would never be the same again. *The Waste Land*, as its
title proclaims, starts in a barren place, at a bleak time (the 'cruel-
lest month', Eliot calls it). The task the poem sets itself is explained
in an essay Eliot published a few months earlier, 'Tradition and the
Individual Talent'. In it Eliot lays out the problem: how to mend a
broken culture. It wasn't a case of simply sticking the leaves back
on the tree. Some new 'modern' living form had to be found, using the materials – damaged and fragmented as they now were –
bequeathed by the past ('tradition'). How Eliot's poem goes about
the task of 'putting it all together again' is illustrated in the section
called 'The Burial of the Dead', which regards London Bridge, in
winter, on a foggy, cold morning. 'Unreal City', says the observer,
adding: 'I had not thought death had undone so many.' What is
described is an everyday scene: commuters streaming from the
railway terminus across the Thames to their offices in the City (the
financial hub of the world), to make the great machine of global
capitalism work. They are, most of them, 'clerks', in the bowler hat,
brolly and briefcase garb of their profession. A dark tide on a dark
morning. But the exclamation 'Unreal City' is, as the well-read
reader was intended to notice, an echo of Baudelaire's poem, 'Seven
Old Men', in *Les Fleurs du mal*:

> Unreal City, city full of dreams,
> Where ghosts in broad daylight cling to passers by!

The workers in Eliot's poem are the 'living dead'. The theme is
intensified by the last line: '... death had undone so many'. It is a
direct quote from Dante's amazed response to the crowds of dead
people he saw on his visit to Hell, in his poem *Inferno*: 'I had not
thought death had undone so many', says Dante, looking at the

massed ranks of the damned. Eliot regarded Dante as one of the giants of literature (Shakespeare was the other). Dante, uniquely, raised literature to the status of philosophy, and his *La Divina Commedia* (the *Divine Comedy*) is one of the masterpieces of world literature. But Eliot is not merely dropping big names to show off his reading; he is weaving a new fabric out of old threads with this kind of allusion, which runs all the way through *The Waste Land*. The poem is Eliot's (the individual talent), but its materials are great literature (tradition).

Ulysses, as Joyce's title signals, connects with Homeric epic: the very starting point of Western literature. But on the face of it, the alignment seems all wrong. The novel is about (insofar as one can ever use that over-simplifying word 'about') one day (16 June 1904) in the life of a Jewish clerk in Dublin – another black-suited desk-slave, like those streaming over London Bridge. Leopold Bloom is married to a woman, Molly, whom he loves, but who he knows is flagrantly unfaithful to him. Not much happens in the day, which is much like every other day – no Troy is sacked, no Helen is abducted, no great battles are fought. But at every point *Ulysses* breaks new ground in literature. On one level (the level largely responsible for the book's long banning in Ireland) it breaks with the old 'decent' inhibitions of fiction – Bloom, for instance, is described on the lavatory. There is the occasional use of four-letter words and vivid descriptions of erotic fantasies. The last section of *Ulysses*, 'Penelope' (named after the undyingly faithful wife in the *Odyssey*), records what is going on in Molly's mind as she slips into sleep. There is, for many pages, no punctuation – it's a kind of stream of subconsciousness. Our minds, Joyce's novel insists, are where we really live, and at every stage the novel explores new ways of making sense of the strange conditions in which all human beings, however ordinary, find themselves.

Like Eliot, Joyce makes heavy demands on the reader. You need to be well read, or have a well-annotated text, to catch the intricate allusions in *The Waste Land* or thread your way through the linguistic and stylistic trickeries of *Ulysses*. But no literature is more worth the effort.

The father-figure behind the great modernist triumph of 1922 was Ezra Pound – '*Il miglior fabbro*' (the greater artist), as Eliot calls him in the dedication to *The Waste Land*. It was Pound who broke down Eliot's first drafts of the poem, creating its daringly new and disjointed shapes. It was Pound, in his role as modernist mentor, who dragged W.B. Yeats out of the nostalgic 'Celtic Twilight' of his early and middle period and made him confront the present state of Ireland with a new, hard style and poems like 'Easter, 1916', reflecting on the bloody Irish uprising and the brutal British repression.

Pound's own poetry found its inspiration in exotic places. He was fascinated by oriental literature and language in which the pictorial and the textual were merged into a single unit. Was it possible to 'crystallise' words into images as the Chinese pictogram did? He succeeded better than anyone in the effort. One of his poems, 'In a Station of the Metro', began as an extended description of the Paris underground. He boiled it down to something as short, brilliant and pictographic as a fourteen-syllable Japanese haiku. You could get it inside a Christmas cracker.

It was not merely modernism on offer to the reader in 1922. At its strongest, the movement was a powerful expression of minority taste in an overwhelming mass culture that was wholly indifferent or violently hostile to what writers like Eliot, Pound, Woolf and Yeats were doing. But time has a way of sifting out the good from the bad. Who now remembers Robert Bridges, the poet laureate in 1922 (he would hold the post from 1913 to 1930)? There were a thousand purchasers of his volume-length 1929 poem, *The Testament of Beauty*, for every one reader of *The Waste Land*, when it was published almost simultaneously in little magazines in Britain and America. Bridges' poem is in the waste-paper basket of literature. *The Waste Land* survives and will be on posterity's bookshelf for as long as poetry is read. The year 2022 will be a great anniversary.

CHAPTER 29

A Literature of her Own
WOOLF

'On or about December 1910', Virginia Woolf famously (and not entirely seriously) said, 'human character changed'. It was then that 'Victorianism' finally came to a close and the new era, modernism, began. The actual moment Woolf specified was when a controversial Post-Impressionist art exhibition opened in London. Woolf was very definitely 'post-Victorian' – an uneasy successor to an age whose values and prejudices were obstinately outliving their historical period.

Virginia Woolf (1882–1941) wrote from within a famous milieu (roughly, a group of like-minded intellectuals) known as the Bloomsbury Group. She was a central member of the group and forcefully articulated many of its leading ideas. She was intellectually powerful and very much her own woman. But without the support of that milieu she would never have been the writer she was. For one thing, the 'Bloomsberries' (as outsiders have belittlingly called them) had, for their time, advanced views on the 'woman question'. Women in Britain would not get the vote until eight years after 1910, the date 'human character changed'. (In the USA it was slightly earlier.) Even then, insultingly, only women over thirty were allowed to vote, being considered too emotionally unstable to handle the responsibility until that age. For the record, Virginia Woolf was twenty-eight years old in 1910. Not yet ready to put her 'X' on the ballot paper – or so the man's world thought.

We cannot seriously discuss Woolf without bringing into the picture two other elements. One, already mentioned, is the Blooms-bury Group in the 1920s. The other is the great reformation in criti-cal thinking about literature which came about with the emergence of the 'Women's Movement' in the mid-1960s, which took her up as a figurehead writer. It did wonders for her sales. During her life-time, Woolf's works sold only in the hundreds. Had she not owned the firm that printed them (the Hogarth Press), she might well have had difficulty getting even those hundreds published. Her work is now everywhere available in hundreds of thousands of copies and everywhere, in the English-speaking world, studied.

It goes well beyond sales figures. Feminist criticism has been especially instrumental in altering the way we now read and value Woolf's works. She herself wrote what became one of the founding texts of literary feminism, *A Room of One's Own* (1929). In this treatise she argues that women need their own space, and money, in order to create literature. They can't reasonably do it on the kitchen table, after they've cooked the evening meal for the man of the house and the children have been safely put to bed. (This is how the Victorian novelist Elizabeth Gaskell, known as 'Mrs Gaskell', wrote her fiction. No one nowadays, incidentally, calls our author 'Mrs Woolf'.) *A Room of One's Own* is infused with flaming anger, and a determination that the sheer unfairness of the inequalities which have unbalanced literature for thousands of years must be put right. The woman's voice must no longer be silenced. This is how Woolf puts it:

> When one reads of a witch being ducked, of a woman possessed by devils, of a wise woman selling herbs, or even of a very remarkable man who had a mother, then I think we are on the track of a lost novelist, a suppressed poet, of some mute

and inglorious Jane Austen, some Emily Brontë who dashed
her brains out on the moor or mopped and mowed about the
highways crazed with the torture that her gift had put her to.

The phrase 'mute and inglorious Jane Austen' alludes to Thomas
Gray's 'Elegy Written in a Country Churchyard'. Wandering and
pondering, looking at the gravestones, Gray thinks how many
of those buried there had poetic talents equivalent to his, but
did not have the social advantages and privileges to bring those
undeveloped gifts to fruition. Yes, says Woolf, but writers like
Thomas Gray could get through. If she had been 'Thomasina Gray',
unless she were abnormally lucky she too would have been 'mute
and inglorious'.

The Bloomsbury Group included among its most notable members the novelist E.M. Forster (Chapter 26), the art critic Roger Fry,
the poet Rupert Brooke (Chapter 27), and the most influential and
radically new-thinking economist of the twentieth century, John
Maynard Keynes. Few milieux have had more 'ideas' circulating
among them.

The group's principal propagandist was Lytton Strachey. It was
he who proclaimed their founding principle: that they were not,
repeat not, Victorians (even though all of them had been born
and raised during that monarch's long reign). For the Bloomsbury
Group the 'Eminent Victorians', as Strachey sneeringly labelled
them in his famous book of that title, existed only to be mocked
and repudiated. But, most importantly, got out of the way.

The Bloomsberries regarded the First World War as the death
throes of Victorianism. It was tragic that so many millions had to
die, but it was 'closure' and made it possible for literature and the
world of ideas to have a wholly new start.

What, then, did 'Bloomsbury' stand for? 'Civilisation', they
might have replied. 'Liberalism' might well have been another
answer. They subscribed to a philosophy that originated with John
Stuart Mill and was reformulated by the Cambridge philosopher,
G.E. Moore. Essentially its basic idea was that you were free to
do anything so long as it did not damage, or infringe upon, the

equivalent freedoms of some other person. It's a beautiful principle, but extremely hard to put into practice. Some would say impossible.

Woolf's life was a mixture of privilege (there was always a servant to clean that room of her own – the servant's interesting biography was published in 2010) and chronic mental suffering. She was born the daughter of a distinguished man of letters, Leslie Stephen, and his equally cultivated wife. The young Virginia Stephen was brought up in fine London houses in the area around London's Bloomsbury Square in central London. That particular square is one of the beauties of the city. Woolf particularly loved it on rainy days when, as she put it, the black, sinuous trunks of the trees looked like 'wet seals'. Bloomsbury itself is also the centre of London's intellectual powerhouse, containing as it does a number of university colleges, the British Museum and, in Woolf's day, a cluster of major publishing houses.

Woolf did not attend university and did not need to. She came into adulthood extraordinarily well read, and well connected with the finest minds of her time. She was writing almost as soon as she could hold a pen in her hand. But even in her childhood it was observed that her mind was troubled. She had her first nervous breakdown when she was just thirteen. Such breakdowns would happen again during her life – finally, fatally.

Aged thirty she made a marriage of mutual convenience with the social thinker (another Bloomsberry) Leonard Woolf. As part of their liberalism the group tolerated previously prohibited kinds of human relationship. Forster and Keynes were gay (at a period when it was criminal). Woolf's passion was reserved for her same-sex relationship with Vita Sackville-West – a fellow writer and creative gardener at her fine country home at Sissinghurst, in Kent. The Bloomsbury Group believed that 'art' could be applied to everything in life – even horticulture.

The relationship between Woolf and Sackville-West was no secret, even to their respective, and similarly open-minded, husbands. It is commemorated in one of Woolf's finest, and most readable works, *Orlando*, a fantasy biography of Vita's family over the centuries with a central character whose sex changes with passing lifetimes. Sackville-West's son, Nigel, called it 'the longest and most charming love-letter in literature'. It was not addressed to Leonard.

Independence was all-important to Woolf – with regards to conventional morality, social restrictions, and the London literary world. She and her husband founded the Hogarth Press publishing firm in 1917, its offices a stone's throw from Bloomsbury Square. She could now write and publish as she pleased. She had begun publishing full-length fiction in 1915 with *The Voyage Out*. Thereafter novels came at regular intervals. They were subtly imbued with her feminist principles but, above all, they were 'experimental', doing things that were new in English literature. The technique with which her writing is most famously linked has been called (not by her) 'stream of consciousness'.

This is how she described it in an essay of 1925 ('gig lamps' are the headlights on a horse-drawn carriage illuminated at night):

> Life is not a series of gig lamps symmetrically arranged; life is a luminous halo, a semi-transparent envelope surrounding us from the beginning of consciousness to the end.

Capturing that 'halo' was Woolf's major endeavour in fiction. Note how she does it in the wonderful opening of her novel, *Mrs Dalloway*. It's the story of a single day in the life of Clarissa Dalloway, the middle-aged wife of a Conservative Member of Parliament, who has planned a party that evening. She is setting out from her house near the Houses of Parliament, alongside chiming Big Ben, to collect some summer flowers to decorate her living room. It is a lovely June morning and she is waiting to cross the road. She feels strangely happy, having just recovered from a life-threatening bout of influenza. A neighbour passes her as she stands at the side of one of the busiest thoroughfares in London, but she doesn't notice him:

> She stiffened a little on the kerb, waiting for Durtnall's van to pass. A charming woman, Scrope Purvis thought her (knowing her as one does know people who live next door to one in West-

minster); a touch of the bird about her, of the jay, blue-green, light, vivacious, though she was over fifty, and grown very white since her illness. There she perched, never seeing him, waiting to cross, very upright.

For having lived in Westminster – how many years now? over twenty, – one feels even in the midst of the traffic, or waking at night, Clarissa was positive, a particular hush, or solemnity; an indescribable pause; a suspense (but that might be her heart, affected, they said, by influenza) before Big Ben strikes. There! Out it boomed. First a warning, musical; then the hour, irrevocable. The leaden circles dissolved in the air. Such fools we are, she thought, crossing Victoria Street.

Who else can one think of who would write so elaborately about waiting for a gap in the traffic to cross a street? It is, of course, exactly what is happening in Clarissa's head, and momentarily that of her neighbour (there are 'streams' of consciousness). Note how the narrative line jumps here and there, following the movements of a mind in motion. Is Clarissa thinking in words, in images, or something that blends the two? What is the interplay between memory (things that happened twenty years ago) and the moment's sense impressions (the booming of Big Ben)?

Not much ever 'happens' in Woolf's narratives. That's not the point. Mrs Dalloway's big event is nothing special – just another party with dull politicians. The novel *To the Lighthouse* (1927), her greatest work, centres on a family (clearly the Stephen family, in the author's girlhood) enjoying their summer holiday at the coast. They plan a trip by boat to a lighthouse. It never quite takes place. Her last novel, *Between the Acts* (1941), is, as the title suggests, about waiting for something to start.

That final novel was written in the early months of the Second World War. The next 'act' Woolf thought, could well be disaster for her and her husband (they had no children). It was feared in spring 1941 that Germany, which had overrun France with no difficulty, could soon invade and conquer Britain. The Woolfs – he was Jewish, both were left-wing – were prominent on the Gestapo death lists and both had prudently made suicide plans. Virginia, who had recently suffered a crippling nervous breakdown and feared permanent madness, went to a river near where they were living in Sussex, loaded her coat pockets with stones, and drowned herself on 28 March 1941.

England would survive to produce, as a nation, more literature. Its greatest woman novelist of the modernist period would not.

CHAPTER 30

Brave New Worlds
UTOPIAS AND DYSTOPIAS

'Utopia' is an Ancient Greek word meaning, literally, 'good place'. If you had used it in conversation with, say, Sophocles or Homer, however, they might well have looked at you oddly. The word was invented by an Englishman, Sir Thomas More, in the sixteenth century as the title of a story that pictured a world in which everything was perfect. The fact that More had his head chopped off a few years later for questioning Henry VIII's marriage arrangements suggests that the England he was living in was something less than perfect.

Literature has the godlike ability, simply using the faculty of the imagination, to create whole worlds. It's helpful to think of putting those worlds on a line, with 'realism' at one end and 'fantasy' at the other. The closer a literary world is to the author's, the more 'realistic' the work of literature is. *Pride and Prejudice* depicts a world which, it's safe to presume, was very like the one in which Jane Austen lived and wrote. *Conan the Barbarian* envisages a world that is entirely different from the seedy 1930s Texas backwater where the author Robert E. Howard fantasised his superhero, and the 'Cimmeria' where Conan performs his superheroics.

Utopias tend, like *Conan*, to cluster at the 'fantasy' end of the line for the very good reason that there has never yet been a perfect society or anything approaching one. Some writers think we are progressing, however gradually, towards that perfection. Their utopias are 'prophetic'. A good example is H.G. Wells's *The Shape of Things to Come* (1933). Wells believed that the extraordinary leaps forward in technology that the late nineteenth and early twentieth century saw would bring about 'technotopia'. A lot of science fiction has been written on that theme.

Others think we are moving away from realising a better world than the one in which we now live. In the nineteenth century there was a yearning for a romanticised medievalism which had been lost to urbanisation and the Industrial Revolution. These back-to-simplicity utopias are nostalgic. One of the most famous, and influential, was *Looking Backward* (1887) by Edward Bellamy. A short-lived American 'People's Party' founded itself on Bellamy's principles.

Whether looking backwards or forwards, all societies have a grand vision of what is, was, or will be their 'good place'. In ancient Greece, Plato's *Republic* imagined a perfect city in which everything would be rationally arranged with 'philosopher kings', like Plato himself, in charge. In societies where Judaeo-Christianity is dominant, images of biblical Eden (in the past) and Heaven (in the future) tend to inspire and colour literature's utopian visions. In ancient Rome it was 'Elysium' (that is, the 'Elysian fields' – a perfect natural world). In Muslim societies, Paradise. For the Vikings, it was Valhalla, a home of great heroes, celebrating their feats in battle. Communism believed, following Marx, that there would come, in the distant future, what he called the 'withering away of the state' and a condition of perfect social equality among men.

These belief systems have all, in their different ways, inspired authors to create imaginary worlds – humanity's 'happy ending'. But the big problem with literary utopias (and More's is no exception) is that they tend to be yawn-inducingly dull. Literature is most readable when it adopts a critical, sceptical or downright quarrelsome position. What is called the 'dystopian' view of things makes for livelier reading, and more provocative thinking about past, present and future societies. The point can be made by looking at some of the more famous literary dystopias which, if you haven't read them yet, are certainly worth seeking out.

Ray Bradbury's *Fahrenheit 451* has a teasing title. It's the temperature at which printed paper spontaneously bursts into flame (a metaphor, you might think, for literature itself). Bradbury wrote it in 1953. He was inspired to do so by the arrival of television as a mass medium. As Bradbury saw it, TV's rise was the death of the book.

Bradbury thought this was a very bad thing. Books, he believed, made people think. They were stimulating. The television set did the opposite. It was a narcotic. And, sinisterly, television made possible a power over the population that no dictator had previously enjoyed – a 'soft tyranny'. Universal mind control.

The hero of *Fahrenheit 451* is a 'fireman' whose job is not to put out fires but to burn any surviving books. (Bradbury was clearly inspired by the Nazi book burnings of the 1930s.) While at work the hero casually picks up a book from a bonfire he has been sent out to start and becomes thereafter, a reader and a rebel. He ends a refugee in the woods, where a likeminded community memorise great works of literature and become themselves living books. Their flame will burn on – perhaps.

What is fascinating about *Fahrenheit 451* is that like other great dystopian literature it is both right and wrong. Bradbury's pessimism about TV is plainly wrong-headed. TV has enriched, not impoverished, culture. Bradbury's dystopian alarm is one of many illustrations of the mixed feelings that society always has about new technologies. The computer, for example, has revolutionised contemporary life, for the better most of us would say. But in dystopian fantasy films like *The Terminator*, the computer 'Skynet' is visualised as mankind's mortal enemy. Cavemen doubtless felt the same about fire. 'Good servant, bad master', as the proverb puts it.

But Bradbury is 100 per cent right in his analysis of how the most effective modern tyranny works. It doesn't have to chop off heads with a guillotine, or exterminate ('purge') whole classes of people, as did Stalin and Hitler. It can work, just as well, by thought control.

The title of this chapter – 'Brave New Worlds' – echoes Miranda's exclamation when she sees Ferdinand and his young companions in Shakespeare's *The Tempest*. Miranda has been brought up on an island where the only other human being is her aged father. When she sees handsome young men, of noble character, like Ferdinand, she jumps to the conclusion that in the outside world everyone is handsome, young and noble. If only.

Aldous Huxley took Miranda's 'brave new world' as the title of his dystopia, which, although published in 1932, remains much read today. The narrative is set 2,000 years hence. According to the calendar of that time it is 'AF632': AF stands for 'After Ford' and, simultaneously, 'After Freud'. What if human beings could be mass-produced in the same way that Henry Ford mass-produced his Model T automobiles – by assembly line? The psychiatrist Sigmund Freud argued that most human neurosis originated in emotional conflicts in the family – what if the nuclear family could be replaced? Huxley came up with the idea of 'ectogenesis': babies in bottles, produced in 'hatcheries' (factories), like Model T cars, needing no parents other than a team of white-coated laboratory technicians.

The result is a perfectly stable society, every member belonging to their assigned upper or lower class and the whole population kept artificially happy with a mass-distributed tranquilliser ('soma'). There is no politics. No war. No religion. No disease. No hunger. No poverty. No unemployment (Huxley, remember, was writing in the Great Depression of the 1930s). And, above all, no books or literature.

Brave New World creates the vision of a utopia, but not one that most of us would want to live in, comfortable as it is. Enter John Savage (the name recalls Rousseau's 'noble savage') who has been brought up on an American Indian reservation with only a copy of Shakespeare's plays to read. This new world is not for him. He rebels, and is destroyed. The brave new world goes on as 'happily' as before. It doesn't need noble savages or Shakespeare.

As with Bradbury, Huxley is both right and wrong in his predictions. There is no likelihood, if one looks at human history, that *Brave New World*'s stable world-state could ever happen. It's way off the fantasy end of the scale. But Huxley's forecast that biological intervention could transform society in worrying ways is amazingly prophetic. The human genome map, IVF (it means, literally, fertilising 'in glass'), and other new biotechnologies make the 'babies in bottles' scenario entirely plausible. It is now quite within human reach to 'make' humans, as Huxley predicted humans one day would. What brave new world will humankind make with that power?

The most argued-over dystopia of the last fifty years is Margaret Atwood's *The Handmaid's Tale*. It was published in 1985 when Ronald Reagan was President of the United States. He was in power, some thought, because of crucial support from the 'religious right' – Christian fundamentalists. This is the starting point for Atwood's feminist-futurist dystopia.

The Handmaid's Tale is set in a post-nuclear-war late twentieth-century. Fundamentalist Christians have taken over the United States which they have renamed the Republic of Gilead. African Americans ('Children of Ham') have been disposed of. Women are again in their subordinate place. At the same time, male and female fertility has declined disastrously. The few women who can bear children are designated 'handmaids' – breeders, at the disposal of men. Gileadian handmaids have no rights, no social life and are given the chattel-name 'Of[their owner]'. The heroine is Offred ('property of Fred'). She was captured with her husband and child trying to escape to liberal Canada (a small chauvinism: Atwood is Canadian). Offred is allocated to a powerful male called 'the Commander'. The novel ends with Offred seeming to make her escape from captivity, although it is written so that we cannot be entirely sure that she will succeed.

It's easy to pooh-pooh Atwood's grim prophecy. From 2009

there has been a 'son of Ham' in the White House and you would be brave or stupid to dare to call Michelle Obama (or Hillary Clinton, come to that) her husband's 'handmaid'. But parts of Atwood's dystopia ring very true – the recurrent attempts of religious pressure groups in America to control the reproductive rights of women, for instance. Those rights were largely won by the feminist movement which began to assert itself by Atwood's own generation, in the mid-1960s. The question raised by Atwood is as relevant today as it was a quarter of a century ago, and for that reason her novel still resonates.

The most influential dystopia of our time has been George Orwell's *Nineteen Eighty-Four*. So influential, in fact, it has added at least one word to our language: 'Orwellian'. The novel was conceived in 1948 and, some would say, is as much about that period as the then-distant year of the title. Britain had emerged from the Second World War exhausted and impoverished. No end was in sight – it would be austerity for ever.

But Orwell had bigger targets in view. The war had been fought against 'totalitarian' states (Germany, Italy, Japan) and their all-powerful dictators. The allies who emerged victorious were 'democratic states'. Their major eastern partner, the USSR, however, was as totalitarian a state as pre-war Germany itself. While the war was going on, that did not matter. He would make an alliance with the Devil, said Churchill, if Lucifer was anti-Hitler. But what about afterwards?

Orwell prophesied that Soviet-style dictatorship and a global balance of co-existing totalitarian superpowers was the shape of things to come. In the novel, Britain is 'Airstrip One', a province in the 'Oceania' superpower. It is under the total domination of a Stalin-like dictator (even down to the famed moustache) – 'Big Brother' – who may or may not exist. Orwell's original title for the novel was 'The Last Man in Europe'. The last man is the novel's hero, Winston Smith, who is destined to be liquidated after he has been 're-educated'. The state is all-powerful and always will be, forever more.

Nineteen Eighty-Four was wholly wrong in predicting a future of continuous, grinding austerity: compared to 1948 when the novel was written, 1984 was a land of milk and honey. And the last totalitarian superpower, the USSR ('Eurasia' in the novel), collapsed in 1989. Orwell was entirely wrong about that. But in other ways the 'Orwellian' future has, indeed, come about.

To take just one example of Orwellian accuracy. Orwell, like Bradbury, was fascinated by the arrival of television. But what, he wondered, if the TV set could watch you? This, the two-way television set, is the principal means by which the 'Party' enforces its tyranny in *Nineteen Eighty-Four*. Which country in the world has most CCTV cameras? You've guessed it. Airstrip One. We live in an 'Orwellian' future. As predicted.

CHAPTER 31

Boxes of Tricks

COMPLEX NARRATIVES

Fiction can do many things other than entertain. It can, for example, instruct. What many of us know about science might have come from reading science fiction. Fiction can enlighten and change minds – as *Uncle Tom's Cabin* changed America's thinking about slavery. Fiction can popularise the central ideas of a political party: what is now the central belief of British Conservatism was worked out in a series of novels by Benjamin Disraeli in the 1840s. Fiction can, if targeted the right way, bring about urgent social reform. In the early twentieth century Upton Sinclair's novel *The Jungle* (1906) about the horrors of the meat-processing industry brought about legislation. In innumerable other ways, fiction can do things that go well beyond keeping the reader turning the pages before they catch their plane or turn off the bedside lamp.

When Anthony Trollope was asked what good all his novels did (he published close on fifty of them), the great Victorian novelist replied that they instructed young ladies how to receive proposals of marriage from the men who loved them. On the face of it, Trollope's remark sounds flippant, but it wasn't. We do pick up things from fiction which help us in our lives – at its very grandest, literature can point us towards what are the most important things in life. Novelists of that kind are the ones who are likely to win the Nobel Prize in Literature (Chapter 39).

One could go on. But one of the most interesting things that fiction does is to explore itself, play games with itself and test its own boundaries and artifices. Fiction is the most self-conscious and playful of genres. In this chapter we'll look at what I've called fiction's 'boxes of tricks'. You could call them novels about novels.

We think of this interest in trickery as a modern thing which, generally, it is. But we can find examples of it as far back as the point at which the novel itself became a dominant literary form, in the eighteenth century, in the work of Laurence Sterne. Critics call the kind of fiction Sterne wrote 'self-reflexive'. It's as if the writer is constantly asking himself, 'What, exactly, am I doing here?'

Laurence Sterne's great work, *The Life and Opinions of Tristram Shandy, Gentleman* (first published in 1759), is as slippery as a basket of eels – which, once you get into it, is its irresistible attraction. Sterne's novel is constantly poking fun at itself and posing conundrums for the reader to wrestle with. Top of the list of conundrums is, as the old proverb puts it, how to get quarts into pint pots.

Sterne was writing when the novel was genuinely novel. It had only just started on its long journey to post-modernism (which, more or less, is where the experimental edge of fiction is now). But the author of *Tristram Shandy* foresaw the fundamental problem for anyone setting out to write a novel: how to fit it all in. It can't be done. Tristram, Sterne's hero-narrator (a comic version of Sterne himself), sets out to tell the story of his life. It's a typical project in fiction. Tristram, sensibly enough, decides to begin at the beginning. But he finds that, to explain how Tristram became what Tristram now is, he has to dig back past his childhood, past his christening (why the odd name 'Tristram'? There's a long riff on that), past his birth, to the moment of his conception – when sperm met egg. By the time he has got back to this starting point, he finds he has used up most of his novel. And so it goes. He has fallen at the first fence. He concludes, ruefully:

> I am this month one whole year older than I was this time twelve-month; and having got, as you perceive, almost into the middle of my third volume [it was originally published in twelve volumes] – and no farther than to my first day's life – 'tis demonstrative that I have three hundred and sixty-four days more life to write just now, than when I first set out.

In other words, Tristram is living his life 364 times faster than he can record his life. He will never catch up.

The problem played with so wittily by Sterne (how to pack everything necessary into the novel for the journey it's about to take when you have ten times more clothes than suitcases) has never been solved. Nor does Sterne himself try to solve it. What he does is to play entertaining games with the impossibilities, for our amusement. Other novelists, of loftier artistic ambition, devise schemes of selection, symbolism, compression, organisation and representation to get round the problem of 'how to get everything in the suitcase'. It all adds up to the art of fiction – more properly, the artifice of fiction. And that, of course, is the point Sterne is making.

This chapter is called 'Boxes of Tricks'. Let's look at a selection of the fictional toys that novelists have offered for our pleasure, and to tease our reading brains. We can start with another basic problem. Narrative presumes a narrator, the 'teller of the tale'. Who is it? The author? Sometimes it seems to be, sometimes it clearly isn't. Sometimes we are left uncertain. Jane Eyre is not Charlotte Brontë, for example, but there seem to be clear connections, biographically and psychologically, between author and heroine.

But what about a modern novel like J.G. Ballard's *Crash* (1973) in which the main character is called James Ballard, who happens to be a man with a wholly sinister interest in car accidents and the unpleasant things they do to human flesh? Is this a confession of some sort? No. It's the author playing a very sophisticated literary game not 'with', but 'against' the reader. It's rather like two friends playing a competitive game of chess.

Ballard's most famous work of fiction (thanks, largely, to Steven Spielberg's Oscar-winning film), is *Empire of the Sun* (1984). It's about a little boy who gets separated from his parents in Shanghai, on the outbreak of World War Two, and finds himself in an internment camp whose horrors will form (deform?) his personality for the rest of his life. The hero is called 'James', and James's experiences match exactly those of James Ballard as recorded in the author's autobiography. So is it fiction? Are we in a 'James = James' situation? Yes and no. Don't even try to work it out, the novel implies. Just take it in.

In his novel *Lunar Park* (2005), Bret Easton Ellis goes even further, with a hero called Bret Easton Ellis (a very depraved fellow, as it happens) who is pursued by the serial sex-killer of Bret Easton Ellis's earlier, very notorious novel, *American Psycho*. (Got it? Neither did I.) Ellis elaborates the trickery by having Ellis (in the novel) be married to a (fictional) film star called Jayne Dennis, for whom he created a straight-faced, apparently real-life website which many readers were taken in by. Martin Amis performs the same trick, just as cunningly, in his novel *Money: A Suicide Note* (1984) in which the hero (called John Self) makes friends with Martin Amis who warns him, as a friend, that if Self carries on as he is, he's going to come to a very bad end. Probably suicide.

Several authors over the years have narrated their novels through the eyes of a dog. Julian Barnes goes one better by having the first chapter of his novel (so to call it) *A History Of The World in 10½ Chapters* (1989) narrated by a woodworm on Noah's ark. It gets zanier.

Novelists are nowadays expert mechanics of the machine they are working with. They love to take it apart and put it back together again in many different ways. Sometimes they leave the job of putting things back together to the reader. John Fowles, for example, in his neo-Victorian but 'new wave' novel, *The French Lieutenant's Woman* (1969), offers the reader three different endings. Italo Calvino, in *If on a Winter's Night a Traveller* (1980), offers ten different openings to the narrative, testing how nimble his readers are on their feet. Are they as nimble as he is as a tale-teller? *If on a Winter's Night a Traveller* opens: 'You are about to begin reading Italo Calvino's new novel, *If on a Winter's Night a Traveller*. Relax.' The joke is you *can't* relax – he's done what post-modernist critics call a 'defamiliarisation' job on you. It's unsettling.

Calvino's opening chapter goes on to ponder ideal sitting positions for 'your' reading of the book. 'In the old days they used to read standing up, at a lectern', advises the novel, but this time why not try a sofa and cushions with a pack of cigarettes and coffee-pot nearby? You'll need them. It dawns on you that 'you' are an actor, not a spectator, in this theatre of reading. Calvino's novel ends with one of its main characters telling the reader to 'turn off the bedside lamp and go to sleep'. There's no point going any further. 'Just a moment', the reader (you, that is) thinks, 'I've almost finished *If on a Winter's Night a Traveller* by Italo Calvino'. But has Calvino finished it? No. In a sense he never started it.

The American Paul Auster is the master of a similar kind of Calvinoesque trickery. *City of Glass* (1985), the novel that made his name, is a 'metaphysical detective story' set in New York. The narrative begins with a midnight phone call: 'It was a wrong number that started it, the telephone ringing three times in the dead of night, and the voice on the other end asking for someone he was not.' The not-someone is, we discover, 'Paul Auster, of the Auster Detective Agency'. The recipient of the call is the thirty-five-year-old author, Daniel Quinn. For reasons Quinn himself cannot explain he pretends to be Paul Auster and takes on the case. It gets even trickier.

The lover of fiction takes the same kind of pleasure in the 'tricksy' novelist as in a conjuring act when a performer comes on stage, states 'My next trick is impossible', and then goes ahead and does it – pulling a dozen rabbits from a hat, or sawing his assistant in half. But sometimes there is deeper significance in the trick. Thomas Pynchon's post-modernist classic (to mix up our terms horribly), *Gravity's Rainbow* (1973), starts with a realistically-described London, in the last months of the Second World War. It's done vividly and accurately. Except for one thing. V2 rockets, which were indeed falling on the city in late 1944, seem to be falling everywhere the American soldier hero, Slothrop, becomes sexually excited. He is controlling the rockets' targeting. It is, of course, 'paranoia' – that disordered state of mind where you think everything in the world is a conspiracy against you personally. Pynchon is fascinated by paranoia. It emerges as the novel's 'theme', insofar as one can simplify things.

More straightforward are the games played by Pynchon's fellow American, Donald Barthelme, many of whose short stories could quite well have come from the pages of *Mad* magazine. In one of them the legendary gorilla, King Kong, is appointed an 'adjunct professor of art history' at an American university. Barthelme's most famous story takes the Snow White fairy tale (originally German, recycled most famously by Walt Disney) and turns the fair maiden-heroine into something very un-maidenly indeed. It's laugh-out-loud funny but, at the same time, Barthelme is shaking to pieces our conventional thinking about literature. Other novelists have *literally* shaken their novels to pieces, like B.S. Johnson, whose *The Unfortunates* (1969) was published as a boxed set of unbound pages which the reader can put together in any order they please. It is literally a box of tricks. *The Unfortunates* drives librarians to distraction. Readers too.

This tricksy type of fiction is very clever and it requires a cleverness on the part of the reader. If we look at the fiction-reading public over the last 300 years, we can see how it has entered into the spirit of the game. There are many pleasures offered by the novel, and trickery is not the least. Laurence Sterne was right.

CHAPTER 32

Off the Page
LITERATURE ON FILM, TV AND THE STAGE

'Literature', as you will know, literally means something that comes to us in the form of letters. That is, something written or printed and taken in through the eye to be interpreted by the brain. But often enough, particularly nowadays, literature comes to us 'mediated', in different forms and through different channels and different sense organs.

Let's play another mind game. If you borrowed H.G. Wells's time machine and brought Homer to the present day, what would he make of the all-action, Brad Pitt-starring 2004 film *Troy* – an epic movie 'based' (as the title and credits affirm) on his epic, the *Iliad*? What would Homer see in that movie as being in any sense 'his'? And could he agree what elements in the film were 'Homeric'?

If you also stopped off in the nineteenth century and picked up Jane Austen (this is getting a bit like *Bill & Ted's Excellent Adventure*, but let's carry on with it), what would the author of *Pride and Prejudice* make of the many TV and film adaptations of her novels? Would she rejoice that, selling only a few hundred copies during her life, she had, two centuries after her death, reached an audience of tens of millions? Or would she see it as a violation and crossly respond: 'Leave my novels alone, Sirs!' And what would the owner of the time machine, H.G. Wells, think of the three films (and innumerable spin-offs) inspired by his 1890s short tale about time travel? Would he say, 'The future has arrived', or 'That is not what I meant at all'?

'Adaptation' is, simply, what happens when literature is recycled in a technology other than that in which it was originated (which is usually print). The word often preferred nowadays is 'versioning'. One sees many such fruitful versionings in literary history. Looking back at earlier chapters, we could argue that the Bible was 'adapted' by the horse-and-cart transport system in the street theatre of the mystery plays. It drove Dickens crazy that there were a dozen stage adaptations of *Oliver Twist* running in competition with his printed novel, from whose producers he received not a penny. 'We are merely "adapting" you, Mr Dickens', the theatrical pirates might have responded. Grand opera adapted ('versioned') classic literary texts for wholly non-literary consumption – for example, Donizetti's *Lucia di Lammermoor* (based on Sir Walter Scott's *The Bride of Lammermoor*) and Verdi's *Otello* (based on Shakespeare's *Othello*).

One could go on. Adaptation as big business began at the turn of the twentieth century, which saw the arrival of the most effective adaptational machine of all: the moving picture. The 'dream that kicks', as it's been called. From the first, cinema swallowed down and spat out vast amounts of literary source-material for the millions of movie-goers it catered for. To take one example of many, in 1897, Bram Stoker, the stage manager of the great actor Henry Irving, decided to write a Gothic romance about blood-sucking vampires and Transylvania. He had never visited the place but he had read some interesting books about it. The vampire was common enough in folklore and there had been some down-market Gothic romances. Stoker's novel *Dracula* did not do all that well until it was adapted as a film, *Nosferatu*, in 1930. Since then over a hundred Dracula films have been made (the actors Bela Lugosi and Christopher Lee are the most famous to have played the blood-sucking count). Dracula has become a 'brand' and the vampire romance a whole genre. Without Stoker's novel, Stephenie Meyer's *Twilight* saga or the similarly blockbusting TV series *The Vampire Diaries* would never have come into being. Adaptation, one concludes, can sometimes dwarf the literary text which gave it birth (not that Stoker's novel sells poorly today – far from it). A single work of fiction like *Dracula* can found a multinational industry.

As a general rule, adaptations of literature are driven by three motives. The first is to exploit 'a good thing' – to make money by jumping on a bandwagon. It is the profit motive, not artistic aspiration, which is often the driving force behind many TV series or, going back a century, the piratical dramatists who adapted Dickens's fiction. The second motive is to find and exploit new media markets or new readerships. Anthony Trollope thought he was doing well if he sold 10,000 copies of his novels. As adapted for television his fiction reaches, in the UK alone, audiences of 5 million and more. Only in a very few cases can printed literature claim such figures. J.K. Rowling sells in the millions. *Harry Potter* films are seen by the hundreds of million. Adaptation creates the-sky's-the-limit opportunities for literature.

The third motive is to explore, or develop, what is buried or missing in the original text. James Fenimore Cooper's *The Last of the Mohicans* has been an American classic ever since it was first published in 1826. But the 1992 film (it was the tenth adaptation for the screen), starring Daniel Day-Lewis as Hawkeye, is infinitely more sensitive to what the extermination of a Native American 'nation' actually meant. The novel is both complicated and enriched by its adaptation and the added dimension that the film (an excellent one in this case) brings. One goes back to read Cooper more thoughtfully.

Another example from Jane Austen, the most widely adapted 'classic' novelist of modern times, is instructive. Her novel, *Mansfield Park*, centres on a large country house and its aristocratic owners. The house itself is a symbol of England and its lastingness over generations. But where does the money which supports the estate come from? Austen does not say, but we see the owner, Sir

Thomas Bertram, going off to put things right in the family's sugar plantations in the West Indies. The 1999 film version of Austen's novel, directed by Patricia Rozema, highlighted the likelihood that Mansfield Park's prosperity came from slave labour and exploitation. 'Behind every great fortune', said the French novelist Balzac, 'lies a crime'. Behind elegant, refined, quintessentially 'English' Mansfield Park lay a crime against humanity, it could be argued, and Rozema's film did just that. It was controversial thesis, but again, the film complicated our response to the original novel, and in an illuminating way. (What is that noise we hear? Miss Austen spinning in her grave in Winchester Cathedral.)

Let's look at another couple of Austen fantasias. In the 2008 TV series, *Lost in Austen*, the young heroine, Amanda Price, finds herself transported back in time to the world of *Pride and Prejudice* and gets tangled, romantically and hilariously, in the relationship between Elizabeth and Darcy. It was done with a light touch (which, one suspects, might have charmed Austen), confident that everyone watching knows the novel.

Lost in Austen's literary game-playing drew on the fanfic vogue on the internet. The website 'The Republic of Pemberley', for example, invites 'Janeites' (as lovers of Austen are called) to come up with alternative and supplementary narratives for their beloved novels (such as, what will the Darcy marriage be like?). But underlying *Lost in Austen* is a more serious question: How relevant, across the centuries, are the novels to the lives (specifically love-lives) we nowadays live? The same question underlies that most far-fetched, and utterly delightful, transposition of Emma Woodhouse to the dilemmas of the Southern Californian 'valley girl' in the 1995 film, *Clueless*. What, this comedy asks, is 'universal and timeless' in Austen?

A central question in the process of literary adaptation is whether it is a service (as I think the above examples are) or a disservice to the text in question. In 1939 the Samuel Goldwyn company produced an immensely popular Hollywood film version of *Wuthering Heights*. It starred, as Heathcliff, the greatest stage actor of the time, Laurence Olivier, whose performance is regarded as a classic. But the film cut out great swathes of the original narrative and pasted a happy ending on to Brontë's story. Unquestionably the film inspired many to return to the original text to discover the real thing but, for the greater number who had not read and never would read the novel, was this not a cheapening of great literature? A disservice? 'Fidelity', one concludes, is as tricky in art as it is in our love-lives.

In the same year, 1939, MGM brought out, with huge fanfare, the film *Gone with the Wind* (GWTW to its millions of fans). It's often voted the greatest film of all time. In commercial terms it was, and still is, one of the biggest ever money-spinners. It was based on a novel by Margaret Mitchell which had been published three years earlier – the only novel this very private woman ever published. There is a romantic story behind it. Mitchell was born in 1900 and brought up in Atlanta, Georgia, in a family who had lived there for generations. There were old citizens in the town who could remember the Civil War, which the South had lost calamitously. There were even more Atlantans who could remember the grim aftermath of 'Reconstruction', as it was called.

Margaret was a young journalist. She broke her ankle at work, and while laid up in bed began writing a 'Civil War novel'. Her husband brought her the necessary research materials, and she polished off the work in a few months before she got back on her feet. Once recovered, she left the manuscript in a cupboard for six years. There it might have remained had Mitchell not been assigned to show a publisher round her town in 1935. He was scouting for new material and, when she mentioned her novel in passing, persuaded her to let him see the dilapidated manuscript. *Gone with the Wind* was accepted instantly and rushed out, with mammoth publicity. It was a runaway bestseller under the slogan 'One million Americans can't be wrong. Read *Gone with the Wind!*' The novel stayed at the top of the bestseller list for two years and won a Pulitzer Prize. Mitchell sold the film rights to MGM for $50,000 and *Gone with the Wind* was adapted, using the new process of Technicolor, by David O. Selznick. It starred Vivien Leigh and Clark Gable.

Even though it remains a very popular work of fiction, for every reader of Mitchell's novel there must be a hundred who only know *Gone with the Wind* as a film. Is the film 'true' to the book? No, it isn't. MGM kept the main outlines of Mitchell's plot but softened the favourable references to the Ku Klux Klan, and omitted the hero Rhett Butler's murder of a freed black man who dared to affront the virtue of a white woman. They took the 'edge' off a very edgy novel. To those who respect the remarkable book, it matters.

There is another objection that we can legitimately bring against adaptation. Unlike many novelists, Jane Austen (to draw on her again) never gives a clear pictorial image of her heroines or heroes. All we know about Emma Woodhouse, for instance, is that she has hazel eyes. This is an artistic decision on Austen's part. It enables the reader to construct their own image. If, however, one watches the 1996 film of *Emma*, Gwyneth Paltrow's face will probably impose itself on every subsequent re-reading of the novel. It's a very nice face – but it's not what Austen wanted.

Translation, it is said, echoing an Italian proverb, is 'betrayal' (*Traduttore, traditore*). Is adaptation, more even than translation, inevitably something of a travesty? Or is it an enhancement? Or an interpretation that supplements our own understanding of the text? Or an invitation to go back and read the original? It can, of course, be any or all of those things. What is fascinating, though, is the question of where adaptation, with its partnering technologies, is going. What will happen, as it will in the not-too-distant future, when thanks to new technology we can enter a virtual world of the literature that interests us – with our sense organs (nose, eyes, ears, hands) activated? When we can literally get 'lost in Austen', not just as spectators, but as players? It will be exciting. But still, one doubts it would entirely please Miss Austen.

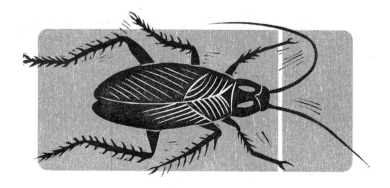

CHAPTER 33

Absurd Existences

KAFKA, CAMUS, BECKETT AND PINTER

If you made a list of the most gripping opening lines in literature, the following would surely make it into the top ten:

> As Gregor Samsa awoke one morning from uneasy dreams he found himself transformed in his bed into a gigantic insect.

It is from a short story, 'The Metamorphosis', by Franz Kafka (1883–1924). It's probable that Kafka did not much care whether we read this sentence or anything that he wrote. He instructed his friend and exectutor Max Brod to burn his literary remains 'preferably unread' after his death – he died prematurely, aged forty, from tuberculosis. Brod, thankfully, defied the instruction. Kafka speaks to us despite Kafka.

The human condition, for Kafka, is well beyond tragic or depressed. It is 'absurd'. He believed that the whole human race was the product of one of 'God's bad days'. There is no 'meaning' to make sense of our lives. Paradoxically that meaninglessness allows us to read into Kafka's novels such as *The Trial* (which is about a legal 'process' which doesn't process anything), or his stories like 'The Metamorphosis', whatever meanings we please. For example, critics have viewed Gregor Samsa's transformation into a cockroach as an allegory of anti-Semitism, a grim forecast of the criminal extermination of a supposedly 'verminous' race. (Kafka was Jewish, and just a little older than Adolf Hitler.) Writers often foresee such things coming before other people do. 'The Metamorphosis', published in 1915, has also been seen as foreshadowing the collapse of the Austro-Hungarian Empire in 1918, after the First World War. Kafka and his fellow citizens in Bohemia, centred in Prague, had lived under that vast empire. They woke up suddenly to find their identities had vanished. Others have read the story in terms of Kafka's problematic relationship with his father, a coarse-grained businessman. Whenever Franz nervously gave his father one of his works, it would be returned unread. His father despised his son.

But any such 'meanings' crumple because there is no larger or underlying meaning in the Kafka universe to underpin them. Yet absurdist literature still had a mission – to assert that literature is, like everything else, pointless. Kafka's disciple, the playwright Samuel Beckett, put it well: the writer 'has nothing with which to express, nothing from which to express, no power to express, no desire to express, together with the obligation to express'.

With that in mind, consider the opening paragraph of Kafka's last and finest novel, *The Castle*:

> It was late evening when K. arrived. The village lay under deep snow. There was no sign of the Castle hill, fog and darkness surrounded it, not even the faintest gleam of light suggested the large Castle. K. stood a long time on the wooden bridge that leads from the main road to the village, gazing upward into the seeming emptiness.

Everything quivers with enigma. 'K.' is a name, but no name (is it 'Kafka'?). It is twilight, that nothing-time between day and night. K. stands on a bridge, suspended in the space between the outside world and the village. Fog, darkness and snow shroud the Castle. Is there anything in front of K. at all but 'emptiness'? We never know where he has come from, nor why he has come. He will never reach the Castle. He cannot even be sure it is there, but it is where he is going.

Kafka, who wrote in German, lived his life in utter literary obscurity. He worked, for as long as his delicate health allowed, in a state insurance office in his native city, Prague. (He was good at the job, reportedly.) He had studied law but was, by profession, a bureaucrat. He had tormented relations with women and his family. He died before his genius could fully flower, and was for decades after his death merely an obscure footnote in the history of German-language literature.

It was not until the 1930s, well after his death, that translations of his works (*The Castle* was the first) began to appear in English. They inspired some writers, but mystified most readers. He was resurrected as a major literary force after the Second World War, not in Prague, London or New York, but Paris.

Kafka was installed as a patriarchal figure in the 1940s French Existentialists' godless universe. It was their philosophy that triggered the 'Kafka Revolution' in the 1960s when everybody discovered the world was either Orwellian or Kafkaesque or possibly both. Kafka no longer mystified, he explained. His time had come.

Albert Camus's opening proposition in his best-known essay, 'The Myth of Sisyphus', is that 'There is but one truly serious philosophical problem and that is suicide'. It echoes Kafka's bleak aphorism: 'A first sign of the beginning of understanding is the wish to die.' Why not, when life is pointless? Camus's essay pictures the human condition in the mythical figure Sisyphus, doomed for eternity to roll a rock up a hill, only for it to fall down again. Pointless. Only two responses are feasible in the face of man's Sisyphean fate: suicide or rebellion. Camus appended a long note – 'Hope and the Absurd in the Works of Franz Kafka'– to his Sisyphus essay, commemorating the writer to whose influence he was indebted.

Kafka's influence is evident in Camus's fictional masterpiece *The Outsider*, written and published under Nazi occupation censorship. The action is set in Algiers, nominally part of Metropolitan France.

The narrative opens bleakly: 'Mother died today. Or maybe yesterday: I can't be sure.' Nor does the French Algerian hero, Meursault, care. He cares about nothing. He has, he confides, 'lost the habit of noting his feelings'. For no particular reason, he shoots an Arab. His only explanation, not that he troubles to come up with explanations, even to save his life, is that it was very hot that day. He goes to the guillotine, not even caring about that. He hopes the crowd watching the execution will jeer.

It was Camus's comrade in philosophy, Jean-Paul Sartre, who perceived, most clearly, what drastic things Kafka had done to fiction's rule book. Generically, as Sartre wrote in a digression in his novel *Nausea* (1938), the novel presumes to makes sense, fully aware that life doesn't make sense. This 'bad faith' is its 'secret power'. Novels, said Sartre, are 'machines that secrete spurious meaning into the world'. They are necessary, but intrinsically dishonest. What else do we have in life other than the 'spurious meanings' we invent?

Absurdity took a long time penetrating the Anglo-Saxon/American world. The moment of penetration occurred in August 1955 when Samuel Beckett's play *Waiting for Godot* was first performed in English at a club theatre in London. Beckett was an Irishman, long resident in France, bilingual and steeped in the Existentialism that dominated French intellectual life in the postwar period.

Waiting for Godot opens with two tramps, Estragon and Vladimir, by a roadside. We don't know who, or where, they are. They talk incessantly throughout the play, but nothing 'happens'. As it transpires the tramps are indeed doing something by doing nothing – they are waiting for a mysterious person, or entity, called 'Godot'. Is this 'God'? Towards the end of the play a boy comes on stage to tell the characters that Godot isn't coming today. Estragon asks Vladimir if they should leave and Vladimir replies, 'Yes, let's go'. The final stage direction is: '*They do not move.*'

It's impossible to exaggerate the impact that *Waiting for Godot* had on English theatre and culture in the mid-1950s. On one actor, who performed in the play in provincial repertory theatre, it had perhaps the most significant impact of all. Harold Pinter went from performing Beckett into writing, as a confessed disciple. Like Beckett, he would go on to win a Nobel Prize.

Pinter's breakthrough play was *The Caretaker* (1960). The action is set in a seedy lodging house with three main characters, two brothers and an outsider – a tramp named Mac Davies. One of the brothers, Aston, has had his brain shattered by 'curative' electroconvulsive therapy. This little community intend to do something – build a garden shed, undertake some random house repairs. They do nothing but quarrel. Mac is constantly intending to get his papers from a nearby government office. He never gets them. None of them carry through their plans, any more than Estragon and Vladimir move along their road. The dialogue in *The Caretaker* is reminiscent of Beckett, but Pinter also cultivates a unique use of silence. The breaks in the dialogue build up a mood of vague menace. Pinter's is the art of the eloquently 'left hanging'.

The least silent of playwrights, Tom Stoppard responded creatively and with firework displays of wit to the comedy in Beckett. Stoppard's first major play was *Rosencrantz and Guildenstern Are Dead* (1967). The action revolves, with dazzlingly clever dialogue, around the two background characters in *Hamlet* who, again like Vladimir and Estragon, do not move. They cannot move. They are only minor characters. All they can do is chatter, which they do incessantly.

The playfulness in the play, and in Stoppard's later works, in some ways evokes the great Italian dramatist, Luigi Pirandello, and plays such as his *Six Characters in Search of an Author* (1921). Playful drama and mind games are, for Stoppard, what Sartre called novels: 'machines that secrete spurious meaning into the world'. But, in Stoppard's case, they are great fun, not nauseating or menacing. Absurdity has its hilarious side.

Literature is always and everywhere a diverse thing. No single container fits all. The Theatre of the Absurd was revolutionary, but it was *avant garde* (or 'cutting edge'), and it happened in Europe, and in circumstances where there are few writers and small audiences. There was, simultaneously, an ultra-realistic new style of British drama that was not absurd but angry, and which from the beginning drew massive audiences, and particularly young ones. The play that launched this new wave in British theatre was John Osborne's *Look Back in Anger*, first performed in 1956, the year after *Godot*, but coming at audiences from a very different direction.

Osborne's hero, Jimmy Porter, is not a Sisyphus figure but an 'angry young man' (as Osborne and his ilk came to be called), raging at 1950s Britain – throwing rocks, not pushing them. It was a moment in British history when things were badly falling apart. The British Empire was in its death throes. The colonial war against Egypt, over the Suez Canal, was its final humiliating moment. The British class system was a dead hand throttling the vitality of the nation. Or so Osborne's play asserts. The monarchy was a gold tooth in a rotting jaw, as one of his characters puts it.

In the play, Jimmy lives in a cramped attic with Alison, the daughter of a colonel who was a colonial administrator before India gained its independence in 1947. Jimmy is anger incarnate. He is university educated, but at an unfashionable (not 'Oxbridge') institution. He cultivates a noticeably working-class lifestyle but is essentially apolitical. His raw anger discharges on Alison, whom he both loves for herself and despises for her class background. Jimmy's anger – eloquently expressed in furious rants – is, we feel, the raw fuel of revolution. But what kind of revolution? The theatre critic Kenneth Tynan called *Look Back in Anger* a 'minor miracle' that presents 'postwar youth as it really is'. It cleared the way for the youth revolution (sex, drugs and rock'n'roll) of the 1960s.

Absurdism never took firm root in the USA, although there was always plenty of anger to be found on the stage. Dramatists like Arthur Miller, in *Death of a Salesman* (1949), followed Henrik Ibsen's example, attacking the falsity at the core of middle-class life under capitalism. Tennessee Williams and Edward Albee were similarly scornful about marriage in *A Streetcar Named Desire* (1947) and *Who's Afraid of Virginia Woolf?* (1962). The great 'Expressionist' American playwright Eugene O'Neill left his play *Long Day's Journey into Night* to be performed after his death (it was first staged in 1956). It portrayed family as a different kind of hell. American theatre, we may say, found its own way to speak about 'meaninglessness'.

There are innumerable things to wonder at in the literature of the twentieth century. But not the least of its wonders is that an unimportant clerk, writing in a European backwater, with no desire to be read should, so long after his death, rise as one of the giants of world literature. Franz Kafka would, of course, have dismissed our marvelling attention, and despised us for it.

CHAPTER 34

The Poetry of Breakdown
LOWELL, PLATH, LARKIN AND HUGHES

On an early October morning in 1800 the poet William Wordsworth went for a walk on his beloved Lake District moors and hills. It had stormed and rained all night but now the sun was shining. It was a new day and a new century. At thirty, William was in the prime of life. To his joy the poet saw a hare running, sending up glistening rainbow splashes of water from the night's puddles in the grass not yet shrivelled by winter. He heard a skylark warbling invisibly. He felt infused with what he liked to call 'joy'. He was as 'happy as a boy'.

It was good to be alive. But then, as often happens, Wordsworth sank into gloom ('dim sadness', he calls it). What caused the sudden change in mood? He had begun to think about the poets of his time and the sorry ends most of them had come to. 'We poets', he reflected,

in our youth begin in gladness;
But thereof come in the end despondency and madness.

He was recalling his close friend, Coleridge (drug-sodden and, for all his genius, incapable of finishing a poem of more than a few lines); Thomas Chatterton, who while still a prodigiously talented teenager had killed himself after being found out in forgery; and Robert Burns, who had drunk himself to an early death. Was this the grim destiny awaiting all poets, the price to be paid for their genius?

Wordsworth's poem goes on to pose a central question in poetry. Are the greatest works conceived and written in 'joy' ('gladness' as Wordsworth puts it, to find a convenient rhyme) and serenity, or in despair – madness even?

It's not easy to come up with a quick or simple answer. It depends where you look. The most recited poem of our own time, for example, is that which is the anthem for the 500 million members of the European Union: Schiller and Beethoven's 'Ode to Joy'. This is how it (rather awkwardly) translates from the German:

> O friends, no more these sounds!
> Let us sing more cheerful songs,
> More full of joy!
> Joy, bright spark of divinity,
> Daughter of Elysium,
> Fire-inspired we tread
> Thy sanctuary.
> Thy magic power re-unites
> All that custom has divided,
> All men become brothers
> Under the sway of thy gentle wings.

The less joyful among us might be inclined to think that the greatest poetry springs not from high spirits, but low. Think, by contrast, of the figure of the poet in T.S. Eliot's *The Waste Land* (Chapter 28). Tiresias is an onlooker on life, doomed never to die but to grow forever older. He has outlived sex (he is androgynous – both male and female). He has seen everything, in its full dreariness, and is doomed to see it over and over again. There is not much joy in Eliot's image of the poet. The implication is: such is life. But while most people (as Eliot put it in another poem) cannot bear very much reality, it is the duty of poets to face it.

The psychoanalyst Sigmund Freud thought that great art was born of neurosis, not psychic 'normality' (if such a thing exists). It could be compared to the irritant grit in the oyster's shell which produces the pearl. This belief has inspired many poets of the last half-century to investigate, rather than try to escape, what Wordsworth called 'despondency and madness', to drill down through the layers of pearl to find the speck of creative grit at the centre.

These explorers of breakdown ('crack-up', as the novelist F. Scott Fitzgerald termed it) consciously transgressed what Eliot laid down as a golden rule for poetry: that 'the more perfect the artist, the more completely separate in him will be the man who suffers and the mind which creates'. Impersonality was the filter through which poetry should be delivered, the author of *The Waste Land* believed. W.B. Yeats prescribed something along the same lines – namely that the poet must write from behind a mask or 'persona' (an assumed personality). He must keep himself out of it. Or become what in Latin is called an 'alter ego' – an 'other self'. The most basic mistake in poetry (particularly modern poetry) is to assume the speaker is the poet. It is also the most commonly-made mistake.

'The man (or woman) who suffers' – that is, the poet's own self – is wilfully the subject of the connoisseurs of breakdown who came to prominence in the late twentieth century. This is poetry without persona. Robert Lowell (1917–77) was an acknowledged pioneer in this exciting, new and dangerous field. One of his very best poems is 'Waking in the Blue' (an *aubade*, or dawn poem). It records the beginning of his (not some Tiresias figure's, or a persona's, but Robert Traill Spence Lowell IV's) day in a closed ward of a New England lunatic asylum. The poem opens with a night nurse, a Boston University student. He has been studying one of his textbooks, and is now doing his patrol of the ward before clocking off. He has been reading, dozily, *The Meaning of Meaning* by I.A. Richards – a critic who, like Eliot, encouraged absolute impersonality in poetry. It's an ironic inclusion, because in this poem Lowell is as personal as can be. It is him in the hospital, already awake, witnessing the breaking day through azure windows. They are blue-glazed to keep out the sun, and strengthened to stop patients breaking them and doing themselves mischief. Lowell looks around the ward at his fellow inmates. The poem concludes:

> We are all old-timers,
> each of us holds a locked razor.

The razors are locked, because none of the patients can be trusted not to kill themselves with ones that are open.

Another of Lowell's poems is called, simply, 'Man and Wife'. A dashingly handsome and wholly unstable man, Lowell went through three marriages, all of which broke up messily. The poem begins with the married couple lying in bed in the morning. The rising sun (it's another *aubade*) bathes them in garish red sunlight. They are calm because they have taken Miltowns a heavy-duty tranquilliser. This is not, we understand, a joyous couple who have enjoyed a romantic night together, but a man and wife on the brink of painful separation. Red, here, is the colour of anger, violence, hate. The drug is the only thing keeping them together.

Lowell taught an inspirational creative writing class at Boston University (where the 'Waking in the Blue' night attendant is a student). One of his most distinguished pupils was the poet Sylvia Plath (1932–63). Her poetry, particularly the extraordinary group she wrote in the period after her traumatic separation from her husband and just before her suicide, take Lowell's ideas about what he called 'life studies' to more of an extreme than even he did. Typical is her poem 'Lady Lazarus', written in her last months. It opens:

> I have done it again.
> One year in every ten
> I manage it –

The 'it' referred to here is a suicide attempt. Lazarus, in the Bible, is the man brought back from the dead by Jesus. Plath was thirty years old when she wrote the poem, and had, she says, attempted to kill herself three times. The fourth attempt would be successful. The poem, less a 'life' than a 'death' study, was published posthumously. It is impossible to read it without a chill to the soul.

Plath was an American who, after her marriage to the poet Ted Hughes, lived and wrote in Britain. Both countries claim her. The English poetic tradition – from Tennyson, through Hardy – is often infused with a broad strain of melancholy. It is gentler than the extremity we see in the work of Lowell and Plath (Wordsworth's 'madness') and more in line with what Wordsworth calls 'despondency'. The laureate of modern poetic despond is, by general agreement, Philip Larkin (1922–85). His English gloom is eloquently expressed in his poem 'Dockery and Son'. It is a poem with a narrative. Larkin returns to his Oxford college in middle age. He is told about one of his contemporaries, Dockery, whose son is now studying there. Larkin has never married and has no children – it would, he bleakly says, have meant not 'increase', but 'dilution'. The poem ends with a magnificently glum meditation on the meaningless of life: it is first boredom, then fear, and whatever you do, it goes. And you die, without the slightest idea what it was all about.

Larkin's 'breakdown', so to call it, took a distinctly Larkinesque twist. Long before his death he stopped writing poetry altogether. It was a sad thing for his millions of admirers. He was asked why he had given up poetry. 'I didn't,' he replied, 'poetry gave up on me'. Call it suicide of the creative spirit.

To return to Wordsworth. At the end of his poem he concludes that what the poet needs, above all, is 'toughness'. He calls it 'resolution and independence' (the poem's title). There has always been that defiant 'I will survive' strain in British and American poetry, – writers who, despite knowing the worst, will not give in. As Dylan Thomas put it, they refuse to 'go gentle into that good night', but fight every inch of the way.

The Yorkshireman Ted Hughes (1930–98) is the toughest of this tough modern school. He accepted that 'the inmost spirit of poetry ... is at bottom, in every recorded case, the voice of pain'. But that voice, he believed, should not be one of surrender or acquiescence, or even too much interest in that pain. This philosophy is expressed vividly in his collection of poems called, simply, *Crow*. The crow is an unlovely bird (no skylark, thrush or nightingale – the birds that inspired Keats, Shelley, Hardy and Wordsworth). The crow is a kind of British vulture. It lives on carrion, rotting things, but is resolutely alive and aggressive (in Britain the birds are commonly seen picking up their food amid the litter alongside thundering motorways). One would back a crow's survival chances against any skylark.

There are many other poets we could bring into the discussion about 'the voice of pain' and how poetry should use it. John Berryman and Anne Sexton, for example, friend and pupil of Lowell respectively, both of whom committed suicide and wrote poetry clearly signalling the act. Or Thom Gunn, more of the Hughes persuasion, one of whose poems thanks all the tough-guys in history, from Alexander the Great to soldiers, athletes and even the rough kids who Stephen Spender was sheltered from as a child, as he explains in his own poem 'My Parents Kept Me from Children Who Were Rough'. But Gunn's poem in its entirety – all his poems, one might argue – are a rejection of passivity and what he thinks of as a spirit of defeat in the work of, say, Philip Larkin. Larkin, on his side, saw Hughes and Gunn as a couple of blowhards, wannabe 'hard men'. He was contemptuous of them in his private letters and conversation. He nicknamed Hughes 'the incredible hulk' and 'Ted Huge', and wrote hilarious parodies of his violent verse. Since Larkin's and Hughes's deaths, however, material has emerged that shows they read each other's work and, from time to time, even used it creatively.

In poetry, then, there is what philosophers call 'dialectic': a clash and a coming together of opposite forces, two schools with very different sets of belief. On the one side are those whom I have called the connoisseurs of breakdown, writers like Lowell, Plath and Larkin, who dig deep down into themselves to mine the pain within. On the other side are those who believe that action and engagement with the external world, and on what Gunn called 'fighting terms', are the proper route. There is searing, powerful poetry to be found on either side, but, it has to be said, little joy among the connoisseurs of breakdown.

CHAPTER 35

Colourful Cultures
Literature and Race

Race is a subject which raises tempers. So too in literature, and discussions of literature. It's something that takes us to uncomfortable places. Is Shakespeare's depiction of Shylock anti-Semitic? Or is it, at heart, sympathetic to a victim of racial prejudice? Those who go for sympathy will quote the lines

> I am a Jew. Hath not a Jew eyes? hath not a Jew hands, organs, dimensions, senses, affections, passions? fed with the same food, hurt with the same weapons, subject to the same diseases, healed by the same means, warmed and cooled by the same winter and summer, as a Christian is? If you prick us, do we not bleed?

Those who think *The Merchant of Venice* is, at heart, anti-Semitic, point to the fact that at the end of the play half of Shylock's property is threatened with confiscation, his daughter is given to a Christian in marriage, and he, Shylock, is forced on pain of losing all his property to convert to Christianity. The image of the Venetian Jew, knife poised to plunge into the heart of a Christian and extract his 'pound of flesh' (a phrase which has entered into common usage), usually tilts the balance towards anti-Semitism. But Shakespeare, we say by way of apology, was no more prejudiced than most in his time and probably less so than many. True, but it is still uneasy-making.

Dickens's Fagin in *Oliver Twist* shows its author as panderiing to gross racial stereotypes – no defence holds up. In later life he regretted Fagin and made changes when the novel was reprinted. He also made amends by introducing a saintly Jewish character into one of his last novels (Riah, in *Our Mutual Friend*). However, Fagin remains for many readers unforgiveable, even in soft-centred films and musical adaptations such as *Oliver!*.

One of the angriest rows in the last few years has been over the head of the dead poet, T.S. Eliot. It was spearheaded by a polemical book by the critic (and lawyer) Anthony Julius who used as evidence remarks made by Eliot in early lectures (later suppressed) and lines in the poems to argue that the poet was anti-Semitic. The evidence is, many objective commentators contend, inconclusive. Eliot has been as fiercely defended as he has been denounced. But the dust kicked up by the row has not yet settled and probably never will.

A useful starting point in thinking about all this is to acknowledge that literature is one of the few places that race is openly discussed, and where the rawest issues it raises are made accessible for debate and quarrel. It's a place where society can work out its attitudes. Most of us would see this as a good thing, whatever our personal opinions or sensitivities, and whatever feathers are ruffled.

Take, as an example of literature going where other forms of discourse fear to tread, Philip Roth's novel, *The Human Stain* (2000). The hero is a Classics professor, of advanced years and the highest reputation, at a distinguished university. He is Jewish. He innocently 'mis-speaks' in class, offending two African American students, and is instructed by a college tribunal to attend a course of 'sensitivity training'. He refuses, on principle, and resigns. It eventually emerges that he is not Jewish after all, but African American. He had hidden his real identity because that was the only way he could, at that time, make a career in higher education. The alternative was to follow his other talent – as a black boxer. He chose to be a white classicist. The novel itself makes the large point about there being 'only one race, the human race'. And another: that we should ignore the political correctness which inhibits us from talking about race. As a novelist, Roth is not one for inhibition.

There is a big difference between how American and European literatures deal with race. America was substantially built, from the ground up, by slave-power, human beings imported involuntarily from Africa (those, that is, who survived the so-called 'middle passage'). It is now seen as one of humanity's great crimes against humanity. Toni Morrison, for example, opens her novel *Beloved* (1987) with the epigraph:

Sixty million and more

It caused huge offence, alluding, as it was generally supposed, to the ('only') six million Jews murdered in the Holocaust and suggesting that there were greater holocausts that America chose to ignore. Morrison's narrative centres on a ghost, from the era of slavery, which can never be exorcised and should never be ignored.

A bloody civil war was fought to abolish American slavery. Abraham Lincoln is supposed to have remarked, on meeting Harriet Beecher Stowe, author of *Uncle Tom's Cabin*, that he wished to shake the hand of the little woman who had started that great war. A modest woman, Stowe might well have replied that actually it was started by brave abolitionists and, if a book was to be congratulated, it should be an autobiography published seven years before hers, in 1845: *Narrative of the Life of Frederick Douglass, an American Slave*. After gaining his freedom, Douglass devoted his life, and his considerable literary abilities, to the cause of the abolition of slavery. The opening paragraphs still have the power to shock, delivered, as they are, in deliberately passionless language:

My father was a white man. He was admitted to be such by all I ever heard speak of my parentage. The opinion was also whispered that my master was my father; but of the correctness of

this opinion, I know nothing; the means of knowing was with-
held from me. My mother and I were separated when I was but
an infant – before I knew her as my mother. It is a common
custom, in the part of Maryland from which I ran away, to part
children from their mothers at a very early age.

British literature's concern with race is linked to the empire which
the home country won, held for centuries, and lost (Chapter 26).
Since the 1950s, when the British Empire was blown away by the
'winds of change', the context of racial discussion has been 'post-
colonial' and radically different. The whole imperial project has
been examined sceptically and, at times, guiltily by British writers
in what is now the most multicultural literary world anywhere
on the planet. This multiculturalism has opened up what some
would say is the richest seam in Britain's recent literature, with
writers such as Salman Rushdie, Monica Ali and Zadie Smith, and
a new interest in such writers as the Nigerian novelist Ben Okri
(a Booker Prize winner) and, originally from the West Indies, the
novelist Wilson Harris and the poet Derek Walcott (a Nobel Prize
winner).

Another British West Indian author, V.S. Naipaul, expressed in
his Nobel Prize-winner's speech the complexities of a post-colonial
writer like himself. His grandfather's generation had been brought
to Trinidad, from India (then a British dominion), as 'indentured
labour', mainly as office workers. Naipaul grew up 'over the bones
of the island's exterminated "aborigines"', and alongside the descen-
dants of black slaves from Africa. Outstandingly clever, he won a
scholarship to Oxford University and made his 'home' in England
as what he called a 'mimic man': English, but not English; Indian,
but not Indian; Trinidadian, but not Trinidadian.

The British live in a post-colonial era, but have colonial
'ownerships' been fully abolished? Not everyone would agree they
have. The greatest Nigerian novelist, many would claim, is Chinua
Achebe (1930–2013). He was christened Albert Achebe, after
Queen Victoria's consort. His first published novel – still the work
for which he is famous worldwide – is *Things Fall Apart* (the title

is a quotation from the Irish poet, W.B. Yeats). It first came out in 1958, in Britain. His later works were all first published in Britain or the USA. In later life, Achebe's main employment was in American universities. Derek Walcott, the most distinguished of post-colonial poets, was also employed in a prestigious American university for most of his career. Can fiction – or poetry – so rooted, or authors so salaried, be truly independent? Or are there still colonial shackles clanking in the background?

The USA is where the most interesting literature centred on racial themes is happening. The classic text is Ralph Waldo Ellison's *Invisible Man* (1952). Unlike his fellow African Americans, James Baldwin and Richard Wright, Ellison wrote not realism but allegory; his fiction is playful in method, but deadly serious in content. He initially planned a short novel and in 1947 published what remains a core element of *Invisible Man*, 'A Battle Royal', in which, for the entertainment of jeering white men, black men are stripped naked, blindfolded, and made to fight each other in a boxing ring for sham prizes. As eventually published, the novel hinges on another conceit: 'I am an *invisible man* ... I am invisible, understand, simply because people refuse to see me.' The USA, the novel says, has 'solved' its racial problem by wilful blindness.

Invisible Man is a jazz novel. Ellison loved the improvisational freedom of the great African American art form – one of the few freedoms his people could lay claim to. Louis Armstrong's '(What Did I Do to Be So) Black and Blue?' haunts the novel like a theme song. As its lyrics lament:

> I'm white ... inside ... but, that don't help my case
> 'cause I ... can't hide ... what is in my face.

Toni Morrison, America's greatest living African American novelist (many would say 'American novelist' *tout court*) is similarly inspired by what is called the one original art to come out of the USA. Discussing her 1992 novel, *Jazz*, she explained:

> the jazzlike structure wasn't a secondary thing for me – it was

the *raison d'être* of the book … I thought of myself as like the jazz musician.

The jazz Ellison loved was 'traditional' New Orleans jazz (hence Louis Armstrong). He disliked Swing and 'modern' jazz, thinking them 'too white'. The jazz that most influences Morrison is the ultra-improvisational, post-modernist Free-Form jazz that Ornette Coleman pioneered in the 1960s.

In general terms one could argue that in Britain (in its literature at least) there has been a kind of 'blending' – a dissolving of racial difference. Toni Morrison has insisted on maintaining angry difference. This anger is at its hottest in her early novel, *Tar Baby* (1981), in which a character concludes: 'White folks and black folks should not sit down and eat together or do any of those personal things in life.' At a conference at that time, Morrison herself roundly declared: 'At no moment in my life have I ever felt as though I was an American. At no moment.' In later years, particularly after winning the Nobel Prize in Literature in 1993, her comments about race have softened, but never to the point that she regards herself as 'American' rather than 'African American'. An angry sense of racial separation burns in all her work.

The endeavour of most politicians and, indeed, most citizens in the USA is to bring about a condition of enlightened colour-blindness. To rise, that is, above the racial division which has caused the country so much pain, and historically cost it so much blood. American literature and its figurehead writer, Morrison, have declined to buy into this. They have used, and still use, the division to explore black identity creatively. To dive into it, that is, rather than float above and forget it.

We find a distinct African American presence nowadays in such literary enclaves as 'private eye' detective fiction. The career of Walter Mosley's black hero, Easy Rawlins, is chronicled in a series of novels, beginning with *Devil in a Blue Dress* (1990), which, in their background, chronicle the history of race relations in Los Angeles. Chester Himes did the same for New York, with his *Harlem Cycle* series of the 1950s and 1960s (which he began writing in prison, and concluded in exile, in Paris). Samuel R. Delany, an African American science fiction writer, has brought a new imput to that genre. There are those who would argue (and I am one) that there is a strong vein of Whitmanesque free verse (Chapter 21) in the blues and, more recently, rap, both of which are African American preserves. In short, there has been no blending out, and American literature is the stronger for its many colours.

What, to sum up, is literature's role in the complex relationships of race, society and history? There is no simple answer. But we can borrow the heartfelt cry in Arthur Miller's play, *Death of a Salesman*: 'attention must be paid'. Where race is concerned, literature is paying attention and we can be grateful for it. But it does not always make for comfortable reading.

CHAPTER 36

Magical Realisms
BORGES, GRASS, RUSHDIE AND MÁRQUEZ

The term 'magic realism' became current in the 1980s. Suddenly everyone seemed to be knowingly dropping it into conversations about the latest thing in literature. What, though, does this odd term mean? On the face of it, 'magic realism' looks like an oxymoron, jamming together two traditionally irreconcilable elements. A novel is 'fictional' (it never happened) but it is also 'true' – that is, 'realistic'. The mass of British fiction, from Defoe, through what has been called the 'Great Tradition' (Jane Austen, George Eliot, Joseph Conrad, D.H. Lawrence), on past Graham Greene and Evelyn Waugh, to Ian McEwan and A.S. Byatt, has tended towards literary realism. So too in the USA, where the mainstream followed Ernest Hemingway's injunction to present life 'as it is'. There were, of course, writers of fantasy like J.R.R. Tolkien and Mervyn Peake, but they resided in a quite separate compartment. Gormenghast Castle is a very different kind of structure from, say, the country houses of Brideshead or Howards End. Magic realism was a new literary hybrid.

Varieties of magic realism had in fact been around for almost half a century before the 1980s. One can see a number of works playing with the idea in an experimental way on the fringes of literature and art. But it was not until the twentieth century was drawing to a close that magic realism took off as a powerful literary genre.

Three reasons can be suggested. One was the recognition in Europe and America that new and exciting things were happening in South American hispanic literature, with Jorge Luis Borges, Gabriel García Márquez, Carlos Fuentes and Mario Vargas Llosa – writers whose international fame, as translation made its impact worldwide, created what was called 'the Latin American Boom' in the 1960s and 1970s. Writers like Günter Grass and Salman Rushdie also recruited mass readerships in Europe. A clear precursor to the boom was Grass's novel *The Tin Drum* (1959); with the publication of Rushdie's *Midnight's Children* (1981), magic realism became mainstream and a literary style without frontiers. The third element that helped make magic realism a style for the time was that it allowed writers, despite the extravagant unreality of their narratives (the 'magic' ingredient), to make what were, in fact, important political interventions. To be players, that is, not merely in literature, but in public life and geopolitical affairs. They came into the public arena, as it were, by a side door that no one was guarding.

It is no accident that two of those mentioned above, Fuentes and Vargas Llosa, were active and highly controversial politicians (the latter came close to becoming prime minister of Peru); nor that Salman Rushdie should have written a novel which led to two nations breaking off diplomatic relations; nor that Grass should have become, when not writing fiction, a spokesman for post-war Germany who regularly, as he put it, 'spat in the soup'.

The writer, proclaimed Jean-Paul Sartre in his influential manifesto *What is Literature?* (1947), should 'engage'. Sartre saw that mission as best achieved through what, in the Soviet Union, was called 'social realism'. Paradoxically, the contemporary fairy stories of the magic realists achieved it better.

The Argentinian Jorge Luis Borges (1899–1986) was the first magic realist to achieve worldwide renown in the 1960s. It helped that he was an ardent anglophile with many friends in Britain and

America. His short, crisply-written stories were collected in 1962 in *Labyrinths* – and it is a telling title: we 'lose' ourselves in fiction, seeking, like Theseus in the Cretan labyrinth, some string to lead us out. These stories translated easily, which also helped.

Borges's method was to fuse surreal imagination with banal human situations and everyday characters. Take one of his most famous works, 'Funes the Memorious' (1942). It tells the story of a young rancher, Ireneo Funes, who after a fall from a horse finds that he can remember everything that happens and has ever happened to him, and can forget nothing. He has, he says, 'more memories in myself alone than all men have had since the world was a world'. He retreats to a dark room, to be alone with his memory, and dies shortly after.

The story is based on a fantastic idea, yet, on another level, it's real. There are such things as super-memorisers. The technical term is 'hyperthymesia', or 'highly superior autobiographical memory' (HSAM). The condition was first clinically described and given a name by psychologists in 2006. Borges himself had a fabulous memory and was in his later years blind. And, for those with any sensitivity to language, 'memorious' (*memorioso* in Spanish) beats 'HSAM' every time.

No one knew quite what to call Borges's strange blends of fancy and fact when they first began circulating widely in the 1960s. But they were recognised as something different and exciting. So, too, was the pioneer magic realist Angela Carter, with works like *The Magic Toyshop* (1967), which merges a bleak post-war Britain with *Alice's Adventures in Wonderland*. Readers did not know what to make of such books, but they responded to a power in them.

Borges was not a political writer, but he created a set of tools for the magic realists who came after. Salman Rushdie enthusiastically borrowed Borgesian devices in the novel that made his name, *Midnight's Children*. It won the Booker Prize in 1981 and went on to become a worldwide bestseller. The novel takes as its (literal) starting point 15 August 1947, when India became an independent country, partitioned from Pakistan – a fact announced to the nation in a radio broadcast by Prime Minister Nehru, as the stroke of midnight approached. It was an event of epoch-making historical importance. Children born in that hour would be different Indians. Rushdie's novel fantasises a telepathic link that connects the children born in the crucial minutes into an 'overmind' – a mental collective. The gimmick, as Rushdie frankly acknowledged, is borrowed from science fiction – John Wyndham's *The Midwich Cuckoos* (1957) comes to mind. (Science fiction is a favourite plunder-box for Rushdie.) But *Midnight's Children* is not set in Midwich – a village as 'unreal' as Brigadoon. It is set in a very real place: the colony which, in little over half a century, would become a superpower. Rushdie, one notes, was born in India in 1947 although not, alas, in the magic hour. *Midnight's Children* has a powerful political charge at the heart of its fantasies, as does all the best magic realism. The author was sued, for libel, by the then Prime Minister of India, Indira Gandhi, and the text was amended accordingly.

One of Rushdie's starting points is, interestingly, that most basic of literatures, the children's story. He has written an illuminating short book on the film version of L. Frank Baum's *The Wonderful Wizard of Oz* – a film which, since childhood, he has loved. *The Wizard of Oz* opens, it will be remembered, in grainy black and white, on a poverty-stricken farm in Depression-era 1930s Kansas: very much the 'real world'. After Dorothy is knocked unconscious by a tornado, she and her little dog Toto wake to find themselves in a Technicolor wonderland, inhabited by witches, talking scarecrows, tin-men and cowardly lions. In Dorothy's immortal phrase, 'Toto, I've a feeling we're not in Kansas any more'. It's a magic world. Magic and realism run together in the film, as they do in the story on which it is based.

The most controversial and provocative of Rushdie's novels, *The Satanic Verses* (1988), opens with a hijacked passenger plane, flying in from India, exploding in mid-air over England. Two of the passengers, Gibreel Farishta and Saladin Chamcha (one with Hindu associations, the other Muslim), fall 29,002 feet to earth. The first line of the novel is 'To be born again ... first you have to die'. They do not die. They land on the beach at Hastings, as did that other foreigner, William the Conqueror, in 1066. They are promptly labelled 'illegal immigrants' (Mrs Thatcher – 'Mrs Torture' in the novel – has decreed a hard line on incomers like them). As the novel evolves, they take on the characters of the archangel Gibreel (Gabriel in the Bible) and Satan. The realism of the terrorist outrage blends, like a potion, into myth, history and religion. This, in a word, is its 'magic'. The Ayatollah Khomeini, Supreme Leader of Iran, did not, as had Mrs Gandhi, bother with libel suits. Nor was he any admirer of magic realism. In 1989 he issued a *fatwa* on Rushdie – a requirement that any truly faithful Muslim should assassinate the blasphemous novelist.

Günter Grass starts from a different place to get to a similar destination. He was born in 1927 and grew up in the Nazi era. When he began his career as an author he accepted as a given that German fiction had to start, after 1945, from a new baseline zero. 'The past must be overcome', said Grass. But without the past, what does a writer do? After Auschwitz, the German philosopher Theodor Adorno had declared, poetry was impossible. So too, it could be argued, was the novel – at least for a German writer. The post-war German writer of fiction could not call on the full orchestra supplied by literary tradition. How could one reach back to Goethe, Schiller and Thomas Mann, across what had happened between 1933 and 1945? Instead of the orchestra, all the author had, Grass proclaimed, was a tin drum. But as *The Tin Drum* depicts, it is an instrument that still has its magic powers. Despite Adorno's grim prophecy, Grass contrived to make great fiction – great magic realism. When he received his Nobel Prize in 1999, Grass presented himself not as a great author but a literary rat. Rats survive anything. Even world wars.

Grass wrote his magic realist works in the aftermath of a period of oppression. The style has also proved useful to writers producing their work while under oppression or censorship. Realism – telling it how it is – can be very dangerous in such circumstances. A case in point is José Saramago, who won his Nobel in 1998.

Saramago (1922–2010) was a Marxist who lived most of his life in Europe's longest-lasting fascist dictatorship, that in Portugal, which lasted until 1974. Even after the overthrow of the dictatorship he was persecuted and ended his life in exile. Allegory – not saying exactly what he meant – was his preferred literary mode. It is, if not magic realism, as close as makes no difference. One of Saramago's finest works, *The Cave* (2000), fantasises an unnamed state dominated by a vast central building. It is a futuristic image of mature capitalism. In the basement of this building is the cave described by Plato, emblematic of the human condition in which chained spectators are destined to see nothing but shadows of the real world projected on the wall. Those unreliable, flickering images are all we have. And in that cave, for Saramago, is where the novelist must work.

As we saw earlier, the most powerful energies within magic realism have been generated by countries in Central and South America. Alongside Borges at the head of this group is Gabriel García Márquez and a novel which, alongside *Midnight's Children*, is regarded as the undisputed masterpiece of the genre: *One Hundred Years of Solitude* (1967). It has a bafflingly shifting narrative, which moves discontinuously through historical time and space.

The novel is set in an imaginary small Colombian town called Macondo and is as much about Márquez's native country as *Midnight's Children* is about India, *The Tin Drum* is about Germany, or *The Cave* is about Portugal. Macondo contains all Colombia within itself: it is a 'city of mirrors'. In a flickering series of scenes, we see flashes of the key moments in the country's history: civil wars, political conflict, the arrival of railways and industrialisation, the oppressive relationship with the USA. Everything is crystallised into a single glittering literary object. The novel is as politically engaged as literature can be, yet remains a supreme artifice.

Magic realism flared up, brilliantly, for a few decades at the turn of the century. It would seem now to have had its day, but history will record it as one of literature's great days.

CHAPTER 37

Republic of Letters
Literature Without Borders

In the twenty-first century, it's safe to say, literature has become truly global. But what does 'world literature' mean if we break the term down? A number of things, as we shall see.

Let's consider, for example, a novel originating in one of the tiniest, most isolated literary communities on earth – Iceland. The first Viking inhabitants arrived on this barren, rocky, freezing island in the ninth century. The following two centuries are called by literary historians the 'Saga Age' (the word 'saga', meaning 'told tale', comes from the Old Norse that Icelanders spoke, and still speak). It's an astonishingly rich body of thirteenth-century heroic poems about the clans who built the country when they weren't, as they often were, feuding with each other heroically.

A century before Chaucer, Norse literature was one of the glories of world literature. But only a few thousand people were familiar with it, stored as it was in their little nation's collective memory and recited lovingly from generation to generation. In 1955, the novelist Halldór Laxness was awarded the Nobel Prize (no writer from a smaller country had ever received one, the Committee said). The award was made largely on the basis of Laxness's 1934 masterpiece, a novel called *Independent People* (a defiant description of Iceland, the reader discovers). It's the story of Bjartur, whose family have been subsistence farmers for 'thirty generations' – since the Saga Age. Bjartur is steeped in his nation's poems, and recites them to himself as he walks the lonely hills with his sheep. His way of life is being changed, forever, by the twentieth century, and an outside world which has suddenly taken an interest in this cold, remote, tiny place.

Bjartur's story is as bleak, heroic and tragic as any of his beloved sagas. In his Nobel acceptance speech, Laxness went out of his way to impress upon his listeners his fiction's connectedness, like a baby's umbilical cord, to the stories narrated by Old Norse *skalds* (poets) in mud huts. Now it was being read in translation all over the planet by millions, and, thanks to the prize, was now 'world literature'. The conclusion one draws? Literature, if it is great or popular enough, and even when it is as deeply rooted in its own soil as Laxness's, is now no longer confined by national boundaries. It can leap over them.

The next example is from the largest literary community in the world, that of the People's Republic of China. Despite its vast size, its population of 1.35 billion, and its millennia-long civilisation, even the best-read Westerners would, most of them, be hard put to come up with the names of more than half a dozen great Chinese writers.

In 2012, the Nobel Prize in Literature was won by the Chinese writer Mo Yan. One of his more significant works is the novel *The Garlic Ballads*. It was first published a few months before the Tiananmen Square protests of June 1989 and was promptly withdrawn from publication. The author has many times found himself in hot water with his country's authorities. 'Mo Yan' is a pen-name he has chosen for himself. It means 'don't speak'.

The Garlic Ballads is dedicated to the remote region where Mo Yan, born into a peasant farming family in 1955, grew up. The story is of a community – cultivating, as they have for thousands of years, a fertile valley – who are ordered by Party bureaucrats to grow nothing but garlic. It's agricultural nonsense. An edict that, literally, stinks. They rebel and are brutally repressed. Garlic it must be, the Party decrees.

The book, like others by Mo Yan, has become an international bestseller. Contrary to his pen-name he does indeed speak – and to the world, not just his countrymen and women. And what conclusions would one draw from this example? It's more complicated than with Laxness. The world is now, all of a sudden, interested in Chinese literature because China has become in an astonishingly short time a twenty-first-century superpower. Napoleon is reputed to have said of China, 'Let her sleep, for when the dragon wakes she will shake the world'. The dragon has woken: China sleeps no more and is no longer ignored, and nor is its literature. Globalism is not just a geopolitical fact, it's a mindset, and literature is now part of that mindset.

The third example is that of Haruki Murakami. This leading Japanese novelist has published a number of works of fiction, successful in both sales and esteem worldwide, and in scores of languages. They 'travel' extraordinarily well and Murakami has more readers outside than inside his country. His major book thus far was the trilogy *IQ84* which concluded in 2010. The final volume was eagerly awaited. In Tokyo crowds queued up for hours to snap up the first copies.

The plot of *IQ84* is, it must be said, totally mystifying. It's magic realist in style (Chapter 36) and includes ninjas, assassinations, Yakuza gangsters, alternative worlds and baffling time-slippages. What is striking, however, is that Murakami knows he is writing for a worldwide public, avid to read and be baffled by him. He chose the title, we are told, because that is what 'nineteen eighty-four' sounds like in Japanese. It's an allusion – one could even call it an homage – to George Orwell. The novel's epigraph, 'It's only a paper moon', is the title of a 1930s American popular song by Harold Arlen. Murakami says elsewhere that he was inspired to write his novel by the Russian novelist Dostoevsky. The conclusion to be drawn here is that Murakami is a novelist who knows he is being read by the world, and is writing for the world. He sucks up influence from everywhere and makes it his own.

When writers are lucky enough to go global, they can earn amounts that rival the revenues of a multinational company. J.K. Rowling, for example, was listed in 2013 as the thirtieth richest person in the UK (and unique, among this select group, in that every penny of her wealth was earned, not inherited). She's not as rich as Coca-Cola, but *Harry Potter* is read in as many places as that fine drink is drunk.

There are exceptions to the rule but globalism, 'without borders', is now the dynamic energy driving literature. How did it happen? By way of the centuries-long growth in communication systems, international trade, and the dominance of certain 'world languages'. It's a long story, but a useful one, because helps us locate works of literature in their historical worlds, and to map the boundaries of those worlds.

For most of literary history, getting from one place to another was limited to travel on foot, by horse or under sail. Literature reflects that. One of the problems we face, as readers of literature often centuries older than we are, is adjusting to the fact that its horizons were far closer. Shakespeare, for example, never anticipated his plays being performed outside London or – at their furthest reach – the English provinces. Now billions of lovers of literature, worldwide, enjoy and study his drama.

The widening of horizons began, dramatically, in the nineteenth century, when mass communication brought people into easier contact within their own countries, and, by the end of the century, connected them internationally. In England in the early nineteenth century, tar-hardened roads made possible W.H. Smith's distribution of newspapers across the country ('First with the News'), using specially commissioned overnight stage coaches. Literature, in magazine form, travelled with the morning papers. Smith's secured what amounted to a monopoly, at mid-century, in the rapid delivery of newspapers and magazines. They were at this period not merely news vendors, but from 1860 also ran a circulating library. You could borrow one of Dickens's novels from the Smith's booth at Euston Station, read it on the ten-hour journey to Edinburgh, and upon arrival return it at the Smith's booth at Waverley Station.

From 1840, the UK-wide Penny Post (one of whose architects was the novelist, Anthony Trollope, in his employment at the General Post Office) meant the whole country could exchange messages daily between the big cities, every few hours. It was almost as fast as email. Authors, typically among the most literate members of society, took full advantage of this new exciting level of intercommunication. Trollope was also instrumental in introducing telegraph communication. The invention of steam power brought drastic reductions in voyage time. It's significant that Trollope partly wrote one of his best novels, *Barchester Towers* (1857), while travelling round Britain by train (aparently on Post Office business) and another, *The Way We Live Now* (1875) – a meaningful title – on a steamship to America, Australia and New Zealand.

The effect of all this progress was to internationalise markets, and make a country's internal market more efficient. When the final 'golden' spike was driven into the railroad tracks to complete the connection between New York and San Francisco, it meant that new books (many of them brought from Europe, by steamship) could be shuttled across the continental distances of the USA in days.

In 1912, when Guglielmo Marconi's radio company laid the ground for a worldwide network, he launched it, on air, with a quotation from Puck in *A Midsummer Night's Dream*: 'I'll put a girdle round about the earth in forty minutes.' Shakespeare himself was now, genuinely, global. The new internationalism was sealed with international copyright agreements (Chapter 11).

Not all authors addressed the new publics which had been opened up for them, but many did. Communications in the late twentieth and early twenty-first century are in a condition of continual evolution. The internet (Chapter 40) is reassembling the apparatus by which we virtually communicate year by year, like an ever-changing literary Legoland. Writers can now see themselves, if they choose, as writing for a global village.

It all sounds very *Brave New World*-ish. But there remains one tricky problem: language. Popular music can cross linguistic borders and be enjoyed by audiences who don't know, or care, what the words mean. Literature can't. Take away the words and there's nothing there. Literature has traditionally been stopped at the border, where language changes. Only a tiny quantity of foreign literature ever makes it across the translation barrier.

Translation (the word literally means 'carrying across') is cumbersome and often inefficient. Ask who are the most important writers of the twentieth century and Kafka's name will certainly come up. But the first English translation of a Kafka novel (an incomplete text) was not available until ten years after his death. Kafka's major works had to wait even longer, and some important languages of the world are still awaiting translations. It's not merely a time-lag. However skilful the translator, and despite the fact that translations can greatly increase an author's income and renown, translation is inherently flawed. Anthony Burgess – both a writer and a linguist – wrote that 'Translation is not a matter of words only: it is a matter of making intelligible a whole culture'. Often attributed to the American poet Robert Frost is the wise comment, 'Poetry is what gets lost in translation'.

It matters less, of course, for popular literature, where the finer points of translation are less important for the reader, who merely wants to turn the pages and enjoy. 'Scandi-noir', as it's called – novels that have followed in the wake of Stieg Larsson's 2005 international bestseller *The Girl with the Dragon Tattoo* – can survive leaden translation, just as the hugely popular Scandinavian TV thrillers can survive their clunky subtitles. Where simple page-turners are involved, fine prose is irrelevant. Functional prose will do very well.

Sadly, in one respect translation is an ever-decreasing problem for world literature. Linguists inform us that a language 'dies' every two weeks; their little literatures of the past, and more poignantly the future, die with them. In the modern era, English has followed world power and is now the 'world language' – as dominant as Latin was 2,000 years ago. The fact that the nineteenth century was 'Britain's century', and the twentieth was 'America's century', has meant dominance by two world powers separated, as George Bernard Shaw put it, 'by a common language'. The twenty-first century may well change that.

Literature is at any one time so diverse that no single generalisation will ever fit all. There are any number of important writers who have chosen to live and work in a small world. Philip Larkin, for example (Chapter 34), never travelled abroad. He joked that he was sure he would not like the 'dust', and his poetry reflects that insularity. Isaac Bashevis Singer, winner of the Nobel Prize in 1978, wrote his fiction in Yiddish, for a small community numbered in the low thousands, in his local New York. A 'fit audience ... though few', as Milton said.

Small worlds thrive, as they always have in literature. But the global world is, like the universe itself, expanding at a huge rate. That is something new, exciting, and, for good or ill, unstoppable.

CHAPTER 38

Guilty Pleasures
BESTSELLERS AND POTBOILERS

There is more 'great' literature readily available to us now than any one person, however ambitious and diligent, can get through in a lifetime – and there is more being added to the pile every year. Literature is a mountain that none of us will reach the peak of; we're lucky if we get through the lower foothills, following our chosen path as carefully as we can, as the summit above us gets ever-higher. To reflect only on authors mentioned in this book, even the best-read of us will go through life not having read *all* of Shakespeare's thirty-nine plays (I plead guilty to being a bit shaky on *Pericles*), or all of Jane Austen's fiction, or every word that Tennyson or Dostoevsky put into print. We can no more read all (or even a large sample) of literature than we can get everything on a supermarket's shelves into our trolley.

But there is an even larger mass to contend with: the less-than-great literature. According to the (distinguished) American author of science fiction, Theodore Sturgeon, 'Ninety per cent of [science fiction] is crud. But then, ninety per cent of *everything* is crud'. There are close to 2 million volumes classified as 'Literature' in the vaults of the British Library and the American Library of Congress. The average literate person reads 600 works of literature in an adult lifetime. If we are honest, a large portion of those 600 are, for most of us, what Sturgeon would dismiss as 'crud'. If you look around any airport departure lounge as people while away the hours of waiting, the chances are you'll see more Dan Brown and Jilly Cooper than Gustave Flaubert or Virginia Woolf. (And this, a primitive fear tells them, might be the last book they read in their lives…)

The 2012 winner of the Booker and Costa fiction prizes (of which more in Chapter 39) was Hilary Mantel, for her historical novel *Bring Up the Bodies*. It sold, within six months, close on a million copies – no previous winner in fifty years had enjoyed such sales success. But let's contrast that with the tens of millions of copies that E.L. James sold over the same period of her 'bonkbuster' (as they are irreverently called) *Fifty Shades of Grey*. Needless to say, it won no great literary prizes and was universally sneered at. Doubtless Ms James cried all the way to the bank (she rather charmingly confided she would use her millions to remodel her kitchen).

We can interpret such figures in two ways. Critics of a puritan cast of mind see it as evidence of the incorrigible cultural depravity of those whom Dr Johnson called 'the common reader' (Dr Johnson, as it happened, did *not* despise them). Those who take a more pragmatic view on the insatiable public appetite for 'crud' see it as healthy, particularly if you look at the big picture. E.L. James, for example, is now published by an imprint of Random House, the same conglomerate conjoined with the supremely 'respectable' Penguin Books imprint. Penguin is one of the main channels to have brought 'high' literature to a mass readership, ever since Allen Lane founded the quality paperback line in 1935. Lane dedicated himself to bringing the best contemporary fiction to the market at the same prices as were charged for cheap reading matter by the chain store Woolworths (in America the 'Five and Ten Cent Store', in Britain the 'Threepenny and Sixpenny Store'). He wanted to offer the highest literature at the lowest price.

Publishers let the sales of 'low' literature pay for the 'high'. That is, these so-called 'potboilers' put bread (or should that be stew?)

on the table. This can work in mysterious ways. Ever since T.S. Eliot was instrumental in founding the firm Faber & Faber in 1929, it has been the most respected publisher of poetry in the English-speaking world. To have its imprint on your volume is, for a poet, the seal of highest achievement. In recent decades the finances of Faber have been helped to stay robustly healthy by – what? Sales of *The Waste Land*, or the works of Ted Hughes and Philip Larkin? No. Most prosperously, it is said, by subsidiary rights revenue from *Cats*, Andrew Lloyd Webber's long-running musical stage adaptation of Eliot's extended joke in verse, *Old Possum's Book of Practical Cats*. No one would call anything that T.S. Eliot put into print 'low' (or, perish the thought, 'crud'). But his *Practical Cats* is not what has made him, by general agreement, the most important poet of his century.

If we are being open-minded it makes more sense to call what isn't 'high' (or 'classic', 'canonical' or 'quality') literature 'popular' rather than 'crud'. 'Popular' implies 'of the people' – that is, not of institutions like the Church, the universities or the government. The fifteenth-century mystery plays (Chapter 6) were popular; the Bible, in Latin at that time, was institutional. We still have institutionally-prescribed literature, forcibly studied at school, college and university.

The novel is the popular genre *par excellence*. When it hits the mark it has always stimulated 'uncritical' consumption. We can see this from the genre's earliest days. When Samuel Richardson published *Pamela* (1740), his chronicle of a pretty maid-servant persecuted by her lecherous employer, it triggered a 'mania' – particularly among women readers of the time. When Sir Walter Scott published one of his novels, there are accounts of purchasers besieging bookshops and tearing the brown paper off the volume to start reading the story in the street. We have seen any number of such 'reader stampedes' all the way to the publication of the seven volumes of the *Harry Potter* series – each of which became a kind of national holiday as purchasers, dressed as wizards, queued up all night outside bookshops. They were not doing so because the book had been well reviewed in that week's *Times Literary Supplement* or was on the A-level syllabus.

The term 'bestseller' is of relatively recent coinage (the first recorded usage is 1912), as is the bestseller list. The first such chart appeared in America, in 1895. One of the persistent British anxieties about 'bestsellerism' is that it represents an unwelcome 'Americanisation' – the bestseller is 'an American kind of book', fine for America, but not for the rest of the world. The British book trade stoutly resisted introducing any authoritative bestseller list until 1975. Books, it was felt, did not 'compete' with one another like horses in the Grand National. Worse than that, bestsellerism cheapened the quality and diversity of books. It worked against the necessary 'discriminations' (this, not that, or perhaps, this then that) which the intelligent reader should make. The argument goes on.

The question is made more complicated by the fact that bestsellers frequently 'come out of nowhere'. *Fifty Shades of Grey*, for instance, was first written as a work of fanfic, online, for an Australian reading group, by an author with no 'name recognition' whatsoever in the book world. Publishing companies have risen to the challenge of developing three strategies (again, mainly in the USA) to minimise the out-of-nowhere factor: 'Genre', 'Franchising' and 'Me too-ism'.

As Chapter 17 suggested, if you go into a bookshop you are free to 'browse' – but the shop will be guiding you toward the kind of fiction that would work for you by racking books of a similar appeal on 'genre' shelves: Science Fiction and Horror, or Romance, or Crime and Mystery. 'Franchising' works rather differently. Readers build up what retailers call 'brand loyalty'. They will buy 'the latest Stephen King' (his name is invariably larger on covers than the title of his latest work) because they enjoyed that author's previous works. 'Me too-ism' is simply 'follow my leader'. *Fifty Shades of Grey*, for example, inspired a veritable tsunami of lookalike covers, titles, themed works and spoofs. (My favourite was *Fifty Shames of Earl Grey*.)

The bestseller list, if one thinks about it, does not merely chart sales, it stimulates them, setting in process a kind of 'herd response'. You read a bestseller because everyone else is reading it. Once the herd is galloping the usual mechanisms of choice and 'discrimination' (some careful thought about what to read) are overridden. Dan Brown's *The Da Vinci Code*, when it was published in 2005, received almost universally negative reviews. Yet for two years it out-sold every other novel. The thundering herd, as always, voted with their hooves. And their wallets.

Most bestsellers quickly come and go. They are, usually, 'books of the day', and this year's bestseller list will contain a different set from last year's. A few, however, enjoy a long life and we can learn a lot about the machineries of popular literature from examining their career through the years – sometimes through centuries. *Les Misérables* is a good example. Victor Hugo published his story of Prisoner 24601's epic struggle with Inspector Javert, set against France's never-ending political upheavals, in 1862. It was initially published in French and ten other languages simultaneously. As a global enterprise, *Les Misérables* was immensely and immediately successful. Hugo's novel was reportedly the most-read book by both armies in the American Civil War in 1861–65. Dramatic versions became staples on the stage, worldwide, for decades after. *Les Misérables* has been filmed no less than twelve times. In 1985 an unambitious musical stage version was premiered at the Barbican in London. Despite poor reviews, it took off, and became what the official 'Les Mis' website describes as 'the world's longest-running musical' – 'Seen by more than 65 million people in 42 countries and in 22 different languages'. At the 2013 Oscars ceremony in Los Angeles, the latest film version (of the 1985 musical) pulled in a creditable three awards.

No one would call Victor Hugo's *Les Misérables* anything less than popular. Neither, if we're being honest, would we call it 'great literature'. It falls into the category of what George Orwell called 'good-bad books'. All the adaptations of the original novel, in different ways and with different degrees of fidelity, retain the core element: the long feud between the prisoner and his jailer and the original novel's social message, what Hugo called the 'social asphyxiation' which causes crime (in Jean Valjean's case, stealing a loaf of bread for his starving family).

Should the long passage of *Les Misérables* through all its different manifestations be seen as cheapening exploitations of the original text? I don't think so. It's more in the nature of a great work of popular fiction being able to evolve, adapt itself, like flowing liquid, to the ever-changing literary-cultural environment of the time. Some works of popular literature can do it, but most can't. Chances are there won't be a musical version of *The Da Vinci Code*, or *Fifty Shades of Grey*, winning any Oscars in 2120.

And what about poetry? Unthinkingly one might imagine that it is always something of minority interest, confined to 'little magazines', slim volumes, and an elite of highly-skilled readers. 'Best-selling poetry', one might argue, is a contradiction in terms – like 'jumbo shrimp'. If we think laterally, however, poetry has never been as popular as it is today. And we hear, over the course of a week, many more hours of it. We live 'in poetry' in ways that no generation before us has done. How come?

The most influential single volume in the history of the form is probably Coleridge and Wordsworth's *Lyrical Ballads*. It helps to unpack the root-meanings of those two words. 'Lyrical' goes back to the ancient musical instrument, the lyre – forerunner of the guitar (Homer is traditonally thought to have recited his epics to lyre accompaniment). 'Ballads' goes back to 'dance' (as does 'ballet'). So what, then, are Bob Dylan's lyrics, sung to his guitar? What are Michael Jackson's, or Beyoncé's, dance and song videos? What is each new generation's recordings of the ballads of Cole Porter? It's not too outrageous a stretch, for those of an open critical mind, to see as much 'literature' in popular music as there was in that 1802 slim volume by Coleridge and Wordsworth. Put another way, look hard and you'll find pearls in the crud.

CHAPTER 39

Who's Best?

Prizes, Festivals and Reading Groups

There have always been prizes for the highest literary achievement, from the ancient world's laurel-leaf crown to the 'biggest ever' advances which (lucky) modern authors receive. 'Laureateships' are prizes of a kind. Tennyson's forty-two-year tenure of the post of British poet laureate (Chapter 22) confirmed his supremacy in the world of poetry, as did the peerage, and the state funeral (in all but name), which a grateful Queen and nation awarded him on his death in 1892.

But systematically organised literary prizes – delivering a jury's verdict that this or that is the best novel, poetry collection or play, or recognising a lifetime's literary achievement – is very much a twentieth-century phenomenon, and of our time. The first such prize to be founded in France, the Goncourt, was awarded in 1903, and the UK and USA followed suit in 1919 and 1921 respectively. Since then, literary prize-giving has grown explosively. It has become like the proverbial Christmas party gift, cynics say: everyone must have one. There are now many hundreds of literary prizes that authors can compete directly for – or be entered for, usually by their publishers – in a large number of countries. And more of them are set up every year.

There is, among them all, a bewildering array of 'category prizes': awards for the best *second* novel of the year (named, wittily, the Encore); for the best detective novel of the year (the Edgar, named after the founder of the genre, Edgar Allan Poe); for the best historical novel (the Walter Scott, ditto); for the best woman's novel (the Women's Prize for Fiction, formerly the Orange Prize and since 2013 the Baileys Prize); for the best any kind of literary book (the Costa Book of the Year); and for the best collection of poetry (the T.S. Eliot). Some give large sums of money, some just 'honour' – and some dishonour (notably the Literary Review's Bad Sex in Fiction award). The biggest cash prize is splashed by the McArthur Foundation's Genius Grants in the USA, giving lucky authors half a million dollars to spend as they please, just for being geniuses. One thing all these prizes have in common is that they do not specify too closely what precise quality they are rewarding, or by what criteria they are judging. Judges and committees have a free hand in deciding what they regard as the worthiest effort.

Before examining a few of the premier prizes, let's ask some important questions. Why has this happened, why now, and why do we need such awards? A number of answers suggest themselves. The most convincing is that we live in an age of competition, where 'winning' is all-important. Everyone, it is said, loves a horse race. The prize system introduces the exciting ingredient of winners and losers into literature. It makes literature a kind of sports stadium, or gladiatorial arena.

In the last twenty years, bookmakers have begun offering odds and taking bets on who will win the Booker, in Britain, or the Pulitzer, in the USA. The big prizes are announced at award ceremonies that each year come more and more to resemble the Oscars. Only the red carpet is missing, and that may come soon.

Another reason for the current obsession with prizes is impatience. As George Orwell observed, the only real judge of whether a work of literature is any good or not is time. When literature first appears, we are very bad judges of how good or bad it is. That includes reviewers, who very often have to make 'authoritative' judgements within days – shooting, as it were, from the hip. Sometimes they miss badly: one early reviewer complained that *The Wind in the Willows* was zoologically inaccurate as to the hibernating habits of moles, which it almost certainly was. Many would have backed Ben Jonson against Shakespeare, in his day. Dickens, discriminating readers believed, was 'low'; you should read Thackeray – much better stuff. *Wuthering Heights*? Don't bother. One could go on. After a few decades, the winners and losers emerge from the fog. They become our 'canon' and are studied in the classroom. Time has done its job. But the reader wants to know *now* who the great contemporary writers are. They won't be around in a hundred years to learn history's verdict. Prizes satisfy that need to know.

The third reason for the profusion of prizes is 'signposting' – giving readers some direction so we might better find our way through the ever more daunting profusion of literature available nowadays. We desperately need guidance. Where shall we find it – the bestseller list? The book all the critics are raving about in this week's newspaper? The book that has the showiest advertisements in the underground station? That 'unmissable' book a friend has mentioned, whose title we can't quite remember? Prizes, judiciously selected by panels of experts who have coolly surveyed the whole field, offer the most reliable of signposts.

For its part, the book trade loves literary prizes. The reason is obvious enough: they help remove the chronic uncertainty which is the bane of their business. The rule-of-thumb ratio often cited is that for every four books that lose money for a publisher, one makes money – and, with luck, pays for the other four. With a prize-winner's medal hanging from its neck, the odds are short-ened that a title (or the next one the author writes) will earn its way. And it's not always necessary for the book to be a winner: to be on the short list, or even the long list, is enough to give the title 'profile'.

Which, then, are the top literary prizes? First in the list, as it was historically first, comes the **Nobel Prize in Literature**, which was set up in 1901. The prize is one of a set of five, each for outstand-ing achievement in a different field. Alfred Nobel was the Swedish inventor of dynamite, the first stable high explosive. It proved to be valuable in the construction and mining industries but also a terrible weapon of war. In his will, Nobel left most of his vast fortune for the annual awards in his name. Some think it was moral reparation. The annual literary selection is made by the Swedish Academy, with (anonymous) expert advice.

Scandinavia has its great writers (Ibsen, Strindberg and Hamsun, for example). But the Nobel net, from the start, was cast worldwide and over anything that could legitimately be called literature. Scandinavia, on the edge of Europe, was ideally placed to be objective and disinterested in its judgements. One of the undeniable achievements of the award has been to 'de-provincialise' our sense of literature: to see it as belonging to the world, not any single country. The Nobel Prize is awarded for a lifetime's achievement and the sole criterion for the prize is that it should go to writers who have produced 'the most outstanding work in an ideal direction'.

The Nobel Prize Committee has always seen itself as having influence in international politics. In choosing to award prizes to Boris Pasternak and Alexander Solzhenitsyn, it was well aware that the USSR would never let them come to collect their award. Disputes over who should have won the Nobel crop up with predictable regularity year after year. Accompanying them is a miasma of (probably apocryphal) Nobel lore. Did Joseph Conrad not get it because of the dynamiting villains in *The Secret Agent*? Did Graham Greene not get it because of the offensive depiction of the Swedish 'safety-match king', Ivar Kreuger, in *England Made Me*? Would the British-born W.H. Auden (widely reported to be a frontrunner in 1971) have won had he not been a US citizen at the wrong time of his life – namely during the bloody Vietnam War? For writers, such gossipy imaginings add spice to every year's announcement. And they are, backhandedly, a tribute to the importance attached to what is undeniably the world's major prize for literature.

The French **Prix Goncourt**, founded in 1903, is the 'purest' of the prizes, from the point of view of literary criticism. It was set up with an endowment by the eminent French man of letters, Edmond de Goncourt, whose high literary ideals it honours. A jury of ten, all distinguished in the literary world, and long-serving, meet once a month in a restaurant (this is, remember, a Parisian prize) to elect a particularly worthy book of the year. Literary quality is all. The cash prize is a derisory ten euros, to emphasise the point that this is not about money. Perish the thought. The lunches probably cost a fortune.

America's **National Book Awards**, nicknamed 'Literature's Oscars', began in 1936 during the Great Depression as an initiative by publishers and the American Booksellers Association to stimulate interest and sales at a low time in their industries. Over the years it has developed a wide array of prizes – almost as many as there are category bookshelves in a city bookstore. In 2012 they even had a niche award for E.L. James's *Fifty Shades of Grey*. It could be argued that the impact of the NBAs is muffled by there being so many of them. Like the Oscars, one yawns as yet another envelope is opened.

No yawning at the annual '**Booker** evening' every October. What is now acknowledged as the world's premier prize for fiction was set up in 1969 as the 'English Goncourt'. Unlike its cross-Channel ancestor, however, it gladly accepted the embrace of commerce and gave handsome cash prizes (and, with the publicity, the knock-on certainty of big sales). Booker McConnell, the original sponsors, had interests in West Indian sugar cultivation. One Booker winner, John Berger, used his speech to attack his 'colonial' benefactors and passed half his prize money to the Black Panther movement. In recent years the prize has been sponsored by a hedge fund and thus renamed the Man Booker Prize. With Anglo-Saxon pragmatism the administrators of the prize have no problem with the deal they make with capitalism.

The long-serving ten Goncourt judges are all from the literary world. The five Booker judges, who serve for one year only, are from the 'real world' – sometimes, controversially, showbiz. The book trade not only likes literary prizes, it likes the controversy which attends them – both before and after the awards ceremony. The administrators' cunningly programmed release of who is serving on the Booker panel, the long list, the short list, all culminate in a night of banqueting, TV coverage, suspense and, usually, fierce debate. A lot of novels, in the process, are bought and consumed. Is literature's contemporary prize-culture a good thing? Most would say it is: if only that it gets literature read. But we should see it as part of what is a changed, and fast-changing, literature scene.

Another twentieth-century novelty is the ever-expanding number of book and literary festivals which began in the period after the Second World War. These events, large and small, bring together congregations of book lovers, and in their genteel way they have become the pop concerts of literature. *En masse*, these fans make their preferences felt to authors, who meet their readers face to face, and to publishers, who pay very close attention to what is selling in the now traditional 'book tent'. Call it a meeting of minds.

Even more recent is the explosive growth of local reading groups, in which like-minded book lovers get together to discuss a series of books they have chosen for themselves. There is nothing overtly educational or self-improving about these groups. There are no fees, no regulations – just a sharing of critical views on literature which is thought to be worth a read, and some lively discussion. Again, minds meet – always a good thing where literature is concerned.

Reading groups have changed the way we talk about literature and have opened up new lines of communication between producers and consumers. Many publishers nowadays package their fiction and poetry for reading groups, with explanatory author interviews and questionnaires. They are democratic in spirit. There is no top-down instruction: it's more bottom-up, and selections are more likely to be titles chosen from 'Oprah's picks' than the book that has got appreciative reviews in the *New York Review of Books*, the *London Review of Books* or *Le Monde*. Reading groups help to keep reading alive and pleasurable. And without that, literature itself would die.

CHAPTER 40

Literature in Your Lifetime... and Beyond

The printed 'book' – a physical thing made up of paper, type, ink and board – has been around now for over 500 years. It has served literature wonderfully: packaging it in cheap (sometimes beautiful) forms that have helped to sustain mass literacy. Few inventions have lasted longer, or done more good.

The book may, however, have had its day. The tipping point has come very recently, in the second decade of the twenty-first century, when e-books – digital things made up of algorithms and pixels – began to outsell the traditional book on Amazon. An e-book, as it's currently marketed for handheld tablets, looks eerily like a 'real' book, just as the early printed books, such as Gutenberg's, looked just like manuscripts. But, of course, it doesn't behave like a 'real' Gutenbergian book. The e-book has the same relation to its predecessor as the horseless carriage (that is, the automobile) had to the horse-drawn carriage.

With an e-book you can alter the type-size, turn the pages with your thumbs (instead of your index finger) at lightning speed, search the text, and extract lumps of it for downloading. In short, you can do a lot more with an e-book, although, as it's routinely pointed out, you can't drop it in the bath. And, of course, the e-book is still evolving – readers won't have to wait 500 years for what comes next. Book apps are already creating new formats and new ways of reading. What forms will literature take in the years to come? What new delivery systems will it use? In the libraries of the future, will we no more see a print-and-paper book than we see a horse-drawn carriage on the motorway?

By way of answering these questions, let's start from three basics that will condition the future world of literature, however it is delivered to us. First, there will be a lot more literature available. Second, literature will come to us in different, untraditional ways (in audio, visual and 'virtual' forms). Third, it will come in new packages.

The first, the 'too-muchness' of literature, is already with us and expanding all the time. Any kind of screen with an internet connection gives its owner access via new (and often free) e-libraries, such as Project Gutenberg, to a quarter of a million works of literature. You hold in the palm of your hand the equivalent of enough old-fashioned books to fill an aircraft-hanger. What's on offer is increasing all the time. Delivery is instantaneous and the material can be customised to your personal preferences for reading it.

This mind-crushing plentifulness creates whole new sets of problems. There are those still living (and I am one) who were raised in a cultural environment whose central features were scarcity, shortage and inaccessibility. If you wanted a new novel, you had either to save up the money to pay for it, or put your name down on a waiting list at the local public library. It was annoying. But, in a way, it made things simpler. You had fewer options.

Now, for relatively small sums, a couple of screen-strokes can procure you anything newly published and virtually limitless numbers of secondhand books. On the Web, a search engine (one of them aptly called 'Jeeves', like the butler) will serve you up any new or ancient poem you want. All you have to do is enter a couple of keywords (wandered + lonely + cloud).

In a single lifetime – mine, for example – shortage has been replaced by an embarrassment of choice. So where, in this electronic

Aladdin's Cave, does one start? More importantly, where should we invest the limited (life-)time at our disposal? It's calculated that someone at school now will encounter some fifty or so works of literature in their school career, and those studying literature at university around 300 more. Most people will probably consume no more than 1,000 works of literature in their adult lifetime. If that.

Where some literature is concerned (books set for examination, for example) we have no choice. But usually it's entirely up to us what we choose to read. We are, as readers in the present time, paddlers in a deluge. In Shakespeare's day there were, it has been estimated, some 2,000 books available to a bookish person like him. You could be, as the phrase was, 'well read'. That is a description for which no one in the future will qualify.

One reading strategy, followed by many, is to fall back on old favourites, the 'Usual Suspects'. In other words the canon, the classics, the works currently topping the bestseller lists, the whole mix spiced up by word-of-mouth from trusted friends and advisers. This could be called swimming with the tide.

An alternative is what we might call the 'shopping trolley' strategy – choosing from the wealth of what is available by defining your own specific needs, interests and tastes, and tailoring your literary diet to what suits you best. When it comes to literature, says William Gibson (pioneer of the 'cyberpunk' science fiction genre), we are 'worms in the cheese'. No worm will consume the whole cheese, and no worm will tunnel through in the same way as any other worm.

The problem of 'managing surplus' is further complicated by the fact that what we have in our hand is much more than a functional text-delivery system. It can go beyond words on the page and also provide music, film, opera, TV and – most insidiously – games. How can the pixel-printed word compete? How do we make time to listen to our favourite music *and* read the latest novel (available, at a relatively painless price, on the same handheld device)?

Whatever else, these days we need to be educated in the intelligent use and investment of time. That, not money, is what we will be short of in the future. How much time does the average working person have for culture, loosely defined, in an average week? Around ten hours, it is estimated. How long does it take to read a new novel by Hilary Mantel (since we've mentioned her), or Jonathan Franzen? You've guessed it. Around ten hours.

At the moment we are in a transitional or 'bridge' moment in our literary world. The electronic 'faux book' format which we cling to is an example of what the critic Marshall McLuhan called 'rear-mirrorism'. What he meant by this is that we always see the new in terms of the old. We hold on to the past because we are nervous about the future or feel unsure how to handle it. Children and comfort blankets come to mind.

Fragments of the old can often be found in the new, if we look carefully enough. Have you ever wondered why films have musical soundtracks but stage plays don't? When Kenneth Branagh played Henry V on the screen, there was thundering music (composed by Patrick Doyle, and conducted by Simon Rattle). On stage, when he plays the same part, there is none. The reason is that silent films – which were all that was available for thirty years – had pit orchestras or, at the very least, piano accompaniment. The music stayed on, even after the 'talkies' came along. Why do the pages of books have such large margins – why doesn't print extend nearer the four edges? Because early manuscript books allowed space for marginal comment and annotation. We still have the margins, though few use them for writing notes in, and libraries get furious if you do. It's a perfect example of 'rear-mirrorism'.

Annotation and comment will, however, thrive in the new electronic margins. What, exactly, do the moors of *Wuthering Heights*'s Yorkshire look like? It would be informative for readers to be able to call them up. Particularly those readers – now that literature is a global phenomenon – who have never been to the wilder areas of the north of England and probably never will.

New technology, will, for a certainty, stimulate the production and consumption of 'graphic' fiction, and 'poetry' (however loosely defined). Literature has up to now been overridingly textual – essentially words on the page. It is one of the things that, regrettably, can render it unattractive to readers (particularly younger readers) whose culture (via screens and game consoles) is richly audio-visual and increasingly 'virtual'. Getting your stories from black marks on a white surface is not so exciting. The graphic novel is exciting, as is poetry set to popular music. All those Guy Fawkes masks, worn by the young agitators of the Occupy movement, were inspired by a graphic novel, Alan Moore's *V for Vendetta* – the masks are directly copied from the illustrator David Lloyd's design. Graphic fiction, like the comic book to which it is related, eases itself into film readily, creating a large knock-on readership. The economic rise of Japan and China, whose writing systems are traditionally pictographic, will add force to this mutation.

Interactive literature, which requires the reader to co-operate rather than passively consume, is already a presence. In the future we can expect what Aldous Huxley, in *Brave New World*, called 'feelies' (Chapter 30) – that is, narratives, poems and plays that are multi-sensorial: felt, smelled, heard, seen. 'Readers', as they formerly were, will be 'participants'. 'Bionic literature' will happen, one may be sure, much sooner than Huxley prophesied. We shall become 'whole body' readers.

'New packaging' is the third of the large 'climatic' changes that will refashion literature. One of the most interesting moves towards it is evident in the explosive rise of 'fanfic' on the web. Fanfic (fan-fiction) is created, as the name suggests, by fans who either want more *of* their favourite fiction, or who want more *from* it. It starts from the premise that works of literature are not 'fixed' things like stone sculptures. The old division between author and reader melts away.

Fanfic thrives on the Web, where there is currently little regulation either of content or copyright. A huge quantity of it is produced – much more than printed fiction. There are vigorous growth areas around classic fiction: as I write, 'The Republic of Pemberley' website, dedicated to 'obsessive' lovers of Jane Austen, has a 'Bits of Ivory' annex in which fans devise sequels to the six novels. Fanfic is not limited to works that are out of copyright. Whole alternative versions of works such as *The Lord of the Rings* have been generated. A lot of fanfic is poor stuff, but some of it is as good as anything you'll find in print.

It is now not unknown for novels that go on to be bestsellers, or otherwise successful, to originate as fanfic productions. As a genre, fanfic is material generated by small groups and intended for circulation among those small groups. It is not commissioned, nor is it paid for, nor is it 'reviewed', nor is it bought. It is not, as the term is usually applied, 'published'. It is fiction written principally for readers who also, many of them, write it – a party where everyone joins in. Fanfic is not a commodity. It is neither commercial nor professional. It is never traded in any kind of market. In many ways, it is closer to a literary conversation – 'talking about books' – than to the printed word. It can also be seen as literature's return to its pre-printed origins. Did the first listeners to the *Odyssey*, or *Beowulf*, or *Gilgamesh* 'pay'? Probably not. Did they join in the literary fun – even suggesting improvements? Quite likely they did.

One of the most interesting things about oral literature, which we explored earlier, is its fluidity. Like conversation it is flexible and changeable; it takes on the personality of whoever is then in charge of it. It flows, like water, over whatever environment it finds itself in.

What this means in practice can be shown by one of the oral-narrative forms that has come down to us over the millennia: the conversational joke. If I tell you a joke, and you think it's a good one, you may well pass it on. But it will not be identical to what I originally told you. You will make it, with any number of small variations, yours – by elaborating some points, or by removing certain details. It may be improved, or it may not. But if you tell the joke, it will carry some of you in it, just as my telling will carry some of me in it. As it passes on to a third person, it will carry some of both of us. We can see something very similar in fanfic. The original fluidities (so to call them) of literature are being recovered. I find that exciting.

Change is inevitable. To play the prophet (always a risky venture), the best thing that could happen to the future world of literature, its practitioners and participants, is that it will recover that quality of 'togetherness'. This book has explored how, taken in its totality, literature is something communal: a dialogue with minds greater than our own; entertainingly-clothed ideas about how we should live our lives; a debate about our world, where it is going and where it should go. This kind of meeting of minds, enabled by literature, is central to our existence now. If things turn out well that meeting of minds will become more intense, more intimate, more active.

What's the worst thing that could happen in the future? If readers were to become swamped – buried under a mass of information they could not process into knowledge – that would be very bad. But I remain hopeful, and with good reason. Literature, that wonderfully creative product of the human mind, will, in whatever new forms and adaptations it takes, forever be a part of our lives, enriching our lives. I say ours, but I should say yours – and your children's.

Index